HOME FROM HOME

BRIAN WILLIAMS

HOME FROM HOME

A WEST HAM SUPPORTER'S STRUGGLE TO
REACH THE NEXT LEVEL

Biteback Publishing

First published in Great Britain in 2017 by
Biteback Publishing Ltd
Westminster Tower
3 Albert Embankment
London SE1 7SP

ISBN 978-1-78590-287-1

10 9 8 7 6 5 4 3 2 1

A CIP catalogue record for this book is available from the British Library.

Set in Adobe Garamond Pro

Printed and bound in Great Britain by
CPI Group (UK) Ltd, Croydon CR0 4YY

MIX
Paper from
responsible sources
FSC
www.fsc.org
FSC® C020471

Contents

Introduction

ON 10 MAY 2016 West Ham United played their last game at the Boleyn Ground, having been there for 112 years. For almost half that time I have supported the club and I didn't welcome the news that we were going to leave.

Having now completed the first season at the London Stadium I'm still trying to come to terms with what, for me, is a major upheaval. To make some sense of it all I set out to compare the final year at Upton Park with the first at Stratford – hence this book. To give the events at both stadiums some sort of chronological order while making the comparison, I've based most of the chapters on the corresponding league fixtures from the respective seasons. Other games in other competitions are mentioned too, but the Premier League matches provided a useful set of signposts.

A very wise friend of mine, who understands exactly how I feel, told me I should find out more about the five stages of grief.

You can't grieve the loss of a football ground, I thought. But I looked them up anyway.

1. Denial: Hmmm, possibly. I certainly left it late before deciding to follow the club to the London Stadium, by which time all the best seats had gone.
2. Anger: You bet I was angry!
3. Bargaining: OK. It's true I spent a long time trying to negotiate better-placed season tickets for me and my family (moaning to anyone who would listen while I did so).
4. Depression: Maybe. When you are so miserable you welcome an international break because it means you don't have to watch your team play, something is definitely not right.
5. Acceptance: Ah. I'm afraid you'll have to read the book to discover the answer to that. I hope you enjoy it.

COYI!

1

Onwards and upwards

London Stadium
Sunday 7 August 2016
Kick-off: 1.00
Final score: West Ham 2–3 Juventus

YOU DON'T GET many clubs bigger than Juventus, yet here they were at West Ham's new home in Stratford. What had started life as the Olympic Stadium had become the London Stadium, and the club I have supported all my life were now its tenants. The showpiece game I was about to witness heralded the move. It was a historic day for my beloved Hammers, but I wasn't happy. Not happy at all.

Before you say anything, let me be the first to admit that relocating from one football stadium to another is not the most serious crisis facing humankind in these worrying times. But it was something that had been troubling me from the moment the plan was first hatched.

It had to be done, we were told repeatedly. Our previous home – the Boleyn Ground to the faithful and Upton Park to the rest of the world – was no longer fit for purpose and if West Ham wanted to progress we simply could not pass up the gold-plated opportunity that had landed on our doorstep. (For those supporters of other clubs who are still confused about the Boleyn Ground/Upton Park thing, the stadium was officially the Boleyn Ground and Upton Park is the geographical area in which it was situated – but don't worry, either will do fine.)

According to the club's owners, moving was the only way to attain football's equivalent of nirvana – the fabled 'next level'. So had West Ham really gone up in the world? I most certainly had. Rather than sitting in row K, as I had done at the Boleyn Ground, I was now in row seventy-three – aka the back row. Not only was it higher up, it was also a lot further back. I only had myself to blame, I suppose.

We, the Williams family, had dithered about renewing our season tickets. Normally, supporters who wish to put themselves through another period of agony the following year renew towards the end of a season. What West Ham wanted us to do prior to the move to Stratford was to sign up for our tickets even before the final season at the Boleyn Ground had begun. To be honest, I thought that was a bit previous.

I suppose, looking back, we were always going to go. We should have just bitten the bullet and got on with it.

I am not a cockney by birth, but I have been going to watch football in London E13 since I was a kid. My wife, Di, is a true East Ender, having been brought up a five-minute walk away from the ground in East Ham. We, along with our son Geoff, were – and still are – season ticket holders. Geoff was perfectly sanguine about the move. However, Di and I, who between us had more than 100 years invested in the Boleyn Ground, were most displeased about leaving a stadium that held so many wonderful memories (and not-so-wonderful ones as well, if I'm going to be brutally honest).

It wasn't just the football itself. We were also being asked to leave behind all the rituals that go with it. A pre-match pint in a proper East End pub, a hotdog outside the ground, an occasional trip to the wonderful Newham Bookshop. Newham is a residential area, with all the amenities that go with it. The same cannot be said of the Olympic Park, which surrounds our new stadium. No pubs, no chippies – and certainly no mobile phone shops like the one in the Barking Road we regularly walked past that proudly announced it also sold baby chickens. All of this was to be replaced by corporate catering within the stadium, and not a baby chicken to be had for love nor money.

However, after much soul-searching (the full extent of which I won't bore you with here), we decided we would not be robbed of the dubious pleasure of watching our football team by owners who will be gone long before we are. Like most West Ham supporters, we do not know the meaning of the word 'defeat' (there are lots of other words we don't know the meaning of either, but then we all went to comprehensive schools).

We bought our season tickets for the new stadium on Blue Monday – the day in mid-January that is said to be the most depressing of the year due to a combination of miserable winter weather and Christmas credit card bills coming home to roost. This is not to be confused with claret and blue Mondays, which crop up regularly during the season and basically involve beating yourself up over West Ham's failure to win at the weekend.

When I was in my teens this would generally involve a Sunday in denial followed by an entire Monday of silent sulking, although I'm much better now. As a man of some maturity, who has qualified for a senior railcard, I only need the Monday morning to get over the disappointment of defeat and rarely snarl at anyone after lunch.

The grandly named West Ham Reservation Centre, the Mecca for anyone wishing to purchase a ticket for the initial season at our new home, was in the Westfield shopping centre. Do not be fooled by Westfield. It may look like a concrete temple built to honour the God of Shopping (the nation's one true god), but it is in fact a spiritual black hole which is gradually sucking every shred of goodness from the universe – having started its feeding frenzy with the soul of my football club.

The Reservation Centre was a glass-fronted unit (aka 'shop') that was harder to find than either Di or I expected. Sitting behind the reception desk, perhaps unsurprisingly, was a receptionist. Above her was West Ham's new crest – redesigned without the castle that represented the ties with the old ground, and with the addition of the word 'London', presumably in case all the new supporters forget where they are.

Well, the club was keen to call them supporters. I beg to differ. Let me quote you these few words from the club's vice-chair Karren Brady, and perhaps then you will understand my disquiet.

'We are ambitious for our great club and aim to set the benchmark for visiting away and neutral supporters from across the globe to come and enjoy the iconic stadium and be part of our Premier League club experience.'

What the hell is a 'neutral supporter'? The whole point of

going to a football match, as I understand it, is to put your heart and soul into supporting one side or the other. I do not want to find myself rubbing shoulders with someone who is ambivalent about the outcome of the game – and is indeed more interested in taking a selfie outside the stadium beforehand. These people are football tourists and belong at grounds such as Old Trafford and Stamford Bridge, rather than at a 'proper' club like West Ham.

Anyway, I consoled myself with the thought that the badge does at least still have the crossed hammers that prompted our nickname and symbolise the club's formative days as a factory team carrying the hopes and dreams of the long-defunct Thames Ironworks and Shipbuilding Company.

Once inside, having completed all the usual formalities, we milled around a bit with several other happy Hammers on a similar mission before being invited to watch a short film.

I anticipated being led into a small cinema to watch the movie. Wrong. Instead, we were shepherded into a compact alcove which boasted a handful of seats – although not enough to accommodate all of us – and a tiny screen that wasn't much bigger than our telly. Still, a film's a film for all that. I wasn't expecting *Star Wars* and I can always watch anything that involves footballing legends in claret and blue. My enthusiasm had to be put on hold for a few moments longer, however, as we were given a short speech by a jolly man in an ill-fitting suit and tie. My hearing is not what it once was, and he was softly spoken, so I didn't pick up as many of his words of wisdom as I would have liked. I think the gist of it concerned the 'West Ham brand' and the exciting journey we were all about to undertake together.

The film certainly confirmed that we were all going on a

journey – a very important journey at that. The voice accompanying footage of West Ham greats, past and present, belonged to none other than Ray Winstone, and he is not a man to be questioned lightly. If he says you are going on a journey, trust me – you are going on a journey.

I'd been told beforehand by a fellow supporter who had been on the same pilgrimage that Winstone's voiceover consisted of nothing more than a string of disjointed words vaguely connected to West Ham United FC. 'Bobby Moore.' 'Sir Trevor Brooking.' 'East End.' 'Pie and mash.' 'Violence.' 'Racism.' But it turned out I was having my leg pulled: Ray Winstone never mentioned racism once.

The film over, we were all introduced to the staff who were there specifically to give us a virtual tour of the stadium and then help us choose our seats. Di and I would have preferred a real tour of the actual stadium but, even though it was relatively close at hand, it turned out this wouldn't be possible. Had we been there before, perhaps to watch the Olympics or a Rugby World Cup match? we were asked. We had not, we replied, with a certain sense of sudden and inexplicable guilt in my case. No matter: the wonders of modern technology meant we'd get a precise image of what it would be like.

The enthusiastic young lady who took us on this virtual tour had an accent that suggested she came from somewhere closer to Botany Bay than Barking, but she knew her stuff. And, unlike us, she had actually been in the stadium itself. We shall call her Kylie.

We began with a series of computer-generated images that showed happy, excited and anorexically thin people in summer shirtsleeves approaching the ground. They did not look like a typical West Ham crowd on its way to a game, but I kept this thought to myself. Kylie asked us how we had got to the Reservation Centre and we replied by train – which was her prompt to tell us that one of the great attractions of the new ground was its accessibility. Having just had my first taste of Stratford International station and then tackled the maze that is Westfield I wasn't so sure – but again I kept my own counsel.

Looking back to the computer screen before us I noticed the Champions Statue, virtually moved from its rightful place near the old Boleyn Ground. Those of you with a passing knowledge of West Ham United FC will recall (although not always admit) that it was us wot won the World Cup in 1966. To commemorate this historic achievement it was decided to erect a statue near the club's ground. The 16-foot bronze creation is based on an iconic photograph of Bobby Moore, hoisted aloft, holding the Jules Rimet trophy in the company of hat-trick hero Geoff Hurst and Martin Peters, the scorer of the other goal (hence the statistically correct score: West Ham 4, West Germany 2).

Curiously, the statue depicts a fourth member of the World Cup winning team in the shape of Ray Wilson, who is there because Moore happened to be sitting on his shoulder when the original photograph was taken. Why royal sculptor Philip Jackson didn't exercise a bit of artistic licence by axing Wilson, who was playing for Everton in 1966, and repositioning Martin Peters so that he was the one who was lending his captain a shoulder to sit on is anyone's guess. Not only would it have meant the effigy was a West Ham only affair, it would have prevented Peters from looking like he'd statue-bombed a historic moment in time. But that's sculptors for you, I guess.

The idea was to move the statue to Stratford, positioning it to the north of the stadium. At Upton Park the north end of the ground – once known simply as the North Bank – ended its days as the Sir Trevor Brooking Stand. This is where the away supporters were housed. The southern end – which once matched its northern twin's simple nomenclature by being called the South Bank – was the Bobby Moore Stand.

However, everything had been turned on its head in the brave new world of the London Stadium. It was decided the away fans should get the south end this time, and it appears the boardroom thinking was that the riff-raff from other clubs must not be allowed to sully the memory of West Ham's favourite son by occupying a stand that bears his name. So, with a twitch of Baroness Brady's magic wand, the Moore and Brooking stands changed ends.

My ability to absorb this staggering piece of information wasn't helped by Kylie constantly flicking from one internal image of the stadium to another – each picture showing row upon row of empty seats. She seemed particularly keen to give us the view from the seats in the lower tiers – before telling us these had all been sold. For the first time in my life I knew how it felt to be a contestant on a quiz show who had missed out on the star prize: 'Look what you could have won!'

As I say, it was our own fault we had missed the chance to sit in the favoured seats. We had been contacted by the club in the summer of 2015 and offered the chance to buy our tickets for the first year at Stratford. We shall brush over the fact that the appointment was set for a day when there was a Tube strike; Geoff and I both had unbreakable work commitments and that the invitation was extended to Di only. The truth is, buying a season ticket for the season after next in a stadium that we weren't sure we wanted to go to wasn't top of our agenda at the time. Our mistake: it clearly should have been.

Even so, I bridled slightly when Kylie adopted the tone of a primary school teacher and reminded us that had we kept the first appointment she had made for us we could have had just about any seat in the house. (I'm not fluent in body language as a rule, but having been married to Di for the best part of thirty years I got the impression she too was not best pleased at being told this.) And I positively bristled when she referred to the new East Stand as 'the Kop'. A Kop at West Ham? Not while there's breath in my body.

We were then given the view from the higher seats. A little over four weeks before we had embarked on our momentous journey to Westfield, the first British male astronaut had headed off to the International Space Station. Two hours after launch someone tweeted Major Tim Peake had just reported that the view from the upper tier of the London Stadium wasn't as bad as the rumours suggested. Somehow that tweet didn't seem quite as funny any more.

In the end we opted for three seats in the back row. The thinking was, that way, we wouldn't have the annoyance of listening to some gobby idiot sitting behind us making inane and ill-informed remarks about the game they're watching. Instead, we would be the gobby idiots sitting behind everyone else.

Credit card processed and tickets purchased, Kylie asked us if we wanted our photograph taken as a memento of our big day out. We may have both been wearing the horrified expressions of an elderly couple who had just escaped from a log flume, but we didn't want to be continually reminded of the experience with a picture. What we wanted was a pub.

Sitting in my new seat, I realised I probably spent too much time in pubs and not nearly enough in the gym. What I needed as I looked down on the pitch far, far, below was oxygen and – very possibly – a defibrillator.

The pint and greasy comestible I'd had on the concourse probably hadn't done much for my fitness levels, and the long climb to the back of the stand had taken its toll. I wondered what was more likely to bring on a heart attack: the 7 million stairs I would have to scale each time I came to watch football, or the price of the hot dogs.

Our season tickets hadn't got us into this game. For the privilege of watching the Betway Cup Final we had to fork out an extra thirty-five quid each. But we did get an opening ceremony as part of the deal. The thirty-minute show included the official opening of the new Bobby Moore and Trevor Brooking stands at either end of the ground. Sir Trev did the honours for the one named in his honour while Freddie Moore, the grandson of England's one and only World Cup winning captain, christened the northern stand.

There was a brass band, bubbles and flames plus a couple of big-screen presentations. We even got an ear-splitting rendition of the national anthem from soprano Laura Wright, who likes to play rugby in her spare time. To be perfectly candid, I found it all somewhat underwhelming. But I'm not a great one for opening ceremonies at the best of times.

Juventus had been Italian champions for the past five years and were destined to go on and win a sixth straight Serie A title. They were supposed to have been West Ham's first opponents at the new stadium, but a bunch of rather ungallant Slovenians by the name of NK Domžale pushed in front of the Old Lady of

Turin and were on the pitch three days beforehand. They were there for a Europa League game. I wasn't, so I missed Cheikhou Kouyaté scoring the first goal at the London Stadium after just eight minutes.

I was there, however, to see the first goal we conceded at the new stadium. Apparently, it was scored by Paulo Dybala, although from my lofty perch it was hard to tell. As I understand it, Mario Mandžukić scored the second goal to be conceded by West Ham United in our new stadium. Again, I would have had trouble picking him out in an identity parade based on what little I saw of him from row seventy-three. And the much-heralded big screens at either end of the ground weren't much help. From where we were, views of both were seriously restricted.

On the plus side, I was able to make out the distinctive frame of Andy Carroll, who scored either side of half time to put us back into the game. I was on the edge of my seat. It was that exciting? I hear you ask. Er, no. I just thought that if I sat on the edge of my seat I might be able to make out some of the players I had paid to see.

Dani Alves, Gianluigi Buffon, Gonzalo Higuaín – that is next-level talent. Juventus also had international striker Simone Zaza, who scored their winner. 'Now that's the sort of player we need to sign if we are going to compete at the top level,' said a tiny voice in my head. But he'd made a complete Horlicks of a crucial penalty against Germany in the Euros, I replied silently. 'Don't you worry about that mate,' said the voice. 'This boy is different gravy. You mark my words.' Which just goes to show, if you do have voices in your head, it might be an idea to get treatment. And, whatever you do, don't build a transfer strategy around them.

All the talk pre-season was about signing a world-class striker. We were told by co-owner David Sullivan, often via his son's Twitter account, that we were in the market for a twenty-goal-a-season goalscorer, and were prepared to spend big to get one. It was all part of the move to the next level. He stated boldly that the club would sign a top striker 'whatever happens'. For the owners, it was a 'statement of intent'.

It certainly would have made a statement. The fact is, no striker (or indeed any other player) has scored twenty Premier League goals in a season for West Ham.

Alexandre Lacazette wasn't interested. Neither was Michy Batshuayi. And, despite a barrage of optimistic tweets from Sullivan Jnr, Carlos Bacca couldn't be persuaded that shopping in Westfield was every bit as pleasurable as a stroll along Via Montenapoleone in Milan.

In desperation, the owners decided to break the club's transfer record anyway. They did that by splashing out a fraction over £20 million on André Ayew. Could he be the man to take us up a level?

The player everyone wanted to see that day was our very own Dimitri Payet, signed at the beginning of the previous season and seemingly on his way to club legend status. There was even a huge picture of our brilliant No 27 on the front of the stadium, complete with our tribute to him (with apologies to Billy Ray Cyrus and his 'Achy Breaky Heart').

We've got Payet, Dimitri Payet.
I just don't think you understand,
He's Super Slav's man,
He's better than Zidane,
We've got Dimitri Payet.

Somewhat embarrassingly for all concerned, at that stage of the season the last line of the mural actually had him down as 'Dimtri'. Ah well, it's better than 'Dimwit', I suppose. The club didn't waste much time before correcting the error, although had they known it would have to come down altogether a few months later they might have saved themselves the trouble.

Little did we know, as we belted out the anthem to honour his appearance for the final fifteen minutes, that he wasn't really Super Slav's man at all. It was a story that would dominate the first half of the season, maybe the season as a whole, but we'll come to that later.

No one was too fussed about losing to Juventus – it was a friendly after all. Those of us who hadn't been to the NK Domžale game were more interested in getting our bearings in the new stadium.

After the final whistle we headed to the bar under the big screen at the Bobby Moore end and considered our verdict on the decision to move to Stratford. That nagging voice, the one which reckoned Zaza was the answer to our problems, was telling me that I wasn't going to like our new home. And this time it sounded a lot more convincing...

2

The last goodbye

Boleyn Ground
Tuesday 10 May 2016
Kick-off: 7.45 (delayed until 8.30)
Final score: West Ham 3–2 Man Utd

GEOFF KNEW THE answer to his question even as he asked it. 'If I had the power to give you one more season at the Boleyn Ground but it would mean we were relegated, would you take it?'

We were in the back streets of east London, on our way to watch West Ham play at the Boleyn Ground for the last time.

It had been an emotional day. It was to be an emotional night. But, when we bumped into friends near the ground a few moments later, we discovered that emotion had to be put on hold for a while because our opponents had been delayed on the way to the stadium.

What were Manchester United thinking about that evening?

It was no secret that this was to be the final game at Upton Park. It was inevitable that a huge crowd would turn out to be part of the occasion, so why did they not allow themselves more time to get from their hotel to the ground? An oversight? I doubt it. Gamesmanship? Possibly. Arrogance? Much more likely.

What was happening on the other side of the ground would dominate the headlines the following morning, but at this stage all we knew was that the team bus was late and the kick-off had been put back. Ah well, if nothing else it provided the perfect excuse for one last bottle of overpriced, tasteless lager in the edifice I had thought of as my spiritual home for more than fifty years.

I'll be honest: it wasn't the first drink I'd had that day, neither would it be my last. Not that I was intoxicated, you understand. Myself, Di and Geoff had merely had a spot of amber throat oil to wash down our pie suppers in the Ruskin Arms, where we had booked a couple of rooms for the night. Splendid pies they were too, although I'm now going to alienate two thirds of the East End by confessing that I had chips with mine. Sorry, but pie and mash doesn't do it for me. It's probably because I wasn't born and raised in east London – pie and mash just isn't in my DNA. Admittedly, there's a lot of pie and chips in my cholesterol, but that's another story.

As we walked from the Ruskin, which is notable for the fact that bands such as the Small Faces and Iron Maiden performed there, Di pointed out a number of personal landmarks to Geoff. These included where she went to secondary school and the place she was born. As a dutiful son Geoff understands the importance of such things and I am glad to report he is rightfully impressed by the East End heritage his mother has bequeathed him.

Inside the ground, once we had necked our beers (Carlsberg – probably the worst lager in the world) we made our way up to row K in the East Stand Upper and took our seats for the last time.

Sorry if the constant use of 'last time' is irritating, but everything we did that momentous day felt like the 'last time'. It was probably the last time we would go to East Ham station. Maybe the last time we would ever find ourselves in E13 at all. And certainly, most painful of all, it was the last time we would ever go to the Boleyn Ground.

Much is talked about 'atmosphere' by football supporters. In an FA Cup game four weeks previously, Manchester United fans had taunted us with 'Where's your famous atmosphere?' after the crowd had been temporarily silenced by a dismal performance from our lot. But, to all those Man U fans who couldn't make it all the way from Surrey for this particular encounter, let me assure you there was enough atmosphere to go round even before a ball had been kicked. If we could have bottled it, we'd have lent you some.

With the start delayed, the air of anticipation grew as we waited for the game to begin at the revised time of 8.30 p.m. The regulars who knew one another chatted among themselves. The not-so-regulars who, while we were drinking our last ever Boleyn Ground lagers downstairs, had busied themselves half-inching the packs containing free T-shirts and wrist bands that had been left on all the seats, busied themselves trying to look innocent. I'm pretty certain that I never would have worn a memorial T-shirt commemorating the closure of the stadium I loved, but I still hope the thieving bastard who nicked mine has to endure a lifetime of piles.

At one point there was a chorus of 'Stand up for the Boleyn Ground'. A strange thing to hear at a football stadium and rather late in the day to save the old place. Perhaps more of us should have done just that when the owners proposed the move, I thought to myself.

I didn't notice the brass band at first. I know, it's hard to miss a brass band on a football pitch, but I never have been noted for my powers of observation. They used to be quite the thing when I first went to football in the late '60s, but not so much now. Honestly, I really wasn't expecting one to turn up. By the time I became aware of their presence they were playing 'Abide With Me'.

In truth, I don't like 'Abide With Me': rather than reminding me of FA Cup finals it always makes me think of the funerals I've been to. I'll admit that, like most people, whenever I'm required to sing it I have to take a surreptitious glance at the hymn sheet to remind myself of the words (much as I now have to take a sneaky look at the programme to remind myself of opposition players' names), but the line 'Where is death's sting? Where, grave, thy victory?' is horribly familiar.

I'd been feeling funereal all day, and the combination of 'Abide With Me' and the images and names of departed West Ham legends being displayed on the big screen opposite me as the rain lashed down did nothing to lighten my gloom. For me, a picture of a young Graham Paddon, who died at the ridiculous age of just fifty-seven, was particularly poignant. He was one of my all-time favourite players and somehow represented the carefree period of my late teens, which were inextricably tied up with the Boleyn Ground.

I'd been interviewed by Adrian Chiles on Radio 5 live in the morning and he had commented on the fact that I sounded unbelievably sad. Well, I say interviewed. It was more a case of listening to what he thought about life and trying to get the odd word in where I could, but he did at least pick up on the fact I was seriously miserable.

My mood wasn't helped by the weather. Earlier in the day, when I was at home in Brighton (well, Hove actually), I thought the damp and misty conditions were down to a sea fret – a meteorological phenomenon that occurs on the coast from time to time. But on the train journey up from East Sussex to London it became apparent that the fog was widespread and my despair deepened. By the time the band got to the final line – 'In life, in death, Oh Lord, abide with me' – I was on the verge of tears. At which point I swallowed hard, wiped my moistening eyes and instructed the inner me to man up. It is, after all, only a game, and moving from one football stadium to another is no big deal.

Only it is for me. It was then, and it still is now we are in our new home. As any serious supporter knows, football is about so much more than the game. Each time we go to watch a match it is an event in itself. The expectation when you wake up and realise it's match day; the superstitions and rituals that precede a game; meeting up with friends you've made because of a common love of the same team; the joy that comes with a victory; the moaning and groaning that follows a defeat – they are all part of the deal. Take away the focal point of all that and things are bound to be different. I liked things just the way they were, thank you very much. I didn't want them to be different. In my experience, different generally means worse.

But, man up I did. You could say I manned up for Man Utd. The incredible rendition of 'Bubbles' that signalled the game was about to start helped. It may have been sung louder at the Boleyn Ground, but if it was I hadn't been there to hear to it. The idea of the free T-shirts, which came in claret or blue, was to ensure the club colours were displayed evenly around the ground the way brutal dictators who have been awarded the Olympics like to decorate their national stadiums in human wallpaper. (Not that I'm comparing West Ham's owners to a brutal dictatorship, you understand. I'm no big fan of the Gold, Sullivan and Brady troika, but even I wouldn't go that far.) Not everybody had bothered to put on their new shirt, and those of us who had been victims of grand larceny didn't have any new shirts to put on, so the visual effect wasn't quite what the organisers had been hoping for. But the singing was a different class.

There was a time, in the dim and distant past, when if you wanted a chorus of 'I'm Forever Blowing Bubbles' you had to sing it yourself. This new-fangled technology malarkey changed all that, of course, and now the first few lines of the chorus are belted out over the club's sound system. When you join in is largely up to you, this is a free country after all. But when you raise your arms to salute the team is critical if you want to avoid looking like a total muppet. Do not, I repeat do not, stand there with your arms aloft from the start. You wait until 'fortune's always hiding'. That is the law at West Ham. That's what we did when I was a kid on the North Bank; that's what my son has done ever since he first went as a six-year-old. If he can learn the drill while still at junior school, so can everyone else. But I digress.

The way 'Bubbles' was sung that night will live with me for ever. What followed was in the couldn't-make-it-up category. Well, you could have made it up, but on this occasion I haven't. In short, Diafra Sakho scored first to put us one-up after ten minutes. Two goals from Anthony Martial appeared to have put a dampener on what was already a damp evening, before Michail Antonio equalised in the seventy-sixth minute. (Trust me – the game really was far more exciting than it sounds here. For those of you who want to relive it, I'm planning on a more detailed description further on in the book – so keep reading!) Then, four minutes later, Winston Reid got his head to a Payet free kick, sending the ball back across David de Gea's goal into the far corner – and sending the West Ham fans wild with unadulterated, undiluted, unexpurgated delight. Sorry – that's probably more than enough uns for one sentence.

What I didn't know at the time was that there was a camera not far from me recording this historic moment. It had been strategically placed in the south-east corner of the ground, high on a ramshackle structure that was used as a pop-up TV studio by presenters whenever the cameras were at Upton Park. It had been put there by award-winning sports photographer Tom Jenkins a couple of hours before the game started. How he managed to get up there without incurring the wrath of the stewards or Sky TV, which was using the box that night, remains a mystery – but that's why Tom is an award-winning photographer (many, including me, believe he's the best in the business).

Tom operated the camera remotely from the other side of the ground when Reid scored, and got himself a brilliant picture. Well, actually, I've got a brilliant picture, because he gave it to me. As you will have gathered, Tom is a mate of mine. At the time we were colleagues on the *Guardian* – I have since retired – and when Tom decided to put together a video documentary for the paper's website about the history of the Boleyn Ground he asked me for a bit of background knowledge. I think he was under the impression that I had been at the first game played there against Millwall in 1904 (we won 3–0, in case you were wondering).

Anyway, of all the tributes to the old place – and there were a shedload in the run-up to the final game – Tom's was easily the best. My contribution was seriously negligible, but Tom presented me with his picture by way of a thank you for what I hadn't really done. It's in a frame above my desk as I write and I find it truly inspirational. Thanks again Tom – I'll even forgive the fact you're a Palace fan.

As I said, there was pandemonium in the ground when Reid scored – the Boleyn Ground rocked for one last time. And then, in the blink of an eye, referee Mike Dean blew the final whistle that marked the end of an era that had spanned my entire lifetime. West Ham United no longer played their football at Upton Park.

In the past, it was not unheard of for supporters to go on the pitch after the last home game of the season. This time – for the last, last game – there had been dire warnings to stay off the sacred turf, and notice was given that any pitch invasion would result in a lifetime ban for those who disobeyed orders.

There was some justification for the edict. The club had organised a farewell celebration featuring past players and black cabs (don't ask – it really was as tacky as it sounds) and they didn't want a bunch of numbskulls running on the pitch and spoiling it for everyone else.

So we sat dutifully in our seats while the players did a lap of honour and then, when the acrid smoke from a bunch of giant pitch-side flares had partially cleared, Sky TV presenters Ben Shephard and Bianca Westwood cracked on with the closing ceremony. Fair play to both of them – they did their best with what was pretty thin material. But it wasn't quite the Greatest Show On Earth, despite the pre-match hype that had hinted at something truly spectacular.

The sound system was terrible. Bianca's voice, in particular, was barely recognisable. Nevertheless, she managed a couple of decent interviews with Marlon Harewood and Carlton Cole, which prompted some of the faithful to exercise their vocal cords. To be honest, none of us at the Boleyn Ground ever needed a second invitation to belt out: 'Always believe in your soul, You've got the power to know, You're indestructible, Always believe in... Carlton Cole!'

Saddest moment of the night was the obvious plight of the once magnificent Martin Peters, who has been laid low by dementia. The taxis came and went, but none of them brought Peters' World Cup winning mate Sir Geoff Hurst. Neither did they bring the man many of us believe to be the greatest Hammer of them all – Billy Bonds. Afterwards, the diplomatic Bonzo said he got caught in heavy traffic and couldn't make it to the ground. Hmmm. It's no secret that Bonzo was never in favour of moving from Upton Park. Still, if he says he got stuck in traffic that's good enough for me.

Interspersed with the cabs and the former players, the big screens were showing tributes from supporters that had been filmed beforehand. And although Bonds wasn't there in person, there was footage of him at his imperious peak.

The commentary that accompanied the pictures had a familiar ring to it.

Just a very classy individual. He gave everything for the club and he was a leader in every sense of the word. He never hid. He had a personal integrity and decency about him. When you think he was actually voted Hammer of the Year when he had turned forty: it's inconceivable that anything like that could happen now. The greatest of them all is Billy Bonds who, for me, embodies everything this club is all about. He is West Ham in my eyes.

As I mentioned previously, the sound system was terrible. I asked Di if she recognised the voice booming out over the loudspeakers and she hadn't got a Scooby. 'That's me,' I told her. And then, to confirm this unlikely fact, my ugly mug appeared on the screens.

Di looked genuinely taken aback, but she wasn't as surprised as Eddy and Barry, who sat in the seats directly in front of us. As soon as they clocked me on the screen they were watching they spun round in unison demanding to know if that really was me. Somewhat sheepishly, I admitted it was. (Honestly, I'm really quite bashful by nature.) By this time, Geoff was getting texts from his mates asking him if he knew his dad was on telly – Sky was broadcasting the closing ceremony live. The bloke who sat next to me was curious too. 'You know someone here?' he asked in the way only an East Ender can pose that question. At that point, Bianca resumed her commentary. 'I know her,' I told my neighbour, which put an end to that particular conversation.

The reason I got to make my brief appearance on that historic night was entirely down to Bianca. She had asked me to join her at Upton Park a couple of weeks beforehand to do an interview for a Farewell Boleyn feature she was putting together for Sky, and while I was there she asked if I'd do a bit for West Ham TV as well.

The interview with Bianca was held outside the press box, in the seats reserved for the fourth estate, overlooking an otherwise empty ground. I think the word 'wistful' best sums up how I felt as I scanned the deserted stadium, knowing we would soon be parted for ever.

The interview with West Ham TV was held in a broom cupboard. I'm serious. On agreeing to speak to the two young men who were keen to film me I was ushered into a tiny, unlit closet and warned not to trip over the vacuum cleaner on the way to my seat.

Briefly, my mind flashed back thirty years to a time when I worked on the *Daily Express* in what was not-so-affectionately known as the Black Lubyanka in Fleet Street. It was a rabbit warren of a building, and when they moved the composing room I had trouble finding my way there. Knowing that my sense of direction is distinctly dodgy, a kindly printer by the name of Reg offered to show me a shortcut. I obediently followed him through a labyrinth of corridors, turning left and right with such frequency that I had no idea where I was going or where I had come from. Then we eventually reached our destination and, ever the gentleman, Reg opened the door and invited me to go first. By the time I realised I was in a cupboard he had shut the door and scarpered.

It took me some while to find my way back. I actually had to go out of the building and start again, taking the one route to the composing room that I was sure of. By the time I got there, every compositor in the room had been made aware of my detour. One hates to think the worst of colleagues, but I've sometimes wondered if the cheers that greeted my arrival that day were a touch sarcastic.

Back in the West Ham broom cupboard, I was now seated

and staring at an incredibly bright light as the interrogation came thick and fast. Who was my favourite West Ham player? What did I remember about Bobby Moore? What was the best goal I'd ever seen? Was I at the game against Cambridge when we got promoted? I was half expecting to be asked: Where were you on the night of the twelfth? At which point I would have asked for legal representation. They kept on about the Cambridge game, which I had been to but didn't regard as one of the greatest encounters I'd ever witnessed. Still, I answered their questions as best I could in the hope of getting a plug for my book and suspecting that I wasn't going to see sunlight again until I had given them everything I knew. When I finally got to ask a question, I quizzed them about when what they had just filmed would be shown. Then they became rather evasive. Never once did they let on that this, along with other footage they had, was destined to be shown on the last night. When it came up on the screens, I really was just as surprised as those around me.

So, interviewed by Adrian Chiles in the morning, and then appearing on Sky TV in the evening? Well, Brian, ain't you Billy Big Potatoes! Go on – I know that's what you're thinking. It's certainly what I'd be thinking. The thing is, all you have to do is knock out a book and the media immediately thinks of you as an expert. That's what happened after I wrote *Nearly Reach the Sky*, available at all good bookshops but not in the West Ham store (can't think why). Once they've got your name – as I was to discover the following day – they really don't let go. Go on, give it a try. Anyone can do it. Just tell the world why you support WHU in 100,000 words and you'll be on 5 live before you know it. Oh, and do pass on my regards to Adrian.

The final act of the closing ceremony was 'Bubbles' performed by Cockney Rejects. I suppose they had to find some way to get us to leave. Despite the threat of lifetime bans, a few characters emerged from what had been the Man Utd end and ran on to the pitch, hotly pursued by stewards. I figured that these weren't Mancs, these were blokes who didn't have tickets and let themselves into the ground as the Manchester fans were leaving. I had an inkling that I might have met one of those blokes, but more of him later. On the screens a guy wearing the club's emblematic No 6 shirt – long-since retired as a mark of respect to Bobby Moore – was shown turning off a switch, and with that the lights went out. 'Mr Moon has left the stadium,' we were informed for one last time. And we all knew he wasn't coming back.

Because of the delayed kick-off it was 11.30 p.m. by the time we left the ground. Most people had no choice other than to head off home. But because of the foresight of my brilliant wife, who had booked our hotel rooms weeks before, and our friendship with Eddy and Barry, who had introduced us to one of the few pubs that had got an extension that night, we were ready to party.

The weather was still pretty damp as we trudged along the Barking Road. When we got to Katherine Road I started to head off on our normal backstreet route towards the wonderfully named Overdraft Tavern, which is a few paces beyond East Ham station. But Geoff vetoed the idea. He wanted to stay with the crowd, savouring the walk up to the town hall, then turning left up High Street North one last time. And he was right.

The Overdraft, when we got there, was rammed. Only regulars were being allowed in and thanks to Eddy and Barry that is what we were now classed as. To be honest, we had expected more pubs to stay open late on what was a momentous night for the area. But we were in, and so were the beers. An East End pub on the night West Ham have beaten Man Utd in the final game at Upton Park. I'm sure you can picture the scene. At least, I hope you can because, to be honest, my recollection of the next two or three hours is somewhat hazy.

What I do recall is standing in the pouring rain outside the pub when they had finally called time and saying our goodbyes to Eddy, Barry and Ashley, an Australian journalist with whom we'd become friendly. And I seem to remember we shared a taxi with Barry, even though the Ruskin is no more than half a mile from the Overdraft. Other than that, it's all a bit of a blank until I was woken by my phone blaring out 'Staying Alive' at a few minutes past seven the following morning. (What do you mean, whose idea was it to have 'Staying Alive' as a ringtone? It was Geoff's actually – and I'll have you know that it is a marvellous ringtone.)

I generally have a pretty fair idea of where I am when I wake up, but on this occasion I wasn't entirely sure at first. What added to my confusion was being told that I had been woken up by the *Victoria Derbyshire* programme, which wanted to see me in their studio in double-quick time. Flattered though I was, I explained that I was in a hotel in East Ham and, more to the point, I hadn't yet had breakfast.

The well-spoken young lady from the BBC wasn't taking no for an answer, and informed me with the air of someone who usually got her way that she could arrange for a car to be outside the hotel asap. I asked her to give me a few minutes while I gathered my thoughts and said we'd talk later. In fact, we texted. I still have the exchange on my phone. 'Many thanks for agree-ing to appear on the programme at 10.40,' she wrote. Again, she mentioned the car, and asked me to let her know what I thought.

What I thought was that I hadn't agreed to anything and that I wanted some breakfast. What's the point of staying in a hotel if you don't have breakfast? I'd rather have a hotel room with no bed than one with no breakfast. Anyway, I declined. Neither was I tempted by the FaceTime or Skype options that she offered by way of an alternative. Instead, Di and I went downstairs, where we met up with Geoff and broke our fast.

After breakfast – which, incidentally, was extremely good despite the absence of bacon – we all went back upstairs to pack, having agreed to meet in the lobby shortly before the check-out deadline. When we three met again, this time without the thunder, lightning or rain of the previous day, Geoff asked me if I'd had the television on while we'd been packing. I told him that I hadn't. He had, though. In fact, he'd been watching the *Victoria Derbyshire* programme, which was heavily focused on the incident involving the Man Utd bus.

It seems there was quite a fuss, complete with pictures of a couple of smashed windows being shown over and over again plus endless speculation about the nature of football supporters – West Ham supporters in particular. Doing his best to defend the reputation of the vast majority of WHU followers was my friend David Blackmore, who also happens to be the editor of the admirable *Blowing Bubbles Monthly* fanzine. David, evidently, had failed to dodge the bullet that initially had my name on it.

For me, it really was a lucky escape. Had I accepted the invitation I would have found myself, without the benefit of a decent breakfast and mildly hungover, being grilled (unlike the absentee bacon) about a subject of which I had no knowledge. That was not an enviable prospect.

I subsequently learned that Man Utd had left their hotel in Canary Wharf at 5.30 p.m., apparently unaware that a large crowd had been gathering in Green Street from 4.00 p.m. Many of the people in that crowd didn't have tickets and those who did wouldn't have been able to get into the ground until 6.30 p.m. anyway. At 5.55 p.m, the coach reached Green Street. With little or no help from the police, who don't provide outriders for away teams playing in London, it took the Mancs seventy-five minutes to negotiate the final 600 yards of their journey. During that time, various cans and bottles were thrown at the coach. The word of choice for the tabloids the following morning was 'pelted'.

What can you say when quizzed about morons throwing things at buses other than no one in their right mind condones behaviour of that nature, but it must always be remembered that the culprits represent a tiny minority of football supporters. You could go on to point out that Man Utd and the police should have shown rather more common sense when considering how best to get a team bus through a large crowd of mainly hostile supporters, many of whom had been drinking for several hours, but that starts to sound dangerously like you are trying to defend the indefensible.

At least I was prepared when 5 live rang later that morning. 'Sorry,' I told Peter Allen, 'think of me as Arsène Wenger: I didn't see a thing. But it was a great game of football if you want to talk about that.' He didn't really. Neither did the independent radio stations that rang throughout the day. It got to the point when I said straight out that if you are calling about the bus don't bother going on because I can't answer questions about an event I didn't witness.

Besides, that wasn't really the question that most concerned me immediately after the final game at the Boleyn Ground. I was wondering what I would make of the new stadium and all that went with it. Just how would it shape up in comparison to the place I loved so much, and to which I had now said my final farewell?

3

The prawn
sandwich brigade

London Stadium
Sunday 21 August 2016
Kick-off: 4.00
Final score: West Ham 1–0 Bournemouth

THE FIRST HOME league game of the season should be a thrill
for any football supporter. When it's at an iconic new stadium it
should be doubly exciting. But I couldn't work up much enthusiasm on the train journey from Brighton.

I wanted to like the new place. Honest! For one thing, I'd
lumped out 800 quid for my season ticket. More importantly,
Geoff had convinced me that if his generation was to ever see
West Ham enjoy the success that I had been lucky enough to
witness, the club needed to make a significant upgrade and the
move to Stratford was the ideal opportunity to do so.

This was part of the conversation that followed his question about whether I'd sell my soul to stay at Upton Park some months earlier. He'd listened to my answer, and then made the case in favour of the move. He was eloquent and powerful. What's more, he was dead right that younger supporters should not be penalised because greybeards such as myself have an inbuilt mistrust of change.

So, despite my misgivings, I was looking to be positive. For a start, the short hop from St Pancras on the high-speed train was a bonus, although the walk to the ground from Stratford International, via the outer edge of Westfield, was a clear reminder of how different things were going to be from now on.

Much of that walk demands that you focus on the stadium itself. 'I'm the star of the show,' it is telling you. 'Forget what you are about to see once you are inside, look at Me, Me, Me!' And you do. However, there is no denying that it is an impressive structure that has a certain wow factor.

Another clear point in the stadium's favour is the toilets. Seriously. I really approve of the toilets. According to the informative literature that came with my new season ticket, there are 995 of them throughout the stadium. At the Juventus game I was rather taken aback by the positioning of tributes to the club's greatest players that gave the impression the urinals had been named after West Ham legends, but now I understood that I wasn't being asked to relieve myself of an expensive bottle of Heineken in the Martin Peters lavatory I felt a lot happier.

The PA system is better than Upton Park's as well, although judging by what I'd heard so far, the club had simply brought its old favourites from E13. If West Ham ever have the funds to update their record collection, I suggest they get themselves a copy of *Led Zeppelin IV*. I'm sure that every supporter making their way to the top of the stands would sing along, albeit ruefully, to the opening lines of one of the album's seminal tracks about a lady who's highly impressed by gold and is purchasing a stairway to heaven.

Strictly speaking, the stairways at the London Stadium are leased. But I can assure you, having made the climb myself, that once you reach the top the afterlife doesn't seem so far away. It's not just that you're up there with the angels, you have a heart rate that would interest any undertaker worth his salt.

The Juventus game had shown me how short of match fitness I was and some changes were clearly in order if I was going to get through the season. I decided to start with a healthier diet. No more hotdogs for me.

There's a handily placed branch of Marks & Spencer at St Pancras station, right by the escalators that take passengers up to the Javelin trains which whisk them off to Stratford International in just seven minutes. Di and I, having arranged to meet Geoff at the ground, slipped in there and bought a selection of sandwiches. It seemed fitting, now that West Ham were looking to attract a new kind of supporter, that at least one of them should be filled with prawns. Soft malted brown bread, of course.

We met Geoff as planned, ordered three pints from one of the pop-up bars opposite the stadium and savoured our oh-so-healthy sandwiches in the sunshine.

There were obviously a good number of people who were there for the first time. Those who had paid £60 or more to have their names, or the names of their loved ones, engraved in the area that had been dubbed Champions Place studied the paving as they searched for their personalised stones. Others simply mingled, taking in their new surroundings. Wherever you looked phones were being used to take pictures of smiling supporters with arms crossed to replicate the club badge.

We tried to enter the stadium using the same turnstile that we had gone through for Juventus, but 'J' was having none of it. Our season tickets clearly stated that we should go in via 'F', 'G' and 'H', and they weren't kidding. So we fought our way round to the designated gates and joined the queues waiting for the obligatory search (why is it, when you are trying to get to a designated spot outside a football ground, everybody else is going in the opposite direction?).

When we got to our seats it was evident that my new dietary regime still had some way to go. I was every bit as knackered as I had been for the Italian champions. I gave myself a few minutes to allow my blood pressure to return to something approaching normal and then began to cast an eye over the people around me.

Immediately adjacent was a father with two young children. The seats directly in front of us were empty, but that didn't strike me as particularly unusual because there were still a few minutes before kick-off. To the left of us there was a standard selection of West Ham supporters, including a guy about my age with whom we'd had a friendly chat during the Juventus game.

The seats in front were still empty when the players came out. I tried to focus on the two teams going through the usual preliminary routine on the other side of the pitch, and reminded myself to never forget my glasses. Without them, I might as well not be there.

What I could make out was that we were back in claret and blue rather than the dark blue strip we had worn for Juventus.

The kit for the showpiece encounter was similar to that worn by Thames Ironworks, a factory side that evolved into West Ham United in 1900. Tipping the club's hat in the general direction of our heritage was a nice touch. However, any brownie points that might have been gained with old-stagers like me two weeks previously were forfeited when I glanced at the freebie that had come with the match programme. This was the *Special Edition Hammers Heroes 2016/17 Sticker Album*, which was to house stickers that would come with the programme every home game. Unfortunately, the marketing geniuses behind this particular venture were not as familiar with West Ham heroes as they should have been. For a start, there was no space for Martin Peters. And, worse still in my eyes, Billy Bonds had been omitted as well. What were they thinking? A West Ham sticker album with no Billy Bonds is like a bacon sandwich with no bacon.

Andy Carroll and André Ayew were both in the sticker book but absent from the team line-up, having been injured the week before. Dimitri Payet was missing as well – the official reason was that he had failed a fitness test. On the plus side, we were about to see some of the summer signings in competitive action for the first time. Arthur Masuaku was in for the injured Aaron Cresswell at left back, Håvard Nordtveit had been drafted into midfield and Gökhan Töre was on the wing. Ashley Fletcher and Jonathan Calleri were on the bench.

The best bit of team news of all was that Slaven Bilić had finally come to the conclusion that Michail Antonio was no right back and had given the job to Sam Byram, who is. Antonio had endured a shocker the previous week at Chelsea in our first league game of the season, conceding a penalty after being caught in possession and later – to his obvious annoyance – being substituted. It was good to see him playing further forward once more.

Bournemouth started well, and Byram was called into action in the opening minutes. At the other end Antonio was starting to look like his old self. He nearly chased down a hopeful long ball from the back, then beat his marker and whipped in a cross that found its way to Töre, who promptly put his shot over the bar. A couple of minutes later Töre got another chance, again after a move involving Antonio. This time our Turkish winger put his shot wide.

Next to try his luck was Enner Valencia. First he had a shot blocked on the edge of the area. A minute later he sent in a piledriver from outside the area, but that too was blocked.

Töre was back in the action when he linked up neatly with Cheikhou Kouyaté on the edge of the box. The ball found its way to Mark Noble, but he failed to pick out a teammate and the move fizzled out. Five minutes later Noble did better with a pass from midfield that might have been interesting if Töre had been quicker to react.

Fifteen minutes had gone and not a shot on target. Of more concern was that Bournemouth were starting to get a foothold in the game. Their best attacks were coming down our left-hand side, where Masuaku looked good going forward but a touch shaky when it came to his defensive duties.

However, West Ham got themselves up the pitch once more and won a free kick just outside Bournemouth's box. This would have been perfect for Payet. In his absence, Töre tried his luck – and put the ball straight into the defensive wall in front of him.

Two minutes later and we were screaming for a penalty as

Valencia went down in the box. Referee Craig Pawson was unmoved. Soon after it was Valencia who was not moving – a crunching challenge had left him in a heap and the on-field treatment took several minutes before our Ecuadorian international was able to hobble to the sideline for an assessment by the medical team.

Thankfully he was fit to continue, and nearly made something of a cross from Masuaku. At least I think it was a cross. It might have been a shot. Our new signing had already let fly from forty yards. The lad was clearly keen to get his name on the scoresheet!

Valencia played a part in the next promising move, laying the ball off to Töre who in turn gave Antonio a shooting chance. Like the previous nine efforts, this was also off target. Four minutes later we finally managed to get a shot on target thanks to Valencia, but his effort was palmed away. Encouraged by that attempt, Valencia had a dig from the edge of the area. It took a diving save to keep it out.

Bournemouth looked to counter-attack, and won a couple of corners that came to nothing. But, other than that, neither goal came under serious threat before Mr Pawson decided enough was enough and called a halt to the first half.

Geoff decided to check out one of the 995 toilets and headed for the stairs. The two young women who took the seats in front of us ten minutes after kick-off and spent the rest of the time checking their mobiles decided to do the same thing. Unlike Geoff, they didn't come back.

Di and I decided to stay put. We asked one another if we felt any better about the seats we had bought. We didn't. But at least we'd got some – unlike fifty-six fellow supporters who had turned up and found they didn't. They had to sit on the concrete floor at the top of the stand and, naturally, they weren't happy about it. Some complained directly to the West Ham owners, but this one wasn't down to them. The failure to put in the seats was the responsibility of the stadium operators, LS185, who duly apologised and agreed to compensate the unhappy Hammers who had been left without seats.

That was the second seating issue in a matter of days. The new stadium had been designed to hold 60,000, but shortly before the Bournemouth game the London Stadium Safety Advisory Group announced that the capacity had been limited to 57,000 because of concerns about supporters standing. To underline the point, season ticket holders had all got a letter from Karren Brady reminding us that we were contractually obliged to remain seated and that anyone who failed to do so faced the very real possibility of having their ticket revoked.

A sizeable number of fans clearly did not take this warning seriously and had stood during the first half – often to the annoyance of those behind them. Below us, in the corner of the stand, the stewards had waded in more than once in an effort to get people to sit down. Their presence appeared to make a tense situation worse.

Several times in the first half the same chant had been heard in various parts of the ground: 'Stand up if you love West Ham!' The not-so-hidden message was: 'Stand up if you love standing up.' Unfortunately, not everybody does – especially those who aren't in the best of health or who have young children with them. It was an issue that was to resurface time and time again during the early part of the season.

The second half saw Bournemouth start brightly and win a corner, which Adrián flapped at before Byram cleared the danger. The keeper did better with a fierce shot from outside the area a couple of minutes later. The away side continued to cause us problems at the back, a free kick resulting in a half-chance for Josh King, then Jordon Ibe made a hash of a more clear-cut opportunity. Adrián was back in action soon after, brilliantly saving another piledriver from King.

The Hammers were struggling to get forward. When we did, good work by Noble was wasted by Masuaku and then Byram. The crowd was subdued, prompting taunts of 'Is this the Emirates?' from the Bournemouth fans.

With almost an hour gone Töre answered them on our behalf with an acrobatic volley at the far post which ended up in the side netting following a beautiful cross from Antonio. Then Noble played a great ball into the feet of Valencia, which he failed to control. That was the signal for Bilić to give him the hook, which did not go down well with the man from Ecuador. In his place we were given loanee signing Jonathan Calleri, who was making his Premier League debut. His initial contributions were encouraging, first chasing down a ball for which he was second favourite then, moments later, giving Antonio an opportunity with an incisive cross.

That said, the game had gone flat. Then Bournemouth's Harry Arter brought down Kouyaté and got a second yellow card with a little under fifteen minutes left. Both managers reacted to the sending off quickly: Eddie Howe's change was defensive while Bilić replaced Nordtveit with Fletcher, who promptly gave our attack some added impetus and set up a chance for Calleri.

The decisive breakthrough came in the eighty-fourth minute, following an attack down the right wing by Antonio. His cross failed to find a colleague in the penalty area, but it was picked up on the opposite flank by Töre. He cut inside and beat his marker, then delivered a lovely cross to the far post, where Antonio converted from close range with his head. Those of us in the stands who hadn't left early celebrated with a mixture of joy and relief.

In typical West Ham fashion we nearly managed to throw away the advantage in the final few minutes, but Reid and Adrián in particular ensured we got the three points that we just about deserved.

After the game Bilić praised us, the supporters, for our part in the victory. 'The atmosphere inside the stadium was brilliant,' he said. 'The fans helped big time with the atmosphere. I was a big fan of Upton Park. You know I'm not paid to hail the new stadium if I don't like it, but I felt it was proper today.'

Thanks Slav. I can only imagine that the atmosphere on your side of the ground was rather more lively than where I was.

At the same press conference we learned that Payet and Lanzini were expected to return soon – hopefully in time for a second leg Europa League tie against FC Astra Giurgiu of Romania the following Thursday – but the news was not so promising about Carroll and Ayew.

'With Andy and André it's long term,' said Bilić. So were we still in the market for a new striker? 'We're going to try to find a good one,' we were reliably informed. That's OK, then. What could possibly go wrong?

Boleyn Ground
Saturday 15 August 2015
Kick-off: 3.00
Final score: West Ham 1–2 Leicester City

As with the first season at the new stadium, the last season at the old ground found the Williams family sitting in different seats. The previous ones were on the end of a row, next to the stairway, just about level with the eighteen-yard line at the Bobby Moore end. We had moved because we'd become fed up with having our view of anything happening to our right blocked by people turning up late and leaving early, both for the game itself and at half time. It was incredibly irritating, particularly when something interesting occurred and the folk who were so keen to be on their way decided to stop and watch the action for a while. I often wondered if these were the same people who slowed down to gawp at an accident on the other side of a motorway. But perhaps that's unduly harsh.

The new seats – still in the East Stand Upper but on the other side of the gangway – were a big improvement. Transferring could have been more straightforward, though. The club set aside a weekend in April 2015 for season ticket holders who wanted to relocate, and I was on the phone shortly after the lines opened. After being told I was one-hundred-and-something in the queue I decided to have a cup of tea and try again in half an hour. When I phoned a second time I was again one-hundred-and-something, only this time the something was an even higher number. However, I opted to stick it out.

It was an hour and a half before I got down to single figures. I tried not to think what the phone bill was going to look like.

But, I told myself, this had to be done. Nine, eight, seven people ahead of me. It was only a matter of time now. Three, two, one… finally, I am next in line to be put through to the ticket office. And then the line went dead.

First I was dumbfounded. Then I was apoplectic. Di suggested another cup of tea, but that didn't quite cover it to be honest. I phoned again, and wasn't surprised to find I was back in the hundred-and-somethings. I didn't put myself through the torture of another countdown. Instead, I grabbed my coat, kissed Di farewell and headed for the station.

It takes the best part of two hours to get from Brighton to Upton Park, which meant my rage had subsided somewhat by the time I approached the ticket office window. Besides, I wasn't cross with the extremely helpful staff who were working there – it wasn't their fault the club had a crappy telephone system, no doubt another manifestation of the owners' decision to spend as little as possible on anything to do with the old ground once there was a move in the offing.

However, the good news was that they did have three seats together. Would I like to see them? You bet I would! Of course, I knew what the view would be like, but I wasn't going to pass up the chance to see the stadium when it was empty.

A steward was summoned to escort me to the East Stand. As we walked around the touchline – I was under strict instruction not to go on the playing surface – he told me that I wasn't the only person who'd experienced problems over the phone. Apparently several people had turned up in person complaining about being cut off after epic countdowns similar to the one I had experienced.

As we passed the dugout my escort asked me if I'd like my

photo taken in the manager's seat. How thoughtful was that? Pictures taken, we continued our walk round the ground. And how did I repay this man's kindness? I let him get a few paces ahead of me and then cut across the corner when he wasn't looking, simply for the thrill of being on the hallowed turf. I'm not proud of myself.

When I sat in the manager's padded chair its rightful occupant was Sam Allardyce. As I sat in my new seat waiting for the game against Leicester to kick off it had become the property of Slaven Bilić.

I, for one, was pleased about the change. After four years of Allardyce we needed something different. Big Sam to his supporters, Fat Sam to his detractors, the departed gaffer had been divisive and we required someone who could unite the fans by offering us some hope of a return to the fabled West Ham Way. Bilić – a former player, occasional rock guitarist, successful international manager and self-confessed socialist with a law degree – seemed as good a choice as anyone else who was available at the time.

Yes, in his playing days he had left us to join Everton in 1997 after being at Upton Park for little over a year, but on the plus side he had chosen to see out a difficult season in an effort to prevent West Ham being relegated. As we finished just two points above the drop zone that seemed more than just an empty gesture. He clearly had some affection for all things claret and blue, which was just as well because the first game of the last season at the Boleyn Ground had been declared 'claret and blue day' by the owners.

I have to admit I rather missed the point of that. To me, every game at the Boleyn Ground was claret and blue day but, hey,

I'm just a supporter and don't have the insight of the owners and their highly trained team of marketing executives. It was certainly better than a sticker book with no room for a sticker of Billy Bonds MBE, former club captain, four-time Hammer of the Year and My Hero.

I did like the retro cover on the programme, though. It described itself as 'a modern representation of West Ham United's Southern League programmes from the 1908/09 season'. Inside there was an informative piece explaining that although Thames Ironworks printed the odd programme, West Ham itself didn't produce any until the 1907/08 season – three years after the move to the Boleyn Ground. The early programmes went by the name of the *Hammers' Gazette* and ran to sixteen black-and-white pages. I bet none of them featured a picture as good as the one on page fifty-three of the modern-day version though. It's hard to do it justice in words, but basically it's a photo of the ladies and gents toilets in the East Stand. I know that doesn't sound all that inspiring, but it has a strange, haunting quality. I still turn to it occasionally when the loss of the old ground becomes too painful to bear.

Bilić had got off to a shaky start with a Europa League campaign that had come unstuck against FC Astra. However, the week before we played Leicester, in his first Premier League game as manager, he had taken West Ham to the Emirates and beaten Arsenal. Star of the show was young Reece Oxford, which prompted a cracking joke along the lines of: 'What do you find in a sixteen-year-old's pocket?' Answer: a mobile phone, fake ID and Mesut Özil.

We did not fare quite so well against Leicester, however, losing 2–1 and seeing Adrián sent off when he went up field for a corner in a last-gasp search for an equaliser. Instead of scoring, he put his studs in Jamie Vardy's chest in a challenge that was reminiscent of the 1970s and promptly got a red card.

Ah well, I told myself as we walked along the Barking Road in the direction of the Denmark Arms, we may be moving grounds but some things about West Ham never change. One week we beat the mighty Gooners, the next we lose to a bunch of no-hopers like Leicester who – let's face it – were never going to win anything.

4

Don't tell Geoff

London Stadium
Saturday 10 September 2016
Kick-off: 3.00
Final score: West Ham 2–4 Watford

BEFORE THE MOVE to the new stadium I'd never left a West Ham game early in my life. Neither had Di. Then came the Watford match and that all changed. Please, don't judge us until I've explained why we did it.

After half an hour we were 2–0 up and cruising. In the twenty days since our less-than-convincing victory against Bournemouth things hadn't gone well for West Ham. We'd been knocked out of Europe by FC Astra, the team that had wrecked our hopes the previous season, and been beaten convincingly by Man City at the Etihad. However, there had been an international break and the rest seemed to have done the team good. Payet and Lanzini were back in the side and loan signing Zaza was making his debut. Two headed goals from Antonio appeared to have guaranteed a comfortable afternoon when I turned to Di and joked: 'Just wait 'til we're 4–2 down. Then we're out of here.'

Despite this being our eighth competitive game of the new season, Payet was actually making his first start since playing so well for France in the Euros. He was outstanding for the first thirty minutes, delivering an out-swinging corner for Antonio to score the first and then bringing out the rabona, wrapping his right leg round the back of his left, to set up Antonio for his second goal of the game and fourth of this Premier League campaign.

'We've got Payet,' echoed all around the ground as our fabulous Frenchman dropped a shoulder here and bamboozled a defender there. Lanzini, Kouyaté, Noble and Antonio took their lead from the master. I swear that in that first half-hour there were more step overs than steps leading up to row seventy-three. Watford were lucky to be just two down. Antonio could have had a hat-trick and Payet himself might have scored in the opening couple of minutes but for a diving stop by Watford keeper Heurelho Gomes. Soon after the first goal, Hornets' defender Daryl Janmaat did his best to gift us a second but his back pass to no one hit the post; next, Lanzini had produced a delicious left-foot shot that just eluded the other upright.

And then it all turned to custard. The Watford fightback began four minutes before the break when James Collins deflected a shot by Odion Ighalo past Adrián, who was diving the other way. More alarmingly, two minutes into stoppage time, the Ginger Pele and our increasingly jittery keeper teamed up to produce a comedy double act that was pure gold. As Adrián charged towards the edge of the box Collins deftly headed the ball over his onrushing partner. Troy Deeney collected the ball, allowed our very own Chuckle Brothers a chance to hurtle back towards the line – and then chipped it over both of them into the far corner. You gotta laugh.

It was reported later that the Watford half-time team talk centred on the fact that they didn't much care to have the mickey taken out of them with rabonas, step overs and all the other flicks and tricks, and that they were jolly well going to show the showboaters that they weren't there to be made fun of. (That may not have been the exact language used, you understand.) Anyway, whatever was said, it did the trick.

Étienne Capoue put the visitors ahead in front of their fans after fifty-three minutes when the ball fell to him at the back post. The ever-obliging West Ham defence gave him all the time he needed to take aim and fire home a left-foot shot. As for the fourth goal, scored by José Holebas ten minutes later, the less said the better. My only advice, if you ever find yourself in the company of Adrián, is don't ask him if he recalls the match.

Bilić's summing up after the game was as succinct as it was accurate. 'We cannot defend like that or we are not going to win a single game.'

It would be wrong to blame one man for the team's defensive frailties, but those players whose terms of employment require them primarily to stop the other side scoring generally take their lead from their goalkeeper. Watching Adrián's performance it was hard to believe that he had spent the international break on duty with Spain. He didn't play in their friendly against Belgium, but he had obviously done enough to earn a place in the squad. He couldn't expect to stay in there for long with displays such as the one we had just witnessed.

One man who knew a bit about holding down a place in the Spanish team was now ideally placed to give him some advice on the subject. Álvaro Arbeloa, who had helped Spain win the World Cup in 2010 and back-to-back European Championships in 2008 and 2012, had signed for the Hammers on transfer deadline day. He hadn't played against Watford, but I was really looking forward to seeing him in action. Admittedly, at thirty-three he was no spring chicken. But this guy had real pedigree – you don't spend seven years at Real Madrid if you're not top quality. Perhaps we were going to the next level after all.

Arbeloa was the thirteenth and final summer signing. Who says thirteen is an unlucky number? All right, we hadn't signed any of the big-money strikers we were chasing but, not only had we bought Ayew, we had tempted Zaza from Juventus with a loan deal that was designed to become a permanent £20 million transfer after fourteen appearances.

We'd also taken up the option to sign Lanzini on a four-year deal from United Arab Emirates club Al Jazira for an undisclosed fee. The 23-year-old Argentinian had completed a season-long loan in which he'd shone alongside Payet. He wasn't exactly a new face, but it was certainly a statement of intent.

Persuading Lanzini to wear a claret and blue shirt at the start of the previous season had convinced us all that Bilić really did have an eye for talent. His biggest coup had been getting Payet to leave Marseille and come to Upton Park. But he'd also signed Antonio, Angelo Ogbonna and Pedro Obiang, as well as Darren Randolph, who had performed heroics in our FA Cup run. If the summer signings that preceded the move to the new stadium were as good we really did have cause to be optimistic.

Of the midfielders, Sofiane Feghouli and Gökhan Töre looked

the most exciting prospects. Feghouli, an Algerian international, had been dubbed 'the new Zidane' as a seventeen-year-old. He never quite lived up to it – who could? – but success in the French top flight earned him a move to Valencia, which is where we had got him from on a free transfer. He had made his debut in the away leg of the tie against NK Domžale and, if the television pictures were anything to go by, he looked as if he could be quite a handful out wide on the right. Better still, he had scored in the return leg the following week in what, of course, was West Ham's first game at the new stadium. That was the victory that had taken us to the Europa League play-offs and another chance to be beaten by the team the fans had nicknamed Vauxhall Astra before the inevitable car crash.

Töre, who is two years younger, had spent a couple of years at Chelsea in the reserves between 2009 and 2011. From there he moved to Hamburg, then Rubin Kazan in Russia before settling in his native Turkey with Beşiktaş, where he worked under Bilić. He certainly had a colourful past, once threatening two teammates from his national side with a firearm over a reported affair with his girlfriend, and the following year getting himself shot in an Istanbul nightclub. If nothing else, he'd be able to handle himself in the pubs and clubs of Basildon.

With more defensive duties in mind, we had acquired Norwegian international Håvard Nordtveit on a free from Borussia Mönchengladbach. As a kid, one of my favourite jokes had always been: Who's the most unpopular person in Germany? Answer – the man at a Borussia Mönchengladbach game who shouts 'give us a B!' Did Nordtveit have a sense of humour, I wondered? Judging by the fact he had spent four years under the hilarious Arsène Wenger at Arsenal without making a single first-team appearance I suspected the answer might be yes. Judging by what we'd just seen from our back four, he was going to need it.

Up front, as part of the hunt for the twenty-goal-a-season striker, we'd brought in Argentinian Jonathan Calleri from Uruguayan club Deportivo Maldonado on a free and purchased Ashley Fletcher from Man Utd for £750,000. Calleri, we were told, had scored goals for fun in South America's continental club competition and was decidedly hot property. Meanwhile Fletcher, who had never actually turned out for the Mancs, had been on loan at Barnsley, where he'd scored five times in twenty-one appearances. Bilić must have seen something in him. Despite the hype, based on what little evidence we had, it was hard to see these two scoring twenty goals between them.

A more intriguing prospect was Antonio Martínez López, known to his friends as Toni Martínez. He had represented Spain at under-seventeen and under-nineteen level, having played for the Real Murcia and Valencia youth teams. We'd handed over £2.4 million for him. Those in the know reckoned he could be one to watch in the future.

Even younger, and an even better prospect if the club's website was to be believed, was Domingos Quina. It described the teenage Portuguese striker as 'outstanding' and reckoned that West Ham had done well to beat some of Europe's leading sides to his signature. And, as we all know, if it's on the club's website it must be true.

Left back Masuaku probably thought he was going to have to wait a while before he saw any serious first team action when he joined from Greek champions Olympiacos for £6.2 million. But Aaron Cresswell's injury in a pre-season friendly had catapulted the Frenchman into Bilić's starting XI for the four Premier League games we'd played up to this point. From what we'd witnessed, he looked good going forward, but suspect when asked to defend. Welcome to West Ham Arthur. Don't worry mate, we've had plenty like you in the past.

While Zaza and Arbeloa were putting pen to paper at the London Stadium in the final week of the transfer window, the lesser known figure of Edimilson Fernandes signed up for a four-year deal after West Ham paid Swiss Super League side FC Sion £5.5 million for his services. In his final season in Switzerland, despite being aged just nineteen, he had made thirty-nine appearances in all competitions, including eight Europa League ties. Sion finished second in their group behind Liverpool, making it through to the round of thirty-two. Don't scoff. West Ham's owners would rip your arm off for the round of thirty-two.

So, that had been West Ham's transfer window. It's fair to say it had left most supporters underwhelmed. One of the big selling points of the new stadium was that moving to Stratford would attract better players. That clearly hadn't happened. The owners had talked a good game, but did they really have the ambition to make West Ham a top club that regularly won trophies and qualified for European football? Time alone would tell.

As things stood after the Watford game, European qualification looked somewhat distant. We had now played four and lost three, with a goal difference of minus four. Everyone tells you that tables are meaningless at this stage of the season, but they don't make for comfortable reading when you are one point out of the relegation zone, with only Southampton, Sunderland and Stoke below you.

Perhaps the atmosphere inside the stadium wouldn't have

been quite so toxic if the results had been better. But, whatever the reason, there was no denying that there were tensions in various parts of the ground. And, on more than one occasion, those tensions erupted into violence.

There were ugly scenes as West Ham supporters fought with Watford fans, stewards and each other at various times during the game. Ten people were ejected, and the club felt compelled to threaten lifetime bans to anyone involved in crowd trouble.

The stewarding came in for a lot of criticism. They were employed by LS185 and many of the 300 stewards who had worked at Upton Park either didn't want a job at the new stadium or didn't have the necessary qualifications. What they did have, though, was common sense – an attribute that seemed to be in short supply in Stratford. There were reports that some people standing in the back row were told to sit down. One supporter complained that he was ordered to get back into his seat – until he explained that he was leaving the ground.

The club wanted the police to work alongside the stewards, but the Met declined the invitation – saying they were unable to do so without a satisfactory radio system in the stadium. Deputy assistant commissioner Peter Terry said: 'Until there is comprehensive Airwave radio coverage throughout the ground, officers will not be routinely deployed within it under a special services agreement.' He added that the issue had been raised with the stadium operators two years previously, but was still unresolved. Well, who needs a radio system in a stadium packed with 57,000 football supporters?

Segregation was always going to be an issue with the way the stadium was designed. I guess it wasn't a problem at the Olympics. I'm no expert on athletics, but it's my understanding that people who follow the sport generally don't get quite as vexed about a Romanian pole-vaulter having the effrontery to come to their manor and pick up the gold medal as followers of the Beautiful Game do when they've just lost at home. Which might explain why football grounds and athletics stadiums are constructed differently.

There was some attempt to keep rival fans apart on the concourse, using internal movable partitions that corralled the away support when closed and which could then be rolled back to restore the original open-plan design at other events. And stewards were positioned between rival supporters once they were in their seats. However, the potential for rival fans to clash appeared to be far greater than it was at Upton Park.

I'll concede that it was not easy to foresee West Ham supporters knocking lumps out of each other, but the standing issue could have been tackled more intelligently than it was.

Like it or not, in two distinct sections of Upton Park supporters had defied the edict to sit down with the tacit agreement of the stewards. If you didn't want to stand you didn't go to the Bobby Moore Lower or Chav corner. It didn't require a genius to know that most of the people who stood at the Boleyn Ground would want to stand at the new stadium. Premier League rules meant that the club could not officially sanction a standing-only section, but if the fans who stood had been able to migrate together, rather than having been scattered all around the London Stadium, there would not have been anything like the number of problems that the inexperienced security staff found themselves having to deal with.

It was evident from my crow's nest in the back row that there was a recurrent problem in the north-east corner below me.

Supporters towards the front stood up, those behind them complained and tempers frayed. Occasionally things boiled over, and punches were thrown. Watching supporters of your own club fight among themselves is a truly depressing sight.

If words alone could have solved the problem, we'd have been home and hosed. Before the game, joint-chairman David Sullivan had penned a piece for the match-day programme in which he said:

> We are expecting another capacity crowd this afternoon, but the demand for tickets has never been higher and we are still seeking permission from the London Stadium safety advisory group to take that up to 60,000. For this to happen we need our fans to remain seated throughout the game.
>
> We fully understand that this is a difficult issue, but the rules on this matter are absolutely clear and persistent standing is strictly forbidden under the Premier League's stadium regulations.
>
> I would therefore ask all our supporters who like to stand to show due respect and consideration for their fellow fans, especially those with disabilities or attending with children who are having their experience at London Stadium ruined by other individuals in front of them.

After the game West Ham issued a statement:

> The club now appeals to all supporters to come together and support West Ham in the famous way we have historically been so proud of. It is important that we recognise the vast majority who have attended the first five fixtures played at London Stadium have been outstanding with their behaviour and support. They, like all

at West Ham United, do not want their reputation or the club's
to be tarnished by the minority.

But what was being done to solve the problem? 'The club is
doing everything possible within its jurisdiction to help provide
a safe and enjoyable environment for all supporters,' we were
told. 'The club is working hard to move like-minded supporters
into areas to enhance their match-day experience.'

This line of defence was supported by the operators. An LS185
spokesman said: 'We remain determined to ensure that all supporters can enjoy the best possible match-day experience in a safe and
secure environment and fully support West Ham's efforts to migrate supporters attending in family groups to dedicated sections.'

But there weren't many seats left unsold to which dissatisfied
customers could be moved. The London Stadium has a capacity
of 57,000; 52,000 season tickets sold; a typical allocation to the
away team of 2,800 tickets – you do the maths (because you will
almost certainly do it better than me). Anyway, there weren't
many seats available.

Some people were moved. We weren't among them, despite
notifying the club of our displeasure with what we had been
sold immediately after the Juventus game. Our problem wasn't
people standing in front of us. In fact, the one good thing about
the back row was that you could stand whenever you wanted –
as long as an over-enthusiastic steward didn't happen to spot you
and decide that rules are rules. We just thought we'd been ripped
off. We had paid for band two seats and what we had bought
simply didn't merit the outlay.

I saw a post on Facebook that compared the view from the
back of the stadium with watching your kid play Subbuteo

while you're in the loft. I'd say that was a very fair assessment. And while that was the biggest problem, there were other issues, too. The deadly lack of atmosphere, for one thing. And the time it took to leave the stadium for another.

It had taken us an age to get out of the ground after the Bournemouth game. Sitting where we did, there were a lot of people on the stairway in front of us at the final whistle. It was a long, slow shuffle to get to the exit. Then, to compound matters, there was a large crowd between us and the station when we were finally out of the stadium, which meant we got caught up in the shambles caused by an army of stewards with stop-go boards who were posted at a strategic point to control the flow of people on Stratford Walk. Being kettled is not a pleasant experience.

A lot of people had already left the ground when I turned to Di and reminded her of the joke I had made earlier. Geoff wasn't with us – he had gone on holiday to Colombia. The things young people do today – I ask you. If he had been there, he'd never have consented to an early departure. (We brought that boy up properly.) But without his puritanical control, we were able to make our own decisions.

We dithered for a while. As I said, neither of us had ever done anything like this before. We weighed up the pros and cons. On the negative side of the equation, we didn't like the stadium, we didn't like our seats, we didn't like the way West Ham had decided to play like a circus team, we didn't like the time it took to get to the exits and we didn't like the stop-go boards. As for the positives: there were none that we could see right then. So we did it. We got up, headed to the gangway and left early. And the world kept spinning.

There must have been about ten minutes left. We were

sure West Ham weren't going to score again. In fact, when we watched the highlights on *Match of the Day* it was Watford who looked more like scoring in the dying minutes. We got back to the station without being kettled, caught the train back to St Pancras and settled down to a couple of well-deserved pints in a nearby pub. We couldn't decide who would tell Geoff what we had done when he returned from South America.

Boleyn Ground
Saturday 22 August 2015
Kick-off: 3.00
Final score: West Ham 3–4 Bournemouth

In the corresponding game at Upton Park Geoff was there, but we weren't. We had gone to a family barbecue instead, and a seriously good time we had, too. However, because this book is essentially an attempt to compare the final season at the Boleyn Ground with the first year at Stratford, I think it is worth recording what happened in E13 that day. So I'll get Geoff to tell the story:

I remember it being a really nice day. Because Mum and Dad couldn't go I went with a couple of friends who don't actually support West Ham. But Kieran (Man City-ish) and Stevan (Leeds) are football fans, and they were both keen to see what they knew was a special ground.

There are few sights like the East End on a glorious summer's day when West Ham are at home, and I remember walking down Green Street and seeing Kieran and Stev being slightly in awe, and then seeing those same expressions when 'Bubbles' was sung as the teams came out.

In an attempt to embrace the proper lads' match-day experience we went to put some bets on the game at the bookies at the end of the East Stand Upper concourse. We occasionally have a punt online, but none of us had actually placed a bet in person before. So after a few minutes of figuring out what we wanted to do, in stereotypical millennial fashion, we decided that it would be easier to just stand next to the kiosk and put bets on using our phones.

Kieran and Stev both backed West Ham so they had genuine reason to cheer on a home win, which I appreciated. I had a feeling that this wasn't going to be the runaway victory that everyone expected – everyone not associated with West Ham, that is. So I thought it would be a good idea to put a few quid (at understandably good odds) on Bournemouth as a sort of insurance policy. Safe to say that the winnings did not cheer me up at all.

Aaron Cresswell was at fault for Bournemouth's first two goals but, impressively, he still wasn't the worst West Ham full-back in that game. That award went to Carl Jenkinson.

It was typical West Ham to be 2–0 down to Bournemouth at home at half time, as I informed Kieran and Stev over a plastic bottle of Carlsberg (which was cold, at least) during the break. They knew.

I was convinced that there were still goals in the game, and despite the score I was optimistic we could get a result. We quickly got it back to 2–2, at which point it felt like the win was a given, but somehow we let them get a third and then Bournemouth sealed their first ever Premier League win after Jenkinson gave away a late penalty and got sent off in the process. It would turn out to be one of the few red cards or penalties given against us that season that I couldn't complain about.

Before the game I was particularly worried about Darren Randolph. I had watched him a bit in pre-season and European qualifiers and he struck me as awful, which is quite hard to achieve as a goalkeeper when you don't have much to do. Perhaps his signing looked particularly bad compared with the others we'd made that summer. To add to that, it was in the news that in his past two games against Bournemouth (yes, Bournemouth) he'd conceded twelve (yes, twelve) goals. Reflecting on the game I actually thought he'd done well, despite conceding four (yes, four) goals. Football is a bizarre game sometimes.

Even though we lost, ultimately I was pleased that Kieran and Stev had been to see a brilliant game (for non-West Ham fans, at least). It had a bit of everything – goals, penalties, a hat-trick, a red card, even a Modibo Maïga goal! If they'd come to see a dull draw or even a 1–0 win from a Mark Noble penalty – the likes of which we'd become accustomed to under the recently departed Sam Allardyce – it wouldn't have done the Boleyn justice.

5

We could have played all night

London Stadium
Sunday 25 September 2016
Kick-off: 4.00
Final score: West Ham 0–3 Southampton

THERE WEREN'T MANY West Ham fans still in the London Stadium when Southampton scored their third and final goal. A couple of minutes later, when referee Jonathan Moss finally put us out of our misery, those who had stuck it out to the end made sure the bedraggled rabble in claret and blue trooping off the pitch with metaphorical tails between their legs were left in no doubt how we felt about their lacklustre performance.

It was a miserable end to a miserable afternoon in what was turning into a miserable season.

Following the last home league against Watford, West Ham

had struggled to beat Accrington Stanley in the League Cup – it took a Payet free kick to produce the single goal of the game in the sixth minute of time added on – and then we got tonked at West Brom.

While we were getting battered by the Baggies at the Hawthorns, Di and I had taken ourselves off for a few days in Palma. What a fantastic city! If you've never been, I can't recommend it highly enough. Be sure to take the wooden train to Soller, a beautiful little town with a magnificent church. But – and here's a tip you'll thank me for one day – catch the bus back. The train isn't particularly comfortable, and the Mallorcan mountains look much the same coming back as they do going out. Seen one mountain and you've seen 'em all if you ask me.

Palma not being short of the odd visitor from the UK, we thought we might find somewhere that was showing the game live, but drew a blank. Instead we watched the humiliation on *Gillette Soccer Saturday* in a pub. Three–nil down at half time, West Ham conceded a fourth in the second period before Antonio and Lanzini added a veneer of respectability to the scoreline.

That defeat, coupled with results the day before our televised Sunday fixture against the Saints, meant we were now in the bottom three. By the time Southampton had finished with us, there were some who were starting to think that would be where we'd spend the rest of the season.

Injuries weren't helping. Not only were we missing Sakho, Carroll and Ayew up front, Masuaku had joined the walking wounded. The good news was that Reid was back after missing the West Brom game. Arbeloa, who had played against the Baggies and made his home debut against Accrington Stanley, came into the side as a makeshift left-back.

The first half started well enough, on the pitch and in the stands. Some supporters were standing. There were announcements that 'customers' who refused to sit down faced the risk of ejection from the ground, and in various places stewards could be seen talking to fans, urging them not to stand. However, the general mood didn't feel as confrontational as it had in previous weeks and the stewarding definitely had a lighter touch about it.

Both teams worked hard to carve out chances, but they all came to nothing. Until the fortieth minute, that is. That's when Ryan Bertrand cut the ball back for Charlie Austin to score with the first shot on target. It had to be Austin, of course. This was the striker David Sullivan had said we wouldn't sign because of concerns over his long-term fitness – in particular a dodgy knee. Austin had called the accusation an 'outrageous slur', and it was evident from his celebration that he took some pleasure in ramming the words back down the throat of our co-owner.

To emphasise the point that both Austin and his right knee were in rude good health, he set up the second for Dušan Tadić with a brilliant first-time ball just after the hour mark. James Ward-Prowse put the final nail in our coffin in the second minute of time added on.

The Southampton fans clearly enjoyed themselves. In fact, it was becoming something of a trademark for the new stadium. The away supporters had a party, while we ended up with a wake. 'We've got more fans than you,' sang our cheery visitors. They also helpfully pointed out that we should have stayed at Upton Park. I concurred.

To be fair to the Southampton fans, the previous year at Upton Park they had come up with one of the best opposition chants I can recall in my fifty-plus years of following West Ham.

Anybody who ever went to Upton Park will know about Mr Moon. Sadly, his services were dispensed with when we moved to the London Stadium, so for the benefit of newcomers and tourists, let me explain. The code for an incident that required the stewards' attention at the Boleyn Ground was: 'Mr Moon is in the ground'. When the incident had been dealt with we were informed that Mr Moon had left the stadium, which generally produced a huge roar of approval. The comings and goings of Mr Moon were reported while we were losing 1–0 to Southampton and not playing particularly well. Which prompted the immortal put down: 'Mr Moon has left because you're shit!' That really was magnificent work boys – I salute you. When, in the second half, West Ham took the lead we responded, to the obvious tune, with: 'Oh when the Saints, go two–one down,' but I have to admit you won the battle of the insults that day.

Di and I didn't hang around to exchange pleasantries with our guests from Southampton. We headed for the station, hoping above hope not to be forced to endure the stop-go experience that was fast becoming part of our new match-day routine. I really wasn't in the mood for the stop-go game.

After the match, Slaven Bilić hit the nail on the head. 'They deserved to win. We didn't,' he said.

Mark Noble told Sky Sports, which had been broadcasting our humiliation to the nation: 'I thought we started all right and then "bang" we conceded a goal and we never looked back in it. If I'm honest it could have been six in the end. Adrián pulled off some good saves and, on the bright side, I don't think it can get any worse. Eleven goals [conceded] in three games is laughable and it's not good enough. I think we could have kept playing until tonight and we wouldn't have scored.'

That man has got a career in punditry ahead of him when he packs up playing if you ask me.

As with previous games, it would be wrong to single out one player for criticism – in this case most of them were woeful. It's true, as our club captain pointed out, that Adrián made some decent saves, but the rush of blood that caused him to come charging out, allowing Tadić to skip round him for the second goal, was another in a string of worrying decisions by the keeper. The team as a whole looked lost and confused. Players who had performed so well the previous season were simultaneously undergoing a startling dip in form. Reid, Ogbonna, Noble, Kouyaté, Lanzini and even Payet all looked like they had barely been introduced to one another. Only Antonio appeared to be firing on all cylinders. As for the summer imports, they just looked like they needed firing: Arbeloa was a shadow of the player I had seen on TV playing for Real Madrid and Spain. Nordtveit, I decided, was well out of his depth in the Premier League. Feghouli was unconvincing and Zaza was hopeless. It's fair to say, we were still some way short of the next level.

Things had got so bad that serious newspapers were starting to publish long, in-depth pieces about the crisis at West Ham. I had been asked to write one myself while in Palma, but declined the commission on the basis that I was on holiday and would rather spend my hard-earned vacation sipping cold beers by a swimming pool than sitting in my hotel room pounding away at the keyboard. I could try to convince you that I was standing up for the terms and conditions of journalists everywhere, but the truth is I am genuinely bone idle.

The press was having much fun at our expense over the fact it was now possible to buy popcorn and ice cream at the stadium, suggesting that we as a club had turned our back on tradition, with pie and mash being one of the early victims. I'll be honest and admit that I'm not a big fan of popcorn. But, then, I'm not a big fan of pie and mash either. I will, however, eat an ice cream in the right circumstances. Does a football match constitute the right circumstances? Well, not for me. But I don't think just because Ben and Jerry's excellent product was now available as a half-time option was, in itself, responsible for West Ham being in the bottom three with one win out of six league games and a goal difference of minus nine. What it did demonstrate, though, was a vision for the club that did not tally with mine.

For me, there was so much to dislike about the new stadium that it was hard to focus on what was important and what was peripheral. I didn't like the fact there was a running track between the supporters and the pitch; I didn't like the design that had produced stands in which the back seats were so far from the action; I didn't like the fact that the ground was no longer in a residential area with easy access to all the amenities that I associated with football. None of that could be changed, at least not without the aid of several bulldozers.

What pained me was that, deep down, I knew that if I was going to continue supporting West Ham in the flesh, these were realities I was simply going to have to swallow. But I didn't have to accept that the ticketing policy was (a) correct and (b) unalterable.

The club had introduced a so-called plus-two policy, which enabled season ticket holders to not only buy one for themselves, but also allowed for two more tickets to be purchased. OK, I understood the business reasons that prompted the club to break an age-old tradition and offer those without a season ticket a chance to buy before those who did have one had exercised their option. I didn't agree with the policy, but I realised they were desperate to fill the place. However, I was having difficulty with whether or not the people who – like us – had left it late before deciding to renew their season tickets were being offered the equivalent of what they had before.

Because the stadium was still being worked on when season tickets went on sale, everyone had to take the club's word for it when it promised that the unseen seats they were buying were equivalent to the ones they had at the Boleyn Ground. Some people were clearly happy with their new seats. Others had every right to feel aggrieved that what they got was not what they were promised.

Also, it had been decided to make 10,000 season tickets available to anyone under the age of sixteen. The popcorn, the ice cream, the sticker book: they were all there for the kids, of course. Now, let me say here and now that I have nothing against children. I've even been rash enough to think I was a fit and proper person to raise a couple of my own. But if a club sells 10,000 season tickets to under-sixteens and then scatters them all round the ground it is going to have a marked effect on the atmosphere. The youngsters may be the future, but I was more concerned about the present.

At the Boleyn Ground there had been a family enclosure, where parents could sit with their kids knowing they were less likely to encounter some of the industrial language and boisterous behaviour that you will find at any football ground. But you can't separate 10,000 youngsters plus parents from the main body of the crowd. There are just too many people for an enclosure. There are too many for a stand!

The under-sixteens season tickets had been sold for just £99 each, irrespective of where they were in the ground. At that price, they had proved extremely popular. The argument was that if existing season ticket holders wanted to bring their kids they would naturally like to sit together. As a result, the under-sixteens were located in all parts of the ground, and they put something of a dampener on proceedings. Children sitting with their parents are unlikely to lend their voices to songs inviting rival teams to stick their blue flag where the sun don't shine or suggesting a disliked opponent has a penchant for older women. Abusive songs may not be everybody's cup of tea but, like it or not, they are all part of this mysterious 'atmosphere' that football supporters are forever banging on about.

What made the junior tickets even more appealing to those who qualified for them was that if you didn't want to bring your little 'uns, the ticket could be upgraded to accommodate a big 'un – not that anybody would abuse this remarkable corporate generosity by acquiring a band one season ticket that normally cost £900 for just £99 and then using it for nefarious purposes. Perish the thought!

In short, the migration of supporters from Upton Park had not been the huge success the club was claiming. Some were disgruntled because the seats they now found themselves in were worse than the ones they had left behind – despite costing the same. Others had the hump because the friends they had made in the Boleyn Ground – often over many years – were now sitting in a different part of the ground and they themselves were surrounded by strangers, who may or may not have had the same idea about what constitutes reasonable behaviour at a football match. And, to cap it all, when you wanted to sing along to a foul-mouthed favourite anthem or let rip at the referee you found yourself biting your tongue because there was a child in the next seat. But what else can you expect when you cease to be regarded as a supporter and are looked on as a customer instead?

So, would I have confined myself to a constructive argument about the ticketing policy had I written the piece I'd been asked to do shortly before the Southampton game? I doubt it. I think I would have kicked off by seeming to be a reasonable sort of bloke and conceding that injuries clearly played some part in our malaise, and pointed out that the summer transfer window had been distinctly substandard. I'd have also agreed that the increased capacity at the London Stadium meant many people who had struggled to buy tickets for games at Upton Park now had a far better chance of getting to see the Hammers. But I couldn't have resisted the temptation of pointing out that they wouldn't be watching them in a stadium that was built for football.

We were all supposed to embrace the move, but I was starting to feel like the little boy who dared to suggest that the Emperor's new clothes weren't all they were cracked up to be.

There was that athletics track for a start. Try as the club did to hide it by covering it up with green plastic sheeting and putting a few retractable seats on the outside lanes, there was no getting away from the fact that we had a running track where a running track ought not to be. They just don't belong in football stadiums.

The atmosphere at Upton Park was never the same after the West Stand development left supporters further from the playing area on both sides of the ground. But at the new stadium the distance from the pitch was that much greater, making it harder still to recreate the cauldron of passion that was once our trademark.

Then there was the unresolved standing issue. The club must have envisaged this problem – it was hardly a big secret that certain sections of the Boleyn Ground stood up as a matter of course. So why didn't we try to persuade the Premier League to change its rule that prevents clubs giving over certain parts of the ground to supporters who prefer to stand?

Before we left E13 David Gold had dropped the strongest possible hint that the club would consider the idea of 'safe standing' once we moved. He said:

> We now don't have the violence we once had and already what exists is unsafe standing. At Upton Park, we currently have unsafe standing that is illegal and anti-social. It's time to give something back to the fans. The fans who want to stand should be given an area to do so.
>
> I'd be stunned if we don't have some form of safe standing experiment soon. Let's face it, it's not very expensive to install and it's safe, very safe, in fact it's twice or three times safer than what we have at the moment.

Just like my colleagues who did write about the state of affairs at the London Stadium, I'd have probably had a sly dig at the popcorn and the ice cream. I'd have even tried to work in a line about the incongruous swan-shaped pedalos on the waters of the Olympic Park. And I would most certainly have taken the opportunity to moan about the terrible view from certain parts of the stand. Indeed, I might well have offered Baroness Brady the chance to join me in the back row to decide for herself. It was an offer I was to make in person a few weeks later.

Boleyn Ground
Monday 14 September 2015
Kick-off: 8.00
Final score: West Ham 2–0 Newcastle

There have been times in my life when watching West Ham play has been about as pleasurable as having a tooth extracted. That was certainly the case when we played Newcastle at the Boleyn Ground for the final time. I'd had a molar removed in the morning – and it was utterly painless. All my fears about finding myself pinned in the chair with the dentist's knee on my chest while she set about me with a pair of pliers were totally unfounded (I really shouldn't have watched *Marathon Man* the night before). Then, in the evening, we demolished a toothless Geordie side being managed by none other than Steve McClaren. Both experiences exceeded my expectations by some distance.

Those mischief-makers who are the fourth estate could not resist the temptation to remind their readers that McClaren had famously faced a team managed by Bilić before. It was the game that resulted in the former England manager being dubbed the 'Wally with the brolly' after he sheltered from the rain under an umbrella while the team he had picked lost 3–2 to Croatia at Wembley, thus ending England's remaining interest in Euro 2008 and his tenure in charge. West Ham fans, naturally, hoped for a similar result in front of the Sky cameras.

We had reason to be optimistic, as well. Although our home results had been disappointing, losing to both Leicester and Bournemouth, our previous match had resulted in a sensational victory at Anfield – after a fifty-two-year wait. We'd then had the annoyance of waiting a further sixteen days to follow it up because of an international break but, despite West Ham's famed ability to lose to struggling opponents immediately after beating one of the big teams, we drove up from Brighton with high hopes.

In recent years I had rarely used the car to get to Upton Park, and this journey was a useful reminder why I generally went by public transport. The traffic was backed up before we got through the Blackwall Tunnel and things never improved after that. In fact, we learned later, the Newcastle bus had been caught in a gridlock in the Barking Road about an hour before kick-off and the players had to walk the best part of a mile to get to the stadium. (Please feel free to make up your own jokes about a Wally who had to park his bus but still lost 2–0.)

We parked, as we usually did when we drove to a game, in the street where Di lived as a child. We just about had time for a swift Mad Dog in Priory Road before taking our seats in the East Stand.

This was the game when I saw for myself just how good Dimitri Payet was. There had been a glimmer of his potential in the first home match of the season against Leicester and, of course, I had seen his televised performances at the Emirates and Anfield. But there's nothing like being there when a quality player really demonstrates what he is all about.

There were some significant contributions from other players as well, notably Kouyaté in central midfield and on-loan Victor Moses out wide. But Payet stole the show.

'He is the player I really wanted from the start,' Bilić said of our new No 27.

I've known the player for a long time and tried to get him to Beşiktaş last season. He's a great player, deciding games, but he makes all the players around him play better. That is the most important thing in football: not only individual goalscorers, but players who raise the game of those around him.

Payet did all of that and more, scoring twice in the process. The first came after nine minutes. Noble won the ball in midfield, then found Sakho, who returned the ball to his captain with a back heel. Noble spotted Payet steaming into the box and squared it for the Frenchman, who bent a first-time side-footer around Newcastle keeper Tim Krul. The goal truly was a thing of beauty.

His second, shortly after the start of the second half, also demonstrated Payet's fantastic technique. Moses raced past two defenders, cut back inside and thumped a shot against the crossbar. The ball fell to Payet, who calmly put it away with a sweet half-volley from just inside the area. The thumb-sucking celebration left a little to be desired, but right then I was prepared to forgive him just about anything.

To rub salt into the Geordie wounds, Slav brought on former Toon favourite Andy Carroll for Moses, prompting some of the ruder West Ham fans to remind our visitors that he had left them because they were shit. Little did they know we would get that back with interest from the Southampton followers later in the season. But, let's be honest, those who live by the puerile insult must expect to perish the same way.

Being an evening kick-off the game was, of course, played under the floodlights – which always seemed to engender a special atmosphere at Upton Park. There wouldn't be many more atmospheric evening encounters at the Boleyn Ground, but I tried desperately to keep the thought from my mind as we

headed back to the car and the inevitable crawl to escape the
back streets of East Ham. It was too early in the season to think
about leaving Upton Park for good – the agony of that would
come soon enough. I had enjoyed a pain-free morning in the
dentist's chair, and I was certainly not going to feel down in the
mouth after a classy 2–0 victory under lights that left us fifth in
the table and which had showcased the incredible talents of a
world class player. I may be a West Ham supporter, but even I'm
not that much of a masochist.

6

The three-course
team talk

London Stadium
Saturday 1 October 2016
Kick-off: 3.00
Final score: West Ham 1–1 Middlesbrough

SIX DAYS AFTER the Southampton debacle Di and I were back at the London Stadium. Geoff was with us, having returned from his holiday in South America. He'd spent some time in the Colombian mountains, so the rarified atmosphere of row seventy-three held no terrors for him. I thought back to the little wooden train that had taken us to the top of Mallorca a couple of weeks earlier and wondered if West Ham could be persuaded to install something similar to get me to my seat.

We'd met for a swift pint at a place near King's Cross station which was showing signs of becoming a West Ham pub on match days. If you timed it right, it was quicker to get from there to Stratford International than it was to walk from Stratford International to the stadium. And we had yet to find a watering hole in Stratford that was crying out for our custom.

During the week, the West Ham players had been out for a couple of pints themselves. After Sunday's defeat, Slaven Bilić had urged Mark Noble to take the players for dinner on Monday as a team-bonding exercise. There were claims in the tabloid press that a couple of them were still boozing the following day.

The club captain wrote about their night out in his programme notes.

> It was a very positive evening, because all the lads came along and we had an honest discussion about where we are and what we're going to do to put things right. When you are in a different environment, like a restaurant having a meal, it helps players who might not otherwise be confident talking in front of the whole squad to come out of themselves and share their thoughts. We've told each other how we feel and we're together as a team and as a squad.

Noble realised that supporters who had seen them out enjoying steak and chips and a few bevvies after the humiliation of the Southampton defeat were perhaps a touch annoyed at a seeming lack of professionalism. 'I appreciate we are in the public eye but this was an evening with a purpose, and that is getting our season up and running,' he wrote.

Noble also took the opportunity to dispel the notion that his remarks about what he had called the 'laughable' performance the previous weekend were in any way intended as a direct criticism of his manager or his comrades in arms. 'I wanted to speak the truth,' he said.

> I have a lot of respect for you all, for the manager, for my team-mates and for all the people who worked so hard to get the club where it is today. Sometimes the truth needs to be spoken and I thought it was the best time to do it after the way we played against Southampton.

You'll get no argument from me about that, Mark. Bilić, too, did his best to rally the troops with a heartfelt column in the programme in which he talked about digging in, working harder and staying positive. And, we were told, the supporters had a big part to play if the club was going to turn things round. 'This is the moment when we need you all,' the manager wrote.

> We feel the fans' support and all that I ask from you is that you stay behind us. It is a big part for us to feel good at home here at London Stadium. We want you to see your team winning and go home happy. It's the same with the players. This is a new ground, and different to the one we played in but we have to make it our home. Together, we will do that, I am sure.

You know things aren't going well when the boss feels the need to tell supporters to get behind the team. Still, I had no complaints about Bilić as manager. He was certainly an improvement on his predecessor, who had been making the headlines during the week, having been asked to quit as England boss after just sixty-seven days in the role.

Sam Allardyce had been snared in an undercover operation by the *Telegraph* that showed him negotiating a fee of £400,000 to represent an overseas firm that was hoping to profit from Premier League transfers. The taped conversations also revealed that he offered advice on how to get around the FA's own regulations on third-party ownership. And if that wasn't enough, he made fun of former England manager Roy Hodgson's speech impediment, said that assistant Gary Neville should 'sit down and shut up', and called the FA's Wembley redevelopment 'stupid'.

However, to his credit, he can claim to be the only England manager to have had a 100 per cent record in charge – albeit that his sole victory was an unconvincing 1–0 win against Slovakia.

Allardyce offered a 'sincere and wholehearted apology' for his actions. Shame he never felt the need to say sorry to West Ham fans for the lack of respect he showed us and the club's traditions during his four years in charge.

In his defence, we were in the Championship when he took over and he did propel us to the next level, the Premier League. But he never really understood what West Ham was all about and, more to the point, he never bothered to find out. In his first season as manager, following a trip to Peterborough, he responded to the repeated chant of 'We're West Ham United – we play on the floor', by saying: 'There has never been a West Ham Way shown to me. I've spoken to a lot of people at the club and no one can tell me what it is.' He claimed that those of us who believed there was such a thing were 'deluded'.

To make matters worse, the season after next he cupped his ear in astonishment as an angry Upton Park crowd booed him off after a terrible performance against Hull. Yes, we had won, but the supporters had rightly expected better against a side that found itself a goal down and reduced to ten men after barely a quarter of an hour. A bemused Allardyce later complained it was the only time he'd ever got a response like that after winning – he just didn't get it at all. Still, this isn't the place to open up old wounds.

Despite the bonding session and uplifting words from both captain and manager, West Ham understandably looked a little jittery in the first half against Middlesbrough. When a terrific effort from Noble came back off the underside of the bar rather than finding the top of the net, the pessimists among us were starting to wonder if it was going to be one of those days.

The pressure is always on to beat a newly promoted side. And when you're at the bottom of the table that pressure is greater still. The Smoggies had finished runners up to Burnley, edging out Brighton on goal difference on the final day of the regular season. They too had started poorly, and had lost their last three games. If our season was going to blossom, the general feeling was that this was the day to get cracking.

I would have so much preferred to have been facing Brighton. I have lived there for thirty years, and in that time I have developed quite a soft spot for the Seagulls (unlike real seagulls, which are nasty, greedy, aggressive beasts and thoroughly dislikeable).

Before moving to Brighton, the closest I'd ever had to a 'second team' was Bristol City. It was a tenuous link. I was born in Bristol but moved away when I was still a babe in arms. Some years later, when the family was settled back in London, my parents took it upon themselves to buy me and my elder brother some football kit for Christmas, which was a curious thing to do because my brother doesn't actually like football. This was before I had taken the conscious decision to follow West Ham – that didn't happen until I'd reached the ripe old age of seven. But even if I had, I don't think it would have made much difference. Mum and Dad had decided to get Chris, my brother, the blue and white quarters of Bristol Rovers while I got the red and white of City.

Parents did things like that back in the early '60s. Not only were Chris and I presented with the colours of two random football clubs who were based 120 miles away along the yet-to-be-completed M4, presumably in the expectation we would follow their fortunes for years to come, we were also lumbered with opposing sides in the University Boat Race. I was Oxford and Chris was Cambridge. We even got given rosettes to wear one year.

Loads of kids of our generation were similarly subjected to this sort of nonsense. Don't ask me why. We just were. My rather mediocre academic qualifications were never enough to take me to Oxbridge, but to this day if I find myself watching the boat race I cheer for the posh boys of Oxford rather than the posh boys of Cambridge, which shows you just how much psychological damage parents can do to their children without knowing it.

Happily, any possibility that Bristol City may have become a lifelong obsession was obliterated when West Ham overcame Preston North End in the 1964 Cup Final, and the choice I made to support the Hammers in the run-up to Wembley was fully vindicated. Who said 'out of the frying pan and into the fire?' Any more sarcastic remarks like that and you will be staying behind after school.

To be honest, I didn't really pay much attention to Brighton's results when Di and I first moved there. This was the mid-1980s, when Brighton and Hove Albion played their games at the

Goldstone Ground. West Ham and Brighton were generally in different divisions, so didn't get to play one another very often. But when they did we would rock up and, naturally, support the Irons.

My attitude changed when Brighton lost their home twenty years ago. It is a much-told tale of skulduggery and duplicity, and I won't go into all the gory details here. But it's fair to say that when Albion went to Hereford to play the final game of the 1996/97 season they were staring oblivion in the face. They had lost their ground, which had been sold to property developers, and they were on the point of losing their football league status – which would almost certainly have resulted in bankruptcy.

On 3 May 1997 West Ham were in Manchester, having already avoided relegation (which is just as well, because we lost 2–0 to Man U). I was in the kitchen, listening to football scores from around the country. And as the half-times came in it was clear that Brighton were in deep, deep trouble following an own goal.

The enormity of what was happening at Edgar Street hit me full in the face. Britain's premier seaside resort – the place that my wife and I had chosen to make our home – was on the point of losing its football team. The parlous state of Albion's finances meant their chances of ever climbing out of the non-league morass were roughly equivalent to an ice cream's prospect of surviving a sunny day on the Palace Pier. Defeat wouldn't just mean the end of league football in the town I loved, there was every chance it could mean the end of Albion itself. The Seagulls may not have been my team, but it was essential there was a team. They simply could not be allowed to perish. Drastic measures were called for.

Worryingly, the reports coming in via the radio were pessimistic in the extreme. Albion had been outplayed in the first forty-five minutes. I abandoned the national stations in favour of local radio to concentrate on the commentary from Hereford. West Ham didn't need me that day, but Brighton clearly needed all the help they could get. I had half an idea forming at the back of my mind, but I decided to give it fifteen minutes to see if they could turn it around by themselves.

Sussex has a proud tradition of devil worship and, let's face it, just about anything goes in Brighton. But hitherto I'd never had any direct dealings with Satan and I'm still not entirely clear why I turned to him when I did. Perhaps it was a reputation for being able to get things done when other supreme beings seem strangely reluctant to get involved. An hour had passed at Edgar Street and it seemed as if Brighton were no closer to scoring than when they began the second period, barely finding the wherewithal to mount an attack at the end which was packed with supporters from the south coast. The commentary, while striving hard to be impartial, was becoming increasingly desperate. That's when I enlisted Lucifer's help.

I wasn't asking for the earth – all I wanted was Brighton to get a point, and I wasn't prepared to sell my soul for that. Not that I'm sure the devil would have wanted it – one previous owner, some wear and tear, would benefit from a respray. However, I was willing to do a deal. My offer was that if Brighton could get out of this in one piece, I would go and support them at least once every season from then on. To convince him I was serious, I agreed that failure to do so would allow the devil to take the most diabolical revenge he could dream up.

Three minutes later Lucifer held up his end of the bargain.

The news reports of the time will tell you that it was a journeyman footballer by the name of Robbie Reinelt who got the crucial goal that kept Albion alive, but I – and I alone – knew the satanic truth that lay behind that goal.

It was two years before the Albion played in Brighton again – from 1997–99 they staged their home games more than seventy miles away in Gillingham. When they did come back it was to a municipal sports complex. I did go and watch them occasionally in the early years at the Withdean Stadium, but it was a depressing experience. There was a running track for one thing. And the atmosphere was even worse than that at the London Stadium. Anyway, to cut a long story short, I stopped going.

Brighton seemed to do well enough without me, climbing through the divisions until they reached the Championship, and getting a terrific new ground for themselves. But every time they tried to take that final step up into the big time, they faltered. After moving to the Amex Stadium they had lost three play-off semi-finals – including one to Sheffield Wednesday after Boro had edged them out of the automatic promotion places. I was beginning to wonder if the devil was exacting his revenge for my failure to keep that promise of supporting them once in a while.

As a rational, intelligent person yourself, who never crosses your fingers, will confidently walk under ladders and isn't in the least bit concerned by the number 13, you will no doubt dismiss my concerns as superstitious nonsense. But I would have definitely been more comfortable had Brighton been promoted rather than Middlesbrough – and that feeling was compounded when they went 1–0 up shortly after the start of the second half.

Adrián saved well from Jordan Rhodes, but from the resultant corner Cristhian Stuani scored with a powerful header which Noble cleared – but from behind the line. The goal stood.

Not for the first time that season I felt as if I was part of a giant balloon that had suddenly deflated. What little bit of atmosphere the diehards had managed to create was sucked out of the stadium in an instant. The only noise came from the Boro end.

It needed something special to get the place off its knees, and something special was what we got. Remember Diego Maradona's goal against England in the 1986 World Cup? Not the 'hand of God' goal. The other one. Well, I'd say Dimitri Payet's effort against Middlesbrough was even better.

It started with a raking aerial pass from Winston Reid, who was deep in his own half. Payet was wide on the left, with Boro's Viktor Fischer in close attendance. Facing his own goal, our No 27 pulled the ball down with his right foot, controlling it instantly. With barely a yard of space between him and the touchline, the only option appeared to be to come back inside. But Payet had other ideas: a flick with the outside of his right foot, a swivel, a stumble, a recovery, another deft touch and he was away down an unlikely corridor that only he knew existed.

The first time he touched the ball with his left foot, it took him into the penalty area – a manoeuvre that left Marten de Roon on his knees. Antonio and Zaza were in the middle, but Payet wasn't looking to pass. A caress with the outside of his left boot removed any hope Antonio Barragán had of making a challenge before an audacious step over took care of Calum Chambers. Another touch with the right foot, then a second, then a third. George Friend was on his backside, Ben Gibson was upright, but nothing more than a spectator as Payet skipped past them both. Having run parallel with the goal line in beating the last three defenders, Payet had actually gone wide of Víctor Valdés' left-hand post, leaving a seemingly impossible angle from which to shoot. The keeper tried to cover his near post, only to see the ball pass him on the other side on its way into the net as Payet cut the ball back – again with that magical right foot.

In all, he had been in possession of the ball for eleven seconds before he got his shot away. In that time he beat five defenders and the goalkeeper. Those eleven seconds were, by themselves, worth the price of a season ticket alone.

Supporters old and new celebrated as one. But rather than go to the crowd and milk the adulation, or run towards Bilić as he had done on so many previous occasions in his first year at the club, Payet headed back towards the centre circle, ordering his teammates to do likewise. As he pulled up his socks, prior to the restart, it was as if he was saying: 'Right, mes amis, our season starts right here, right now. Let's show the world what we're all about.'

Sadly, his call went unheeded and the game finished 1–1. Four points after seven games represented the club's worst start since 1988–89, a year in which the Hammers were relegated. As we trooped away from the stadium, delighted with the goal but disappointed with a result that kept us in the bottom three, the black sky behind the massive Westfield shopping centre was brightened by a rainbow. I've supported West Ham for too long to know there was no pot of gold at the end of it.

Boleyn Ground
Saturday 26 September 2015
Kick-off: 3.00
Final score: West Ham 2–2 Norwich

Supping our pints in the Denmark after a 2–2 draw with Norwich at the Boleyn Ground, Di, Geoff and I contemplated whether our metaphorical glasses were half empty or half full. It was a game that we had gone to hoping to win, but had left happy with a draw after falling behind twice.

Since the game against Newcastle, West Ham had travelled to Man City and pulled off a totally expected 2–1 victory, then lost by the same score at Leicester in the League Cup. I was really disappointed by the result at Leicester. This, of all seasons, would have been the year to get to Wembley, but I suppose I should have known better. West Ham and the League Cup have never exactly been on the best of terms.

The Man City result was fantastic, though – not least because it was entirely deserved. Di and I watched the game on a huge screen in a pub in Brixham on the Devon coast. The woman behind the bar was from Essex, and more than happy to make sure we had a front-row view. It's a great spot is Brixham, and I can thoroughly recommend the food at the hotel we stayed in. If I can ever remember its name, I will let you know.

The victory at the Etihad meant we became only the fourth team in Premier League history to win away at Arsenal, Liverpool and Manchester City in the same season. Our away form was outstanding, but we continued to disappoint at home. Some pundits put our lethargic start against Norwich down to the fact that we had to play extra time at the King Power Stadium.

Whatever the reason, we gave away a terrible goal after just nine minutes when Noble under-hit a square ball to James Tomkins, allowing Robbie Brady to take full advantage.

Norwich could have been four up by the time Diafra Sakho equalised in the thirty-third minute. The decisive cross, needless to say, came from a certain Frenchman who – at that time at least – was better than Zidane in the eyes of every West Ham fan on the planet.

West Ham didn't start the second half too brightly, either. Adrián was forced into a fingertip save to deny a long-range effort – then he used his face to block a point-blank shot. Bilić described the save as 'unbelievable'. History does not record what Adrián thought about putting his boat race in the line of fire.

At the opposite end, Sakho went close a couple of times before Andy Carroll came on in place of Lanzini to join him up front.

With seven minutes left, Nathan Redmond put Norwich ahead and the doubters in the crowd headed for the exits. Those of us who stuck it out to the end got our reward when West Ham did what West Ham so rarely seem to do and scored in the dying seconds. Payet, from a free kick on the right, sent over a cross. Keeper John Ruddy was unsettled by Carroll's presence in his penalty area and flapped at the ball. His limp punch hit Carroll and fell to Kouyaté – who gleefully rammed the ball into the back of the net before charging off to accept the heartfelt congratulations of the Bobby Moore Lower.

Back in the Denmark, our actual glasses were empty so Di headed off to the crowded bar to get them refilled. It was 'old school' in there, with the sort of blokes who were happy to let a lady go first no matter how thirsty they were. As a result, she always seemed to get served quicker than me. That, at least, is my story and I'm sticking to it.

When she got back we pondered the fate of the injured pigeon that had landed on the pitch in the second half, before being tenderly carried to the sideline by Norwich's Jonny Howson to cheers from all parts of the ground. Inevitably, there were questions about what Delia Smith would do with it if she got the chance. I'm guessing she didn't encase it in shortcrust pasty, which meant Howson's intervention was almost certainly the first time a Canary has ever rescued a pigeon.

We also contemplated the delights of being third in the league. How did it feel? With most of the pub singing along to 'Sweet Caroline', you didn't have to wait long for the answer. 'So Good! So Good! So Good!' we bellowed in unison.

If only good times didn't have to end…

7

And the brand played on

London Stadium
Saturday 22 October 2016
Kick-off: 3.00
Final score: West Ham 1–0 Sunderland

IT HAD BEEN three weeks since we were last in the London Stadium and, quite frankly, I was grateful for the time away. You shouldn't feel like that about going to watch your football team. But I did.

I had been saddened by reports of fighting at the stadium immediately after the Boro game. There were allegations from the away supporters that bottles and other missiles had been thrown into their end during the game, and there were ugly pictures of rival fans squaring up to one another outside despite a large police presence. Grown men throwing punches and children in tears? That's not what a day out at a football match is supposed to be all about.

Then, just when I thought my spirits couldn't sink much lower, Lady Brady proved me wrong. Speaking at a sports business conference, she hailed the move to the London Stadium as a triumph – in corporate terms, at least. 'We are ranked fifteenth in terms of brand values,' she told the summit. To be honest, I'm not really sure what that means, but apparently we were 115th when Karren joined the club, so that's clearly a move in the right direction if you're keen on brand values. Also, it turned out, West Ham were now twentieth in the Deloitte Football Money League, which essentially ranks clubs based on the amount of revenue they generate. I know I should have been pleased by this piece of news, but I was rather more concerned by the fact that we were eighteenth in the Premier League.

Call me unduly suspicious, but I was mildly alarmed that she made this speech to the Leaders Sport Business Summit at Stamford Bridge of all places. Now there's a club with a brand, and it's not one I want any part of, thank you very much. I was also surprised that the Baroness clearly doesn't own a map. The London Stadium was – in her words – 'less than, sort of, a mile away from' Upton Park. Er, no it isn't. Not even 'sort of'. Still, what's the odd mile or two between friends? Branding: that's what we should be concentrating on here.

'Rebranding ourselves was really important with our stadium,' according to Lady B. 'We're in the London Stadium. We added the word London to our crest because we felt it had real global appeal. Nobody else does it.'

Sorry to interrupt Karren, but have you ever wondered why nobody else does it? I don't claim to be the greatest at geography but I really don't need to be told where we're from. I'm sure it's much the same for other supporters of the club. Still, that's a small point, I know. Please, carry on.

'We are in the heart of London, in the foothills of the financial sector.'

Sorry, but I'm really going to have to stop you again. The Olympic Park is not in the heart of London. More like a pimple on the capital's right buttock if you ask me. OK, that was uncalled for. I promise not to interrupt again.

'We have the best stadium – there are some great stadiums in this country but there is only one Olympic Stadium and it's ours.'

Hmmm, strictly speaking it isn't, is it? The club has a ninety-nine-year lease, and pays rent of £2.5 million a year. As I understand it, the stadium is owned by E20 Stadium LLP, an organisation set up by the London Legacy Development Corporation and Newham Council, and run on a day-to-day basis by LS185, a UK-based subsidiary of the French construction giant Vinci. And whether or not it's the best stadium in the country is debatable. I'm guessing the '185' represents the number of medals won by UK athletes at the 2012 Olympic and Paralympic Games, but I'm sure you can put me straight on that if I'm wrong.

Still, there's no denying a lot of people bought into the idea of moving to Stratford. 'We sold the stadium out to 52,000 season-ticket holders,' Brady said. 'We have 10,000 under-sixteen-year-olds who come week in, week out. We have completely sold out hospitality. I have 50,000 people who have paid to join the waiting list to be able to buy a season ticket. We have 36,000 members.'

As someone who had paid the same amount as I had the previous season for a seat with a worse view I struggled to agree with the next assertion. 'We have this great stadium and much better prospects and facilities than in our old stadium but we charge a lower price. We offer a more dynamic product at an inferior price. It's been so well received and it comes back to our values and our culture.'

Well received? Not in my bit of row seventy-three, it wasn't. And there was a good deal of confusion over quite what she meant by the word 'culture', which she also used in her speech when talking about the club as a whole at the time it was bought by the Davids Gold and Sullivan.

> There were two interesting things about it [the club]. One, it had £100 million worth of debt. Two, it had no what I would call culture. At football clubs we don't make anything, we don't manufacture anything, we don't really produce anything other than more players. So getting the culture right, being a place where something is expected of you, having discipline, planning and process and strategy. That wasn't there.

Many supporters took this as a direct criticism, although to be fair to Brady I think she was talking about a business culture rather than laying into the fans. 'If you're always driven by money, you lose your traditional values and what you're there for,' she said. 'The stadium and the league are not what makes a club. It's the people who support it. Protecting their traditions and their values and their integrity in their own brand is very important.'

Ah, there's that word 'brand' again. We're fifteenth you say? Do we get into the Champions League of Brands if we get into the top four?

There were no Premier League games on the Saturday after Karren Brady's speech due to an international break. The two World Cup qualifiers were Gareth Southgate's first matches in charge following the departure of Big/Fat Sam, and he'd called up Michail Antonio – who, the previous week, had demonstrated that he is as much of a star off the pitch as he is on it by personally delivering his West Ham shirt to a charity, set up following the death of a little girl due to a heart defect in 2013 when she was just two weeks old.

He had promised Libby Mae's Little Angels a signed shirt to help raise money for neonatal units in the Birmingham area but then realised that, having missed the post, the only way he could get it to the auction on time was to take it himself. So, still wearing his match-day tracksuit, he jumped in his car immediately after the Boro game and drove to the Midlands, before meeting up with family in Manchester and then joining the England squad at St George's Park in Staffordshire. As it was, Antonio didn't get picked for either the 2–0 win against Malta on the Saturday of the international break, or the 0–0 midweek draw in Slovenia. But his time will come, mark my words.

The following Saturday the Hammers were at Selhurst Park. The game was live on BT Sport, and despite Palace being considerably closer to where I live than most Premier League grounds – including Stratford – I chose to watch it from the comfort of the couch using my souped-up Amazon Fire TV

Stick. Reception was less than brilliant (and possibly not entirely legal) but I did catch Lanzini's winning goal and Cresswell's controversial sending off. Talking of soup, I must try to get to the Palace game next season, if only to check out Geoff's assertion that the Eagles actually call their cut-price version of Bovril 'Meat Drink'. I sometimes wonder if he really has inherited the thirst for accuracy that you would expect from the offspring of two journalists – although I can fully understand why he has no thirst for Bovril.

The thing was, I'd woken up on successive Saturdays and my immediate thought had been, thank heavens I don't have to go to Stratford today. Never, in all my life, had I felt like that about Upton Park.

Nobody makes me go to football, of course. I am well within my rights to simply turn round and say to myself, don't do it Brian – if you don't want to go you don't have to. But the thing is, football is what I like to do. Come to think of it, that's not strictly true. West Ham is what I like to do. I am not a football fan: I am a West Ham supporter – and those who don't understand the difference might as well stop reading now because the rest of this book will be meaningless to anyone who doesn't get that distinction.

I know most fellow supporters – whichever club they support – will get my drift, even if they have a broader based love for the Beautiful Game than me. True club supporters, even if they follow their national team more closely than I do or can contentedly watch a match that doesn't involve their club, will understand the obsession – possibly even addiction – that goes with the territory. It's not like swapping Tesco for Sainsbury's, or the *Daily Mail* for the *Express*. (Why not try the *Guardian* if you really want a better newspaper?) People like me can't simply say we're going to try another brand – much as the Lady Bradys of this world may wish it were so – we either pay to watch our team or we watch no team at all.

The truth is, the owners of football clubs hold the whip hand – they know however badly they treat us we will invariably come crawling back for more. No doubt the Marquis de Sade would have an explanation for it all. Maybe E. L. James could give us *Fifty Shades of Claret and Blue*. But I most certainly can't fathom why people who are normally sane and sensible individuals willingly queue up on a regular basis to be humiliated with football's equivalent of bondage gags, nipple clamps and riding crops.

Despite what many folk who don't share our obsession may think, football supporters are a pretty savvy bunch as a rule. Of course, every club has its share of knuckleheads, but they are in the minority. At least, that's certainly the case at West Ham.

You've only got to look at the number of terrific books about the club to see that there is a huge demand for well-informed, considered and comprehensively researched literature. People such as Steve Marsh, Brian Belton, John Northcutt, John Powles, Robert Banks and Pete May are among those who try to satisfy that need with some brilliant writing. (And for those who prefer an intemperate rant, I'm here for you.)

The wit and wisdom of West Ham supporters also shines through on the plethora of websites, podcasts and Facebook pages that allow people to have their say about the club they love so much. My favourite podcast, partly because they invite me on to have a moan from time to time, is *STOP! Hammer Time* – hosted by the estimable Phil Whelans and Jim Grant. Seriously, if you've not heard it before you really do need to check it out.

Phil and Jim, who are a first-rate double act by themselves, also have some fantastic guests – not all of whom abuse their hospitality by constantly grumbling about the move to the London Stadium. The podcast is supported by a Facebook group with well over 5,000 members – and the quality of debate on there puts most politicians to shame. If Parliament could consider the nation's problems with the same degree of courtesy and intellectual rigour that S!HT members have displayed when discussing the continued absence of a decent striker, or which of our two principal goalkeepers is the least accident prone, this would be a better country by far.

In many ways the various social media forums have gone some way to replacing the terrace humour that was such an integral part of watching football at Upton Park before Lord Justice Taylor decided the tragic events that unfolded at Hillsborough on 15 April 1989 meant we all had to sit down for our own good. Don't ask me why, but football supporters are funnier when they're standing up.

That said, on the S!HT Facebook page there are always some very funny people saying some very funny things. More importantly, for me at least, is that fellow supporters understand that it is possible to be critical of the way West Ham is run while remaining totally loyal to the club and its traditions.

A couple of days before the Palace game I was invited to appear on something called Fan TV, which hitherto had been an organisation of which I was totally unaware. For those who are as unfamiliar with Fan TV as I was, the idea is that supporters of various clubs are invited to sit on a lime green sofa and engage in what I believe is now known as 'bantz' while the programme is screened live on Sky, YouTube and Facebook.

I was on the couch with fellow *Blowing Bubbles* contributor Greg Richardson, who had a considerably more upbeat view of the new stadium than me. Our host was Toby Tarrant, son of Chris, and clearly someone who was totally at home in a broadcasting studio. He certainly had some very perceptive questions – not least whether there would have been quite as much disillusionment among supporters had we been fourth in the league, rather than eighteenth. For those of us who felt the way we did, we could have been top and still not liked the new stadium.

Interestingly, Fan TV had held a snap poll to gauge the feeling among supporters about the move, and found a tiny majority in favour. (Small majority in favour of a huge decision that is going to change your life in unexpected ways you may not like – sound familiar at all?)

I enjoyed the encounter with Greg – not least because I was so angry about the move I was having trouble seeing the wood for the trees. Having to put my muddled fury into words in front of a TV camera, albeit with an audience that ran into hundreds rather than thousands, helped me clarify my thoughts.

The new stadium had enabled Greg, like so many other people, to buy a season ticket whereas at Upton Park he had trouble getting to see games. I will readily agree Stratford can chalk that up as a major point in its favour. I'm not so convinced by the claims that it's easier to get to than Upton Park – that rather depends where you're coming from. As to whether the stadium is fit for purpose, I remained convinced that it wasn't – and believe it never will be while it still has a running track.

In other news, Greg and I readily agreed that West Ham were not going to get relegated, despite the traumatic start to the season. In fact we both – correctly as it turned out – predicted

that we would finish eleventh. I also foresaw the victory at Selhurst Park – although I went for 2–1 rather than 1–0. Ever the
optimist, that's me.

Having beaten Palace the week before we played the Mackems,
natural-born optimists such as myself could have been forgiven
for thinking that we might have put a very poor Sunderland side
to the sword. Maybe not the 8–0 thrashing that we dished out in
1968 at the Boleyn Ground, but something pretty comprehensive which may have finally kick-started our season.

For the first twenty minutes that's the way it looked. Dimitri
Payet was particularly threatening. His first effort went tanta-
lisingly wide; next he overcompensated and placed his shot too
close to goalkeeper Jordan Pickford; then he hit the post from
the edge of the box after an exquisite demonstration of his technique on the ball.

In what appeared to be a brilliant piece of timing, Payet was
one of the four Hammers Heroes stickers that appeared in the
programme, waiting to be extracted and then stuck in the official
book. And who would have argued with his hero status right then?

This is the sticker book, you may recall, that had somehow
forgotten to include Martin Peters and Billy Bonds. It did, however, have space for Jermain Defoe.

It's fair to say that some West Ham fans bear a grudge. These
are people who might have nominated Defoe for a slot in a *Special Edition Treacherous Bastards Sticker Album*. I'm not like that,
you understand. But I did raise an eyebrow when I read the
caption that accompanied his picture.

Lively striker Defoe began his senior career with the Hammers
having joined as a youngster from Charlton Athletic. Breaking

into the first team as a teenager after a profitable spell on loan at Bournemouth, the youngster was superb in his first full season, scoring fourteen times. Joining Spurs after two more excellent campaigns, Defoe ended his Hammers career in 2004.

What it fails to mention is that in 2003 Defoe demanded a transfer just twenty-four hours after we had been relegated. The request was turned down, so he stayed – getting sent off three times in the early part of the following season before finally securing his move to Tottenham.

Sir Trevor Brooking, who was caretaker manager at the time of the request, doesn't blame the lad himself, suggesting instead that his mother was the driving force. The trouble is, Mrs Defoe hasn't turned out in opposition colours cheerfully scoring against us on a regular basis, so we never got the chance to boo her. Jermain, however, has – which explains the less-than-cheery welcome he can expect whenever he plays against West Ham, despite his inclusion in the *Special Edition Hammers Heroes Sticker Album*.

Thankfully, Defoe hasn't scored against us for quite a while – Geoff used to back him to do so, knowing that a Williams wager is a sure-fire way of preventing something happening, but he doesn't bother now. Much to our relief Sunderland's main goalscoring hope didn't really look dangerous on this occasion either. To be fair, for the remainder of the first half, no one did after those initial Payet attempts.

The visitors started the second half brightly. Defoe looked more like his old self, Jack Rodwell went close with a header and Wahbi Khazri fluffed a decent chance, his tame shot comfortably saved by Adrián.

The West Ham support, like the team itself, lost all its early intensity. The atmosphere was flatter than piss on a plate, as my old granny used to say. With ten minutes left there was a steady stream of disgruntled humanity heading for the exits. Sunderland replaced two of their attacking players with defenders in an attempt to hang on to what they had. Respect the point and all that. Sam Allardyce would have approved.

As the ninetieth minute ticked by the scores were still level, but those who had stayed to the end finally got their reward in time added on. A short corner enabled Payet to pick out Winston Reid on the edge of the box – and the big defender smashed it through a sea of bodies into the net. Job done, I suppose. However, as a game, it was definitely one to forget.

Boleyn Ground
Saturday 24 October 2015
Kick-off: 3.00
Final score: West Ham 2–1 Chelsea

There was nothing forgettable about our encounter with Chelsea in the final season at the Boleyn Ground. Goals, yellow cards, red cards, blue flags being inserted in anatomically unlikely places, the Special One banished to the stands, his assistant sent off, a fabulous late winner – the game had the lot.

I detest Chelski. I fully understand that for most West Ham supporters the primary hate figures are Tottenham, but for me it's the Stamford Bridge mob. My loathing started when I was brought up in the Berkshire new town of Bracknell, which is west of London and therefore has more than its fair share of the blue flag brigade. My intense hatred was cemented when Roman Abramovich bought the club and several trophies, which prompted a number of people who'd never been to a football match in their lives to suddenly remember that they had been Chelsea supporters all along.

Chelsea, it should be noted, were the defending champions. And, to the joy of football supporters everywhere, they weren't making much of a fist of their defence. In fact it was their worst ever start to a Premier League campaign.

They began the game against us well enough, but that all changed with barely a quarter of an hour gone. Payet's trickery won him a free kick twenty-five yards out, which Chelsea keeper Asmir Begović managed to palm over the bar. Payet, seemingly both bemused and amused that he hadn't scored, jogged over to take the corner – and whipped in a beauty which the Chelsea defence couldn't handle. The ball fell to Mauro Zárate, who promptly stuck it in the bottom corner.

According to the statisticians, this was the first goal we had scored against the hated Chelski in 467 minutes of football. But that wasn't what Di, Geoff and I were thinking about as we hugged one another and jumped up and down in the East Stand. Then we hugged Barry and Eddy, but as they were in the row in front of us jumping up and down wasn't an option. Not that Eddy would have been worried about that. He was just happy to have the chance to hug Di. In fact I think if he'd had his way they would have still been locked in an embrace when Lanzini, having been put through by another piece of Payet brilliance, chipped over the bar with only Begović to beat twenty minutes later.

Kouyaté, as usual that season, was having a storming game in midfield. Matić felt the best way to stop his progress was by crudely hauling him back, and was booked for a professional foul by referee Jonathan Moss.

Chelsea believed they had equalised soon after, even though Zouma's header was cleared scrappily by Lanzini. They thought the ball had crossed the line. Mr Moss thought differently. And, crucially, Mr Moss was proved correct by goal-line technology. Then, following a West Ham corner, Chelsea counter-attacked and Cesc Fàbregas put the ball in the net – only to be ruled offside. He wasn't happy, and neither was José Mourinho, who'd had a face like a bag of spanners ever since some of the less tactful spectators had suggested he was going to get sacked in the morning. It was tight, but from where I was sitting it looked like a good decision. If nothing else, it balanced the scales of justice following Chelsea's winner in the corresponding fixture the previous season, when Eden Hazard was so far offside he was lucky not to have been charged for admission to the Bobby Moore Lower.

Things got even worse for the visitors when Matić dragged down the impressive Sakho by the touchline and earned himself a second yellow card. Several Chelsea players surrounded the ref in a mob-rule protest orchestrated by John Terry. Diego Costa and Fàbregas were booked – others were lucky not to join them. Then, on the other side of the pitch, Chelsea coach Silvino Louro got himself sent off for monstering the fourth official. Chelsea were a shambles. It was beautiful to behold.

Chelsea came back in the second half, but Mourinho didn't. It turned out he had been sent to the stands after confronting Mr Moss during the interval. Judging by the response from the more raucous element in the crowd, it appeared a referee's decision had gone down well for once.

The merriment subsided somewhat when Gary Cahill

equalised from a corner, and the jitters began to spread as ten-man Chelsea started to look the more likely winners. But in Slav we trust. With twenty minutes to go he sent on Andy Carroll, and the tide turned once more. The winning goal came moments later. As with the first goal, Chelsea made a mess of clearing a Payet corner, and the ball fell to Cresswell. His perfect cross was manna from heaven for Carroll, whose towering header gave Begović no chance.

Andy headed towards the East Stand and celebrated with his version of a Lancaster bomber coming in to land. As he went horizontal we were distinctly vertical – jumping up and down in much the same way we had done in the first half.

The final minutes were pure joy – spent alternately advising the Chelsea fans where to stick their blue flag and praising the brilliance of Payet, confident that we were good enough to hang on to all three points. It doesn't get much better than that for West Ham supporters – or certainly not this particular West Ham supporter.

I was still ecstatic as we strolled along the Barking Road. The victory meant West Ham had made their best ever start to a Premier League season, taking an astonishing twenty points from ten games. But that wasn't the big issue for me – the key thing was we had defeated the team I dislike more than any other.

Yet there was a fly in the ointment. This was the last time we would ever play Chelsea at Upton Park. This was the last time we would ever beat Chelsea at Upton Park. I'd been trying to ignore the fact we were going to vacate the stadium at the end of the season. But now, for me, there was no denying that the clock was ticking. It felt as if I had just been robbed of something very precious.

8

Light the blue touchpaper

London Stadium
Saturday 5 November 2016
Kick-off: 3.00
Final score: West Ham 1–1 Stoke

JOURNALISTS CAN'T HELP themselves when a football match is played on Bonfire Night. The scorer of the winning goal is usually said to have provided the fireworks; his shot was almost certainly a rocket and one of his teammates would have sparkled. The game against Stoke, however, was a damp squib. (Many years ago I worked for a chief sub-editor who was adamant that the phrase is actually 'damp squid' – and on two separate occasions changed headlines accordingly. He didn't continue in the role long enough to change a third.)

Right then, let's review the highlights. This isn't *Match of the*

Day – we're not going to wait until it's past your bedtime then give you such a brief snippet it makes you wonder why you bothered staying up so late.

In the first hour of play West Ham had one serious attempt on goal – a bullet header by Angelo Ogbonna that called for a decent save – and saw the sort of free kick that Dimitri Payet was scoring for fun the previous season disappear over the bar. The unenthusiastic support matched the lethargy of the performance.

When Bilić finally decided the time had come to change things, he was spoilt for choice about which players to replace. With the possible exception of Pedro Obiang, none of them could have complained if they'd got the hook. In the end he settled on Manuel Lanzini and André Ayew, who was back in the side for the first time since being injured three months beforehand. On came Ashley Fletcher and Edimilson Fernandes, and the 4–4–2 formation they brought with them made a difference straight away.

After sixty-four minutes we won what was only our third corner of the game. Payet's delivery was cleared but the ball fell to Mark Noble. He promptly gave it back to the Frenchman, who shimmied towards the penalty area and sent over a flighted cross for Michail Antonio. Having scored five with his head since the start of the season, Antonio didn't hesitate in trying to make it six – and might well have done if his deft header hadn't been diverted past goalkeeper Lee Grant, via the post, for a Glenn Whelan own goal.

Stoke made a double substitution of their own. But their goal came less from tactical acumen and more from another goalkeeping clanger by Adrián. A hopeful ball by Charlie Adam to the corner of the penalty area looked harmless enough, but

Adrián saw things differently and came charging off his line like Don Quixote with a particularly provocative windmill in his sights. Jonathan Walters's hooked pass over the Spaniard's head left the goalkeeper stranded in the middle of nowhere and Bojan Krkić volleyed home – thus saving referee Andre Marriner the bother of awarding a penalty for Adrián's illicit challenge on Walters shortly after the striker had got rid of the ball.

That left ten minutes to play, which was just enough time for Adam to test the jittery Adrián with a long-range free kick. By that time, the stadium was half empty.

Afterwards, Slaven Bilić didn't pull any punches. 'It's a mistake by Adrián. It looked like he was never going to get to the ball. We gave that goal away very cheaply. We were 1–0 up with fifteen minutes to go. A very cheap goal has cost us a win.'

Playing Cheikhou Kouyaté in midfield rather than in a three-man defence might have made a difference, but what do I know? I'm just the bloke in the back row. We have a highly paid manager to make decisions like that.

Would the game have been more enjoyable if it had been at Upton Park? Of course not – turgid football is turgid football no matter where it is played. The big difference at the Boleyn Ground was that it held memories I could call on when the going got tough. For Stoke, those memories included some great moments – such as Billy Jennings's hat-trick at the back end of 1975, which I cheered to the rafters of the Chicken Run. There were the not-so-great moments, too: Gordon Banks saving Geoff Hurst's penalty in front of the North Bank to deny West Ham a place in the League Cup final of 1972; Hurst returning to Upton Park as a Stoke player twelve months after the missed spot kick and scoring in front of what had until so recently been his adoring fans, me included. But those recollections – good and bad – were part of my life. They were part of my attachment to the club. The new ground, because it was a new ground, had nothing similar to offer me – and possibly never would.

On the plus side, there was no trouble at the Stoke game. The same could not be said of our previous match at the London Stadium.

Four days after the tedious victory over Sunderland we had entertained Chelsea in the League Cup – and it all kicked off. It was a great game – easily the best we'd seen in Stratford. But the quality of the football was overshadowed by violence.

Before the game I had hoped it would be the turning point in our season, and used my regular column in *Blowing Bubbles* to urge all those in claret and blue to forget their differences in the name of unity. 'In some parts of the ground the atmosphere is toxic,' I wrote. 'West Ham United? We're West Ham Divided right now.'

I took the opportunity to spell out the difficulties as I saw them.

It's no secret that some supporters are angry that they can't stand up. Equally, others are upset because there are people directly in front of them defying the club's instruction to remain seated and obstructing their view of the game.

There are problems all over the place. A lot of season ticket holders don't like their new seats. Many people feel the stewards are heavy-handed. Traditional match-day rituals have had to be abandoned. Ben & Jerry's doesn't feel right in a football stadium. Popcorn is unthinkable. The kids that the new merchandise is aimed at appear to be bored out of their minds. Hardcore supporters sitting next to the little 'uns are having to mind their language while Håvard Nordtveit misdirects yet another pass. The only thing we seem able to agree on is that our early season form is woeful.

For many diehards the low point came when, for the first time in the club's history, we started a game without a single Englishman in claret and blue as the Academy hopefuls – the lifeblood of the club – were overlooked in favour of a bunch of very ordinary imports in a League Cup fixture.

That fixture, of course, was against League Two small fry Accrington Stanley in the previous round – a game that West Ham should have won easily but instead had to rely on a magnificent free kick from Payet in the ninety-sixth minute. However, I tried to be uncharacteristically positive and wrote: 'His moment of brilliance has given us all a chance to forget the grumbles and shelve our differences by setting up a fourth-round match that should unite us all.'

Not for the first time I detailed my specific dislike of our opponents – a team owned by a Russian billionaire who, I believe, has done more than anyone to convince supporters of all clubs that success can be bought at the expense of a club's heart and soul.

Chelsea. The very name ought to fill any West Ham supporter with revulsion. There may be much we don't like about what is happening with our own club at the moment, but we *really* don't like Chelsea. Not one bit.

I have my own reasons for disliking the Stamford Bridge club – I grew up in an area with a large Chelsea support and occasionally found myself in playground scraps for having the temerity to wear my West Ham colours. However, my childhood problems pale into insignificance when you look at what has happened in the Abramovich era.

In the thirteen years since the unholy Roman empire was established in West London, Chelsea have won a lorry-load of silverware – yet the way they have achieved that success has made them one of the most despised clubs in the country.

It's hard to put your finger on what, precisely, constitutes 'class' at a football club. I see it as a combination of style and the ability to handle success. Liverpool certainly had it in their heyday. Leeds didn't. Man Utd, under Busby, had class; under Ferguson, not so much. Arsenal, for all their annoying ways, have always been a classy set-up. Chelsea never have been and never will be.

Here at West Ham, the argument in favour of moving to the new ground was that it will eventually provide the funds for better players and more success. We all want to see that, but we must make sure our identity isn't buried in the rubble of Upton Park in an attempt to match the roubles of Stamford Bridge.

There are problems at the new stadium, but they can be sorted out over time. Safe standing; a reallocation of season tickets so like-minded supporters can be grouped together; a family enclosure – it is all doable. I can even put up with the popcorn if that's what it takes.

Of course, nothing will help more than stringing a few results together, and none would be sweeter than a victory over the club we must vow never to emulate. Win that game and the London Stadium may finally start to feel like home. Stand up if you love West Ham? Well, only if you are prepared to have your season ticket revoked. But sing up – and sing together – if you want to see the hated Chelsea put to the sword. United we stand, divided we fall!

However, I wasn't suggesting that the West Ham faithful rip out the seats and lob them at the blue-flag boys.

Let's deal with the football first. There was some real passion behind 'Bubbles' as the game began, and it hadn't subsided ten minutes later when Antonio was fouled by Gary Cahill. The free kick led to a corner, which came out to Noble. His cross was aimed at Kouyaté, who outjumped John Terry to score. West Ham supporters live for moments such as these.

Fuelled by the best atmosphere we had managed to create all season, the team tore into Chelsea. Antonio put a shot just wide, then created an opportunity for Lanzini. A Payet free kick brought out a decent save from Asmir Begović, then Obiang tried out the keeper from distance. We should have led by more than a single goal at half time.

Three minutes into the second half we did. Fernandes beat Ola Aina, moved the ball on to his left foot, then swept it past Begović into the bottom corner. Euphoria.

Chelsea threw on the big guns they had chosen to rest – Diego Costa, Eden Hazard, then Pedro were all called into action. But it was one of those nights when West Ham were not to be denied, and even though Cahill took a little gloss off the scoreline by bundling in a corner with the last kick of the game, we never looked like losing.

But the media wasn't terribly interested in what happened on the pitch that night. It was the fighting that made all the headlines.

There were reports of trouble outside the ground before the

game kicked off – and Chelsea supporters were critical of the way the police handled things after hundreds of their fans were held at Highbury and Islington station on the way to the game.

They were then marched slowly from Stratford to the stadium by police. They didn't get in until midway through the match. One of them later told the *Evening Standard*: 'They were clueless, the police – they didn't know what to do. They had no plans whatsoever. They just wouldn't let us through, and they didn't give us a reason. It was quite scary; they were running around like headless chickens.'

But the real problems started inside the stadium and then spilled out on to the streets afterwards. Any game between West Ham and Chelsea has the potential to generate trouble, no matter where it's played. Police were deployed inside the ground for the first time, and there were extra stewards on duty. There was even a ban on the sale of alcohol (like people didn't have plenty of chance to get tanked up before an evening kick-off?). The authorities had every right to expect trouble of some kind, and they got it.

Precisely who launched the first missile will always be a matter of considerable debate. But whoever started it, there is no denying that plastic bottles, coins and even a few seats were exchanged by the warring factions.

One Chelsea season ticket holder told the BBC that he was at the game with his eight-year-old daughter. He said: 'My daughter was hit with seven coins all over her body. We were watching the game in the front row near to the home fans – suddenly there's a whole load of coins coming over. Other kids were hit, it was not just my daughter.'

Personally, I think anyone who takes an eight-year-old child into the away end at a London derby should have their head examined. Apparently he had been taking her to football since she was two. Who takes a two-year-old to a football match? But I am by no means condoning anyone pelting them with coins, of course.

The major flashpoint came towards the end of the game, when a Chelsea fan wriggled his way through a line of stewards and broke into the area that divided rival supporters. He then scaled the seats that were covered by a claret tarpaulin and abused the West Ham faction. His picture appeared in just about every national paper you can think of the following day.

That was the cue for the two sets of fans with violence on their minds to head for the stadium concourse, where they surged towards one another. The stewards needed the support of riot police to prevent a serious punch-up.

When a semblance of order was finally restored, the bulk of the Chelsea fans were escorted into Stratford by the police, but there were isolated skirmishes nevertheless. In all, seven people were arrested on the night. Thirty others, it turned out, had – in the words of the police – 'been prevented from attending the match'. The following day the West Ham management threatened to ban 200 supporters as a direct result of the trouble inside the ground. In the end they settled on forty-eight, explaining that eighteen individuals they thought were involved could not be identified by the CCTV footage, while several other people successfully appealed against their exclusion orders. With twenty-three people banned already, that took the number of people who were no longer welcome inside the London Stadium to seventy-one. I couldn't help wondering what proportion of those were Upton Park old-stagers, and how many were part of the new intake.

When the dust had settled Police Commander B. J. Harrington said: 'There were a minority of people who attended the match that were clearly intent on being involved in confrontation and violence.' He was right. I was vaguely familiar with one of them.

Di and I first met Australian journalist Ashley Gray at the end of the final season at the Boleyn Ground. Ashley, Aussie born and bred, was – and still is – a lifelong Hammers fan. We were keen to make the acquaintance of someone who lived on the other side of the world yet had decided of their own free will to sign up for the life of turmoil that goes with following West Ham.

Perhaps at this stage I should make it crystal clear that Ashley was not one of the people Commander Harrington was referring to. He was at home in Sydney going about his entirely lawful business on the night of the crime. Honestly officer, I can vouch for him. Please, bear with me for a moment and his part in all this will become clear.

Ashley had got in touch before flying over from Australia to write about the final two games to see if I could provide him with a couple of contact numbers. I was happy to offer any help I could – let's face it, if a man is prepared to fly from Australia to support the Irons he deserves all the help he can get.

By the time of the Swansea game Di, Geoff and I had become match-day regulars in the Overdraft, and thought Ashley might enjoy the warm East End welcome that was guaranteed to one and all in there (provided they were dressed in claret and blue, natu-rally). We met up on the corner of the Barking Road and Priory Road and headed off to the pub, naturally discussing the match as we went. Inside, the place was busy as usual with good-hearted souls falling over themselves to get the drinks in. People like Barry and Eddy didn't let a small detail such as never having met some-one before prevent them from buying him (or her) a drink.

An hour later Di noticed that Ashley was deep in conversa-tion with a bloke we'd not seen in there before. 'Do you think he's all right?' she asked.

'Sure,' I replied, a pint in both hands because Barry had just taken it upon himself to get another round even though it wasn't his turn. 'He's fine – what are you worried about?'

Then I gave the matter some thought, and realised there was plenty to be worried about. I'd only just met Ashley and had no idea if he was familiar with East End characters who can suddenly take offence at the least little thing and glass you. Do they have individuals like that in other countries? From what little I'd seen of *Neighbours*, Australians all seemed thoroughly nice people, albeit with a tendency to become slightly cocky when the subject turned to cricket. I was suddenly struck by the thought of Ashley innocently mentioning Shane Warne's first delivery in his debut Ashes Test – the one that spun sideways and did for Mike Gatting – then finding the bridge of his nose making sudden and unexpected contact with a bony cockney forehead. (I don't know if you've ever been nutted before, but I can testify that it is extremely painful.)

Don't be fooled by the tip from 'The Shoop Shoop Song' that 'It's In His Kiss'. Not when you're dealing with hard cases, it isn't. It's in his eyes. And the guy Ashley was talking to had the sort of eyes that gave me the distinct impression that here was a man not to be messed with. I absolutely agreed that it was time to bring my new-found friend back into the fold before he floated even further away from us on the tide of humanity that was ebbing and flowing within the pub.

You know how it is with some people – you just hit it off straight away. Ashley and I became mates in a very short space of time and have kept in regular contact since he returned Down Under. What I could not have predicted was that he also kept in touch with the guy he met in the Overdraft. We shall call him Dave, although that's not his real name. And I shouldn't have worried about Ashley being an innocent abroad – he recognised that look from the moment he first saw it.

'It was the eyes that gave him away,' Ashley said when I asked him to recall that evening. 'It's a common football affliction. Crazy four-pint slits working in tandem with randomly aggressive pronouncements about a club's future. In this case, of course, it was West Ham's future.'

I remember that he was adamant he was going to the last game at the Boleyn Ground despite not having a ticket. Was that the booze talking do you reckon?

Dave was no ordinary beer bard. He had his own 'firm'. So when he growled stuff like: 'We don't need fucking tickets' to get into that sold-out final Upton Park game against Manchester United, you believed him. And when he later sent me a video of him and his crew sledging 'cuntz', ie United fans, in the away end, you knew he was probably the real deal.

From what I could tell he was a bright guy. Hard, but definitely not stupid. How would you describe him?

Street tough – but charming and smart in that way hard guys who lead other hard guys have to be. He resented the Boleyn's demise and the rise of the football tourist it so brazenly encouraged.

He wasn't keen on the move, was he?

'I'm not going to sit in silence and eat a prawn sandwich at the new ground,' he told me over the phone. Never a truer word was texted.

So not only did he get into Upton Park for the Man U game as he had promised, he was also at the Chelsea League Cup tie at the London Stadium?

That really hammered home his authentic but brutal love for West Ham. He called Chelsea fans 'The Russians'. When the violence erupted, Dave's firm was at its bloody heart.

How can you be sure?

He was texting me as it happened. And sending videos. They flew as thick and fast as the punches and coins aimed at the Russians. I've still got them. 'We tried to storm their end. Their arses fell out.' 'Fuckin' disgracing the English flag, we'll fuckin go to war with them two-bit shit cunts.' 'All we need is West Ham vs Isis.' Only one more came after that. 'The police have us locked in a pub.'

Do you know what happened to him?

No mate. But I guess it was someone else's turn to look into those eyes.

I for one am certain that Dave would not have been the one to blink first.

Boleyn Ground
Saturday 7 November 2015
Kick-off: 3.00
Final score: West Ham 1–1 Everton

Wonderful though Upton Park was, there is no denying the place was perfectly capable of staging very ordinary football matches. The game against Everton in the final season was one of them.

It boasted a brilliant goal by Lanzini, an inevitable goal by Romelu Lukaku and a series of crude challenges on our more skilful players that should have, on their own, prompted a sustained frenzy of rage in the stands. Yet someone forgot to bring the matches and the blue touchpaper never got lit. It happened at the Boleyn Ground from time to time. I guess it must happen everywhere.

Perhaps it would have been a better game if Payet hadn't hobbled off five minutes after the restart – the victim of a disgraceful first-half scissor tackle by James McCarthy from which he never fully recovered.

In the early stages it appeared that the Everton players were lining up to kick Lanzini and Payet. They probably would have kicked Victor Moses as well if they could have caught him. Referee Paul Tierney should have done more than he did. The yellow card he showed McCarthy was too little, too late. It should have been red, and it shouldn't have been the first card of the afternoon.

Payet was replaced by Enner Valencia – who was stretchered off twenty minutes later with injuries to both ankles after some more robust tackling. 'The first was a bad challenge,' Bilić said later. 'The second was... English'.

There was an old boy sitting a few rows in front of us who,

every game, leaped from his seat and brandished an imaginary card every time a member of the opposition committed the slightest misdemeanour. He had a busy afternoon.

We all knew Lukaku was going to score that afternoon. It was the seventh consecutive game in which he'd done it. He went on to do it twice more before finally failing to put the ball in West Ham's net. Perhaps he'd got bored by then.

Lanzini's goal came as more of a surprise. With half an hour gone Moses powered his way into the penalty area and tried his luck. The shot was blocked and then cleared, but the ball fell to Lanzini thirty yards out. The Argentinian edged forward, took aim – and then curled a fantastic effort into the top corner with his right foot. It was a belter.

The goal made him the first West Ham player to score against both the major Merseyside teams since Bobby Zamora in the 2006–07 season. In fact, 2007 was the last time we'd beaten Everton in the league at Upton Park.

Want to know the memory that I hung on to as, time and again, we got chewed up and spat out by the Toffees? I'll share it with you anyway. It was Colin Foster's winning volley in an FA Cup quarter-final in 1991. We were in the West Stand back then. I'd barely exchanged three words with the bloke in the next seat all season, but when that goal went in he hugged me like I was his long lost brother. Such was the passion of his embrace, he bent my glasses.

Having my spectacles twisted in a spontaneous act of sheer joy is not something I can see happening at the London Stadium any time soon. But perhaps I'm being unduly pessimistic here.

9

This is gonna hurt

London Stadium
Saturday 3 December 2016
Kick-off: 5.30
Final score: West Ham 1–5 Arsenal

I SUPPOSE THE one group of away supporters we didn't ever expect to taunt us with 'is this the Emirates' were the Gooners, but that's precisely what they did as a deathly hush descended over Stratford. Given that we were witnessing a massacre, the silence was almost excusable for once. But we'll come to that later.

So much had happened since I'd last made the long haul up to row seventy-three it was hard to catch your breath – in more ways than one in my case.

The week after the Stoke game was an international break. England hammered Scotland 3–0 at Wembley in a Friday night World Cup qualifier without the aid of Michail Antonio, who had failed to make the squad. England's next fixture was a friendly against Spain, who omitted Adrián from their 25-man party. Quite frankly, at that stage of the season he would have been a borderline choice for the Fox and Firkin third XI, let alone the Spanish national side. The good news for West Ham fans was that Aaron Cresswell made his England debut, coming on as a late sub in a 2–2 draw.

The following Saturday West Ham had gone to Tottenham, and lost after twice being in front. Adrián had been replaced in goal by Darren Randolph – and many of us felt the change hadn't come a moment too soon.

From what I could see on the live stream I was following, West Ham played well before hitting the self-destruct button. Michail Antonio gave West Ham the lead – another headed goal – before a young Tottenham player, who goes by the unlikely name of Harry Winks, equalised. (I fear that boy is going to come in for more than his fair share of abuse from opposition fans with a moniker like that.) Things were looking good when Manuel Lanzini restored the lead from the penalty spot. Then, with victory in sight, another Harry – this time Kane – got an equaliser. At this point, the stream I had been following froze, which gave me the perfect excuse to walk away from my desktop computer in disgust. No, I do not accept this is the same as leaving a game early: it's a different matter entirely. Anyway, when I turned on Sky Sports to confirm that we had dropped a point I discovered we had in fact dropped all three – thanks to a moment of madness from Håvard Nordtveit, who had conceded a last-gasp penalty, which Kane had of course converted. To make matters worse (how much worse can they be? you may ask), Winston Reid had been sent off after picking up a second yellow card. The Williams' family feline took one look at my face and wisely headed for his cat flap at a rate of knots.

Next up was Man Utd. Again it was an away game, and again West Ham played well. Randolph kept his place – he had clearly been earmarked as first choice for the league campaign. Diafra Sakho scored a great goal after just two minutes (all goals against Man U are great goals). Zlatan Ibrahimović equalised twenty minutes later, and shortly after that our old friend José Mourinho provided a little light entertainment of his own by kicking a water bottle in frustration at the perfectly justified decision to book Paul Pogba for diving and was duly sent to sit on the naughty step for the rest of the game by the ref. I'd have gladly settled for the one-all draw that we left with had I been offered it before the match.

Three days later West Ham were back at Old Trafford – this time in the League Cup. And we got off to the worst possible start when Ibrahimović scored within two minutes. Adrián was back in the side – one of five changes – but could count himself lucky to stay on the pitch after employing a swinging right leg to clean up the Swedish striker, who took several minutes to recover sufficiently to gingerly celebrate his goal.

Ibrahimović should have doubled the lead soon after but Adrián foiled him with a double save. Other chances came and went. Former West Ham player Michael Carrick (why's he in the sticker book when Martin Peters isn't?) pulled the strings as the Man U attack threatened to tear our defence to shreds.

An equaliser looked about as likely as the West Ham faithful taking Wayne Rooney to their hearts but, astonishingly, one came after thirty-five minutes when David de Gea spilled Dimitri Payet's shot and Ashley Fletcher did the rest from six yards. 'He's one of our own' the travelling support cheekily informed the Stretford End before explaining precisely why the lad had left Old Trafford in the first place. The TV sound engineers hurriedly tweaked their various buttons to ensure the explanation didn't offend the delicate ears of sensitive souls such as myself watching the game at home.

What was needed in the second half was a decent start, backed up by a totally committed, disciplined performance from every man in an away shirt. Which was precisely what didn't happen. Anthony Martial smacked the ball into the roof of the West Ham net three minutes after the restart, and the Hammers fell apart. Martial scored again and Ibrahimović got his second in stoppage time.

Slaven Bilić was angry. 'At half time when we were back in the game I said we cannot make the same mistake again, but we did. Exactly the same start to the half.' But he was diplomatic enough not to mention any players by name. If he had, Dimitri Payet would have certainly merited a king-size bollocking for his performance. His half-hearted pass out of defence gave Man U the chance for their second goal and his failure to show any real interest in his defensive duties placed an added burden on his already overstretched colleagues. If you didn't know better, you might have been forgiven for thinking that he didn't actually want to play for West Ham.

However, there was one bright spot in that this was the game that produced what was generally considered the worst shot of the season in all competitions. Shortly after coming on as a substitute, Simone Zaza let fly from inside the Man Utd penalty area – and the ball went out for a throw-in level with the eighteen-yard line. When the ball came to a standstill it was considerably further from the Man U goal than when it started. In effect, it went backwards to provide an everlasting nugget of comedy gold. I was starting to have my doubts that Zaza really was the man to take us to the next level after all.

Conceding four goals at Old Trafford is bad enough. Letting in five at home is another matter entirely. Happily, it is not a humiliation I have had to endure all that often. West Ham may get beaten at home more than they should, but we don't usually let the opposition run up a rugby score. The last time we conceded five at Upton Park was in 2002, when the visitors were Man Utd (to put it in context, it should be noted we scored three). There was a 1–5 thrashing at the hands of Leeds three years before that game, which is best forgotten, and in 1987 there was a crazy League Cup tie against Barnsley which we contrived to lose 2–5 in extra time after being 2–0 up.

Generally, though, things don't get out of hand that badly all that often. In 112 years of trying, Arsenal never scored five against West Ham at Upton Park. But that's what they managed on their first visit to the London Stadium. I'll be honest: it hurt.

I would like to say that three of Arsenal's goals were offside, one never crossed the line and Alexis Sánchez should have been sent off in the first minute for wearing gloves. In truth, the Gooners were the better side from start to finish.

Such was their dominance, it was hard to believe they only scored once in the first half. Losing James Collins after just seven minutes didn't help. West Ham were forced to switch to four at the back, rather than Bilić's preferred system of three, and Nacho Monreal spent the rest of the afternoon giving substitute Álvaro Arbeloa the runaround. But if anyone was to be blamed for Arsenal's opener it had to be the normally reliable Angelo

Ogbonna, whose mistake enabled Sánchez to gift Mesut Özil a tap-in. What had been a less-than-hostile atmosphere became even more subdued. There were boos as the players traipsed off at the break.

Half time was brightened by a pitchside interview with Marlon Harewood, who had scored the winner in the corresponding fixture ten years beforehand. Rather than talking to the likes of me, marooned in the back row because I couldn't face the long haul down to the bar and back, he should have been getting stripped off. Judging by what I'd seen in the first forty-five minutes, he was more likely to score than the isolated Ashley Fletcher.

We hung on gamely for twenty-five minutes in the second half. Those West Ham fans who left after seventy minutes – and there were several – must have known something we didn't. Because two minutes later the wheels came off in spectacular fashion. Sánchez controlled a long ball from Shkodran Mustafi, skipped past Arthur Masuaku and sent an angled shot past Darren Randolph from twenty yards. Fourteen minutes later he had a hat-trick. His second was a half-volley. The third came after he feigned to shoot then, when Randolph bought the dummy, he lifted the ball over the diving goalkeeper. For the record, that one was offside.

In between hat-trick goals two and three, Andy Carroll had pulled one back with a headed effort from close range after a Payet free kick cannoned off the bar, and then Alex Oxlade-Chamberlain scored Arsenal's fourth of the afternoon with another high-class finish from distance.

Remarkably for a London derby of this magnitude, there were some empty seats scattered around the stadium at the beginning of the match. There were even more come the end. Many, many, more. Di, Geoff and I were among the few who stuck it out to the bitter end. With a mauling like that you have to, don't you? I may not like the London Stadium, but it is my home ground. I'm not leaving it with a bunch of Gooners claiming they can see me sneaking out. It's a badge of honour.

Whisper it quietly, but the Hammers have always regarded Arsenal as something of a role model. In his comprehensive and compelling history of the club, simply entitled *West Ham United*, Charles Korr traces this respect back to Syd King, the long-serving manager who took the Irons to the White Horse Final of 1923. More than thirty-five years later, in 1960, manager Ted Fenton published a book in which he likened King's achievements to those of Arsenal supremo Herbert Chapman – a man generally thought to have ushered association football into a new era. Korr writes:

Chapman, the hugely successful manager of Arsenal Football Club, revolutionised the game, while King was only a mildly successful manager of a fringe club with no claims to tactical innovations. What therefore was the basis of Fenton's remark? It must have been that King thought in terms of putting West Ham on the football map. Chapman had accomplished this with Arsenal; he had established a tradition that saw the club through even when its performance on the field fell below standard. Fenton shared a feeling with many of his players that Arsenal was *the* London club. It 'was always something special' to go to Arsenal's ground at Highbury for a match. No one at West Ham would admit they wanted to copy Arsenal, but they certainly wanted to be like it.

Ten years before West Ham upped sticks and moved to a new stadium, Arsenal had done the same thing. There were differences of course – not least that the Gooners actually paid for their new gaff rather than rented it. And our north London neighbours put their iconic clock in a public place where people could readily see it, while West Ham chose to put Upton Park's emblematic John Lyall gates in the club store which, to me, smacks of having to leave a tourist attraction via the gift shop. But I wondered if there were lessons to be learned for supporters who, like me, were having trouble adjusting to new surroundings. So I asked my friend Dee for her thoughts. This is what she told me:

> Like many Gooners, I was glad that Arsenal found a site for its new stadium so close to historic Highbury and admired its state-of-the-art design, snooker table pitch, efficient crowd circulation routes and good sight lines. I was particularly chuffed at the toilet provision – it's the only public entertainment venue I've ever been to where men, not women, have to spend most of half time queuing to get comfy.
>
> We Arsenal supporters had been told that a move was essential to allow the club to compete in the world of modern top-level football. The existing ground inspired admiration and awe with its marble halls and small pitch, with close proximity to the crowd, which created a great atmosphere and made it such a challenge for visiting teams. But its 38,400 capacity did not bring in enough revenue and could not meet the demand for tickets.
>
> So in 2006 we moved to the 60,432 capacity Emirates, just over 500 yards away as the crow flies: a steel, glass and

concrete arena that perches neatly over and around the East Coast Mainline and a local commuter route. The old Highbury, shoehorned equally neatly behind north London Victorian terraced houses, was converted into luxury apartments priced (like most Arsenal tickets) beyond the pockets of most Arsenal supporters.

And there's the rub. The stadium that was supposed to increase access for fans has done the opposite. Despite the highest season ticket prices in the Premier League (£891 for 2017/18, compared with £1,014 in 2016/17 because of a Europa League discount) and the second highest in Europe after Paris Saint-Germain, there is still a years-long waiting list. Most major matches (Premier League, FA Cup, Champions/Europa League) are season ticket only. To stand a chance of buying returns (when season ticket holders make their seats available if they can't attend) or for 'lesser' matches such as the League Cup, fans usually need to be a red member (cost £34 a year, minimum) and tickets mostly need to be bought in advance. No rocking up on the day because you and your mates have a last-minute whim to see some footie.

The main increase in provision at the Emirates was for even more expensive grades of tickets (club class, executive boxes, fine dining…), which bring in much prized VIP and corporate revenues worth apparently even more than that from the punters in the 'cheap seats'.

So has all this extra dosh brought Arsenal even greater success? No. Since 2006, Arsenal have won the FA Cup three times (which is not to be sniffed at) but have failed to really challenge for the Premier League title or the Champions League, in marked contrast to the ten Wenger years immediately before the move (1996/7 to 2005/6), when they achieved the Champions League final in 2006, won the Premier League three times and the FA Cup four times.

I was told by one of the accountants who drew up the business plan for moving to the Emirates, which was without funding from oligarchs or Middle Eastern royals, that the redevelopment relied on Arsenal selling their best player each year for ten years and qualifying for the Champions League. And this is what happened: bye-bye to Ashley Cole, Cesc Fàbregas, Thierry Henry, Alexander Hleb, Samir Nasri, Robin van Persie, Robert Pirès... Admittedly we qualified for the Champions League, which meant fans could watch some of the best teams in Europe run rings round us.

The Emirates has been criticised for lacking atmosphere compared with the grounds of other top clubs – in fact, a friend sitting in the top tier was told to shut up by those around him when he burst into song. But that's hardly surprising when players who fans admire (often demonstrated by buying costly replica shirts with their name on) are sold on because of an accounting strategy.

Don't get me wrong. I'm not starry-eyed about 'awesome Arsenal'. I cut my teeth as a Gooner at the age of nine, standing at the old Clock End with Dad in the 1960s, watching the Gunners grind out 0–0 draws or 1–0 wins against Leeds United or Wolverhampton Wanderers. Those were the days of 'boring Arsenal', but that didn't really matter because often we'd have decided on the day to go and tickets were affordable, even for a print worker.

I'd meet Dad at my grandparents' flat in Hoxton, after he'd finished Saturday morning overtime and I'd run some basic errands (paying Nan and Granddad's paper bill, buying a loaf). We'd drop in to see Dad's brother Charley and, if he and my cousin Lawrence were up for it, we'd catch the bus to Highbury for the match (usually fuelled with a lunch of boiled beef and carrots from Auntie Doll). We didn't support Arsenal out of respect for the Herbert Chapman glory days (and certainly not for the less-than glorious facilities of old Highbury), but because they were our local team and we identified with the likes of Pat Rice, who'd been to nearby Gifford Street School, and Charlie George, who drank at the Admiral Mann pub off Brecknock Road, plus all the other players from further away who stuck with us.

It's hard to identify with a stadium called the Emirates, majority owned by an absentee US billionaire, which is run as a business rather than a local source of pride and passion. However, I'm a third-generation Gooner so, like many supporters across the country, I'll keep paying for my half of our jointly owned season ticket, travel to our corporate ground and sing my heart out. In 2017/18 we haven't qualified for the Champions League (for the first time since 1998) and Arsène Wenger says he will not sell his best player (Alexis Sánchez). Maybe football is finally challenging the accountants. I hope so. We may have moved just 500 yards, but in many ways it's a million miles.

For me, Dee, the leap that West Ham has made feels even further.

Boleyn Ground
Sunday 29 November 2015
Kick-off: 2.05
Final score: West Ham 1–1 WBA

For the final visit of West Brom to Upton Park security was tight following the appalling terrorist attack on Paris that had taken place earlier in the month. Bags were checked assiduously – and rightly so. Just over two weeks had passed since that terrible night which saw the deaths of 130 innocent people of all classes, colours and creeds in the heart of one of the world's major cities, and nerves were still raw.

West Ham had played one game since the attack – an away fixture at Tottenham. As a mark of respect, the French national anthem was played beforehand – as it was at all league grounds that weekend. Then both sets of players lined up together for a joint team photograph, which appeared across a double-page spread in the match-day programme that was produced for the West Brom game. Football so often gets these things wrong, but this picture was spot on. The two teams, randomly intermingled, reminded me of two sets of mates about to have a kickabout in the park. It completely encapsulated the spirit of unity that we all need to feel after such senseless acts of horrific violence.

For the record, West Ham had got well and truly stuffed at White Hart Lane, going down 4–1. But even a defeat of that magnitude against our fiercest rivals paled into insignificance compared with the atrocities that had taken place in the French capital. Football more important than life and death? It was a great line in its day, but we all know that it isn't true.

The West Brom fixture, played on a Sunday, came with the

rather bizarre kick-off time of five past two. Whatever happened to three o'clock on a Saturday? Not that time had much meaning in Upton Park any more: the clocks inside the ground appeared to have stopped working. Sadly, I couldn't say the same about the upturned egg-timer in my head that was monitoring the sands of time that were fast running out for the Boleyn Ground.

Before the game, the club wheeled out a battery of former players they had dubbed 'cult heroes' as part of the season-long farewell party. There were eighteen in all, spanning five decades. Some had contributed more to the West Ham cause than others, but they were all applauded vigorously. There were certainly some favourites of mine among them – not least Peter Brabrook, who had provided the cross for Ronnie Boyce to score the goal that had cemented my love affair with the club more than fifty years ago.

Memories, memories, memories. As I stood and applauded the old-stagers, so many recollections came flooding back. John Moncur sent on as a substitute against Newcastle and getting booked before he'd actually touched the ball; Dudley Tyler's one and only goal for West Ham in a 5–2 thrashing of Leicester; Ludo's giant clearances (Di and I both desperately hoped he'd score with one of them); Devo's brilliance for so many seasons (despite matchstick legs and questionable tonsorial choices, one of the all-time greats); Mad Dog's ferocity (plus a peach of a goal against Liverpool); Ian Bishop's leadership in the promotion season of 1990–91; Matty Etherington's stunner against Ipswich in the play-off semi-finals.

Could I parcel up these memories in bubblewrap then ship them off to Stratford, or were they so rooted in the turf of the Boleyn Ground they would disappear along with the stands when the bulldozers arrived to do their abominable business?

In his programme notes, Bilić had earmarked one of his current squad as a potential cult hero in the making. However, everyone's favourite Frenchman was still missing as a result of the diabolical tackling to which he had been subjected in the previous home game against Everton. In all, he was to be out for the best part of ten weeks.

Also missing was club captain Mark Noble, who had been booked at Tottenham and picked up a one-game suspension under the totting up procedure. The bloke in the seat next to me had been on Noble's case for most of the season. I felt much of the criticism was unfair, and had said so more than once. At one stage, when West Brom were on top for a spell, my increasingly anxious neighbour gave full rein to his feelings. 'Where's the midfield?' he demanded to know. I couldn't resist the temptation. 'He's suspended,' I told him with a grin. Fair play to the guy – he had the good grace to laugh.

The first half was all West Ham, with Manuel Lanzini at the centre of things. Salomón Rondón could have scored for the visitors in the thirteenth minute with a wicked shot that went past the far post. But, other than that, the Hammers were on top. The deserved breakthrough came four minutes later when Gareth McAuley was adjudged to have fouled Diafra Sakho. Mauro Zárate curled the free kick into the top corner from twenty-five yards.

We could and should have scored again. First Cheikhou Kouyaté's glancing header went wide. Then Lanzini forced goalkeeper Boaz Myhill into using his feet to save a long-range effort. Lanzini had another effort saved five minutes later then Sakho and Victor Moses failed to make the most of passable chances.

Geoff fancied a half-time beer. Di joined him while I stayed in my seat, chatting with Barry and Eddy. We rued the missed chances, knowing all too well that if you don't take them when you're on top you can live to regret it. Which is exactly what happened. Five minutes into the second half Darren Fletcher chested the ball to Rickie Lambert, who had been brought off the subs bench, and his shot found its way past Adrián via Winston Reid.

After that, either side could have won it. Sakho nearly converted a great cross by Aaron Cresswell, then Adrián had to pull off a superb save to deny Rondón. Zárate took another wonderful free kick which Myhill pushed away. The Baggies had the majority of possession – hence my neighbour's enquiry regarding the whereabouts of our midfield – but West Ham looked good on the break. In one counter-attack Moses sprinted fifty yards with the ball before giving it to Sakho, whose shot from just inside the area was diverted into the side netting. Soon after, the Senegalese striker had to leave the field with a thigh injury.

Andy Carroll, who had been brought on to replace Pedro Obiang, had a sniff in the closing minutes, but in the end we had to settle for a point. It wasn't the worst game I had ever seen, but I'd hardly put it in the 'unforgettable' category. Just as well in some ways. The afternoon had made me realise there wasn't much room left in the section of my memory bank reserved for Upton Park reminiscences.

10

And the winner isn't…

London Stadium
Wednesday 14 December 2016
Kick-off: 7.45
Final score: West Ham 1–0 Burnley

IT HAD BEEN a sad week for West Ham fans of my generation. Four days before the Burnley game, one of my boyhood heroes had died.

If it hadn't been for Peter Brabrook, I might not have been a West Ham supporter at all. He was a key member of the 1964 FA Cup winning side. I was three weeks short of my eighth birthday at the time and, despite having no connection with east London whatsoever, had adopted the Hammers as my team after they had beaten Manchester United in the semi-final.

I'm sure you hardly need me to remind you that it was Brabrook who, in the closing minutes of the Wembley final against Preston North End with the scores tied at 2–2, collected the ball on the right-hand side of the area, composed himself, then played the perfect cross for Ticker Boyce to steer home the header that meant West Ham had won the cup for the first time in their history.

In later years I began to ask myself if I would have stuck with West Ham had we lost that game. As I say, I knew nothing about the East End – I'd never even been there – and seven-year-olds are not renowned for their loyalties to lost causes.

I like to think I would have kept the faith, but who knows? Of course, my fate was sealed the following year when West Ham won the European Cup Winners' Cup: no prepubescent glory hunter can resist success like that.

Contrary to David Sullivan's programme notes, Brabrook was not a member of the team that beat TSV 1860 Munich 2–0 at Wembley in 1965. A series of injuries restricted his European campaign to a single appearance in a first-round second-leg tie at Upton Park. His No 7 shirt went to Alan Sealey – the man who went on to score both goals in the final. He was, however, in the side that beat Chelsea 3–1 at Stamford Bridge in the autumn of 1967 – the first time I saw my personal Hammers Heroes in the flesh. I was eleven, and there was never any question that I would be anything other than West Ham 'til I die by then. For the record, 1967–68 was Brabrook's last season at West Ham. His place was eventually taken by a certain Harry Redknapp.

As a West Ham supporter himself, Brabrook was desperate to secure a move from Chelsea to the club he loved. He even turned down an offer from Everton that would have been worth double the salary Ron Greenwood was prepared to pay him. When his drawn-out transfer saga was finally completed he made an instant impact, laying on a goal for Geoff Hurst in the first minute of his debut.

Mr Sullivan may not have been totally spot on with Brabrook's CV, but the programme did at least feature him on the cover. He's wearing what I still think of as the iconic West Ham shirt: long, light-blue sleeves with three claret bands around the cuff, plus a blue crew-neck with a single claret band. You know the one. (Oh, and there's no badge – and no sponsor's name emblazoned across the front.)

To misquote Hans Gruber in *Die Hard*, I could talk about Peter Brabrook and football fashion all day, but I realise you are busy people. Before we move on I should just point out that, coincidentally in the circumstances, Brabrook's first appearance in claret and blue was against Burnley. To the programme's credit, the unnamed author of that piece knew their facts.

The club had arranged a minute's applause by way of a tribute before the game. I was still making the trek up to row seventy-three as that went on – thanks to another inept performance by the security staff on the turnstiles. We had got to Stratford International shortly after 7.00 p.m. – it was a 7.45 p.m. kick-off. Yet we weren't in our seats in time to pay our respects to a West Ham legend because it took an eternity to get into the ground.

I understand the importance of checking bags for explosive devices, but I really don't see the need to pat down every single supporter to ascertain if they have come tooled up for aggro. It's time-consuming and moderately offensive. I didn't hide razor blades in the collar of my coat when the Teddy Bunter Firm and the South Bank Crew were in their heyday, and I don't do it now. Neither do my wife and son (at least, that's what they tell me). What Di does take with her is a bottle of water, which is clearly regarded as an offensive weapon if it has a top on it. So the top is confiscated. Now I probably shouldn't be telling you this, and I would be grateful if you don't let on to the stewards, but my wife has a cunning plan that gets around the problem of a topless bottle. She takes a separate, identical top with her, which she puts back on the bottle once she's in the stadium. I'm guessing that no more than 30,000 people have hit on the same ruse. All she's got to do now is devise a cunning plan that allows her to identify which sprawling queue of supporters will find a female security guard waiting for them when they've finally shuffled to the front.

West Ham really needed to beat Burnley. A draw at Anfield three days before had lifted us out of the relegation zone, but we were only one point and one place above the bottom three. Payet had looked more interested than he did at Old Trafford in the League Cup tie, and equalised Liverpool's first goal with a free kick that really should have been saved. Michail Antonio had given us the lead before half time, but Darren Randolph gifted the Mickey Mousers a second goal when he dropped an innocuous cross. He did, however, make up for his error with a stunning save that left Jordan Henderson looking more be-mused than usual.

Despite the slight improvement in our league position there had been stories in the red-top press suggesting Payet would be allowed to leave if West Ham were relegated. Where had they got that from, I wondered? And why were they running the story with more than half the season yet to play?

As so often happens, floodlights seemed to lift the spirits of the West Ham faithful. There were empty seats towards the back of the stadium, but for once there was a fair amount of noise rather than the polite silence that so often seemed to follow 'Bubbles' in our new home.

It helped that West Ham attacked with urgency from the outset. Andy Carroll, who was making his first start since August, went close in the opening stages. Payet should have done better with his shot from a dangerous position. Antonio nearly got on to the end of a Mark Noble cross at the far post. We might have had a penalty when the ball made contact with the arm of a Burnley defender in the box. Then Pedro Obiang hit the post with a rasping shot from twenty-five yards.

When Noble's curling shot from twenty yards rebounded off the woodwork after forty-five minutes I began to fear it might just be one of those nights. Although I felt a lot better two minutes later when referee Bobby Madley ruled that Ben Mee had fouled Winston Reid and pointed to the spot. Noble's low penalty to keeper Tom Heaton's left was saved, but the captain made no mistake when the ball came straight back to him. His tap-in gave us a much-needed and well-deserved lead.

We were nowhere near as impressive in the second half. Randolph was called into action more than once and Sam Vokes missed a sitter. The stadium got increasingly jittery as the game went on – not that the tension prevented a steady procession of supporters leaving before the end. Those of us still there welcomed Mr Madley's final whistle with a roar of relief and made our own exits. We even managed to skip past the stop-go boards without let or hindrance.

Sadly, the minute's applause for Brabrook wasn't the only emotional tribute paid that night. During the opening spell, in the thirteenth minute, the crowd applauded the memory of young Jack Howard, who had died of kidney cancer aged just twelve. Well-wishers had raised £250,000 that enabled Jack to undergo experimental treatment in California which, tragically, was unsuccessful. He finally succumbed to the vile disease he had fought so bravely at the beginning of December. His aunt, Keely Howard, told us in the match-day programme: 'He was with his mum and dad in bed when it happened and is now in peace with his West Ham shirt on.' What can you say? There are no words.

Boleyn Ground
Saturday 12 December 2015
Kick-off: 3.00
Final score: West Ham 0–0 Stoke

Ain't it typical. You wait all season for a goalless draw, then two come along at once. The Saturday before we played Stoke at Upton Park, West Ham had left Old Trafford with a point and the plaudits. The 0–0 scoreline was repeated against a very useful Mark Hughes side in the penultimate home game of 2015.

Tell someone that you've just witnessed a game without goals and they usually give you a sympathetic look and shake their head knowingly. But the encounter with Stoke was highly entertaining, and both sides were applauded off at the end.

Being a 3.00 p.m. Saturday kick-off, we had time for a leisurely pint in the Denmark followed by a hotdog in Priory Road before the game. Never let it be said the Williams family doesn't know how to have a good time.

The West Ham injury list was getting longer by the day. The latest casualty was Winston Reid – the victim, according to his manager, of rock-hard conditions at the Chadwell Heath training ground. Slaven Bilić decided the time had come to act and brought forward a proposed move to Rush Green, which wasn't due to happen until the start of the following season. Former West Ham favourite Matty Etherington, who was no stranger to the treatment room himself, agreed with Slav. 'It was like training on a road for two hours every day,' he wrote in a blog for thewesthamway site. 'Eventually your muscles say enough, then come the injuries.' Given that Matty left the club in 2009, it rather begs the question why it had taken so long to rectify the problem.

Payet was still missing following the clogging he'd been given by Everton, although Enner Valencia, who had also been roughed up in that game, was on the bench. Manuel Lanzini, Victor Moses and Diafra Sakho had sick notes. The good news was that we got to see Michail Antonio make his first start since signing from Nottingham Forest.

Andy Carroll had a right old battle with Ryan Shawcross all afternoon, but couldn't break the deadlock. In the first half our best chance fell to Cheikhou Kouyaté, who saw a fierce drive saved by Jack Butland. Then Mark Noble was gifted the ball by Shawcross in a promising area before the defender recovered with a well-timed tackle.

At the other end Chelsea loanee Marco van Ginkel wasted a glorious chance from seven yards following one of a series of dangerous crosses from Stoke's right by Ibrahim Afellay. When Afellay drifted into a more central position and got in a shot of his own, James Collins deflected it for a corner. Then a cross from West Ham old boy Glen Johnson set up Marko Arnautović, who put his shot wide from inside the box.

The second half was more even. The service to Carroll improved, and he produced a dangerous glancing header after getting the better of Shawcross for once. A few minutes later Antonio could have scored his first goal for the club with a volley: sadly, Butland had other ideas. Adrián, too, was kept busy. Having thwarted Afellay in the first half with his feet, he once again called on his lower limbs in twice denying substitute Mame Biram Diouf.

After withstanding a good deal of pressure despite missing several first-choice players, West Ham finished the stronger of the two sides. Mauro Zárate hit the post and then, in time added on, Kouyaté had a header cleared off the line.

Apparently, there were thirty-four attempts on goal in all. Tell that to the bloke with the patronising smile and wobbly head next time you talk to him about 0–0 draws.

On the Monday before the Stoke game I had been to the swanky St Pancras Hotel for the Football Supporters Federation annual awards. I was there because *Blowing Bubbles Monthly*, the magazine I had written for since the first edition when it was simply called *Blowing Bubbles*, had been nominated for fanzine of the year.

It was a great night. I was on a table with *Bubbles* editor David Blackmore, fellow contributor Bianca Westwood and the man who puts it all together, the tireless Simon Osborn. On the next table was a big contingent from Knees Up Mother Brown (KUMB), whose podcast was also up for an award. I was delighted that the West Ham alternative media was so well represented at such a prestigious ceremony.

Bubbles has, in part, changed the course of my life. The columns I wrote in the early issues formed the basis of my book *Nearly Reach the Sky* and while being an author is hardly lucrative (not in my case, anyway) it does give you the opportunity to meet a lot of fantastic people you wouldn't have otherwise encountered. There was a time when being approached in an East End pub and asked if I'm Brian Williams would have given me considerable cause for concern. Now, on the odd occasion it happens, it's truly heart-warming. Better still is being contacted by someone who hasn't picked up a book since they left school but rediscovered a taste for the written word after reading yours.

Not only is David Blackmore the editor of *Bubbles*, he is also the man who created the publication in the first place. I asked what made him do it:
The idea was conceived on a particularly restless night in July 2012. My eldest daughter had just been born and I was on a rather firm sofa bed downstairs to ensure I got enough rest to get me through the working day as a journalist on a regional daily newspaper.

But I was frustrated. I wasn't going to get a promotion any time soon. I yearned to become an editor. I craved being able to shape a publication my way and produce something that I could be proud of. It needed to be something I was passionate about. But what? And that's when the cogs starting grinding.

I always sleep with a notepad next to my bed for these very nights. Sad, but all my best ideas come during sleepless nights. Slowly but surely I started to join together a few thoughts from the days and weeks preceding that night.

I'd spoken to a fellow journalist working on a boxing magazine about how reading a magazine on a tablet was 'the way forward'. I'd also been flicking through a copy of the then long-standing West Ham fanzine *Over Land And Sea* (*OLAS*), and thinking about how I'd edit it differently. Put these elements together with my desire to become an editor, and suddenly my notepad was alive with ideas for creating a West Ham fan magazine that could be read on computer, tablet and mobile.

Did a title spring to mind immediately?
I listed all the words you'd associate with West Ham. It was a long list, but 'Blowing Bubbles' stood out for some reason.

How about finding people to write for it? For example, before you launched *Bubbles*, we had never met before.
I created a Twitter account and typed in 'West Ham journalist' and 'West Ham writer'. It didn't take long to find a team of willing contributors. Some of them still write for every issue. Lucy Woolford and Geoff Hillyer have been with me since the beginning – as have you Brian.

But there's more to a magazine than just the words, of course. What about the design? Did you know how to host it online? And what about publicity and marketing?
These were all questions I asked myself. But deadlines are a great way to focus the mind. The first game of the new season was a month away: Aston Villa at home, 18 August. I spent the next month working every night to get it right. Come the hours ahead of the first match day of the 2012/13 season I was stood outside Upton Park with 1,000 copies of my 64-page fanzine. I'd done it, I'd achieved what I'd set out to do. Except, I didn't want to stand on street corners in the pouring rain trying to sell a hard copy – do you know how much it costs to print these days? I wanted to be purely digital.

What sort of reaction did you get on that first day outside Upton Park?

With the first copies being handed out, *OLAS* editor Gary Firmager approached me. He flicked through the magazine, smirked and said: 'I'll give you eight issues before you quit'. If it wasn't for that comment, I don't think we'd be having this conversation now.

Blowing Bubbles **has changed a fair bit over the years.**

Looking back through issues from our first season, you can see the evolution. How I put my stamp on the magazine but also how our team of contributors excelled in writing for a publication that was quickly getting a very good reputation.

What made you decide to focus more closely on printed editions? Let's face it, the rest of the media business has taken the exact opposite view!

As word spread among the West Ham community so did the calls for hard copies. You speak to anyone in the media world and they say the same thing: newspapers are dead. Print is so twentieth century. But niche publications are surging and hyperlocal newspapers are thriving. *Blowing Bubbles* is part of this trend and we've had to evolve to survive.

It must have been quite a struggle in the early years?

The first two seasons were tough. We came out ahead of every home game and I often spent many a Sunday working through to the early hours of Monday, pulling together the next issue to ensure it got to the printers on time and back to me to stuff into envelopes and post to our ever-increasing subscribers.

The start of the 2014/15 season saw *Blowing Bubbles* change again. The arrival of long-suffering friend and fellow Hammer Simon Osborn to the team saw us become monthly, and it proved a massive success. He altered the layout, we agreed fixed features, we were able to secure exclusive interviews, our articles were more considered, and we were able to secure fresh photographs every month from a lovely snapper who, like most of the team, I was able to persuade into helping me.

And the changes made a difference?
The next two seasons saw the magazine grow its audience beyond recognition: from thousands of online readers to tens of thousands. There was also cause for celebration in May 2016 as we said farewell to Upton Park with a print run that would have blown the mind of my 2012 self.

When we moved to the London Stadium you decided to 'do an *OLAS*' and sell *Blowing Bubbles* outside the ground. Aren't you the man who vowed never to stand in the pouring rain flogging hard copies?
When *OLAS* announced that it was closing there was a gap in the market. It was an opportunity not to be missed. *Blowing Bubbles* has never stood still. It has changed every season, every month, almost every issue. So, come August 2016 we were ready with a renewed marketing campaign that involved giving away 10,000 free copies in Stratford. We wanted people to read what our contributors were writing.

You always refer to *Blowing Bubbles* as a magazine rather than a fanzine. Why is that?

I've never been a fan of the old Stratford shopping centre (my friend Angela once returned to the car park to find her 2CV had been turned on its roof by a group of local ne'er-do-wells) but it is still a recognisable part of the capital city. But then go through Westfield and it is a different story. The Olympic Park – now officially known as the Queen Elizabeth Olympic Park – is about as connected to London as Donald Trump is to reality.

The place is, to quote The Donald, fake news. When you're somewhere that feels compelled to put up signs saying things like 'The Future Is Balanced' you know that all is not well. It's artificial. They even had to give the area its own postcode – choosing to replicate the E20 which had already been created for the fictional borough of Walford in *EastEnders*. The stadium itself is the jewel in a plastic crown. And even then it's made of zirconia.

Back with the online rant, I was warming to my theme:

It's supposedly taking us to the next level. I don't know whether the next level is up, back or sideways – but I don't like it. It's not for me at all. I can't tell you how distraught I am about what they've done to my club. It doesn't feel like my club any more.

As I recall, I whinged on in much the same manner for quite a while. A fair bit of my diatribe has been edited out. But here is some more of what got left in.

Nobody ever knows what to do with an Olympic stadium. Wherever you go around the world after an Olympics the talk is about regeneration. The idea that Barcelona was regenerated by the Olympics is nonsense. Barcelona regenerated Barcelona. This [stadium] hasn't regenerated Stratford. It's a massive great white elephant that the football club could see that was sitting there going begging and they got it.

If Dave and Max are looking for another project, there's an interesting piece to be done on what happens to Olympic stadiums once the games have moved on (they could call it 'Not A Legacy To Stand On'). The starting point would have to be Athens, the Olympics' spiritual home. After staging the summer games in 2004 at a cost of £7 billion, the giant Hellinikon Olympic complex was left to rot and is now a testament to dereliction rather than regeneration. And there are plenty of other venues that tell a similar story.

West Ham, of course, are not the first football club to move into a disused Olympic stadium. In Rome, host to the 1960 summer games, AS Roma and SS Lazio still play in the Stadio Olimpico. And in Germany, following the 1972 summer games, Bayern Munich relocated to the Olympiastadion, where some years later they were joined by TSV Munich 1860 – the team the Hammers beat to win the European Cup Winners' Cup in 1965. However, when the clubs were offered a new home at the purpose-built Allianz Arena in 2005 both of them jumped at the chance. Which brings us back to Barcelona, so often held up as the city which was given a new lease of life by the Olympics. Try telling that to supporters of Espanyol, who found themselves under pressure to spare the local government's blushes by taking possession of the Catalan capital's very own pallid pachyderm, born out of the 1992 summer games. After five years of civic arm-twisting they moved from their heartland to the Olympic stadium at the summit of the Montjuïc hill – much to the anger of the fans. The supporters never warmed to their new surroundings, rarely missing an opportunity to make their feelings known. And, twelve years after being marched up the hill, they marched back down – to a working class suburb that really did feel like home. And may they prosper there for evermore.

I wasn't the only one in the film not completely sold on the new stadium. Criticisms included the lack of atmosphere, problems with the pitch and the fact that too many of the new intake didn't understand the passion that was required of a West Ham supporter – or were there simply to say they had been inside the new stadium and had no intention of coming back the following year. Even so, those who had their doubts regarded the problems as little more than teething troubles. 'I wasn't convinced at first, but it's growing on me,' said one.

Others embraced it wholeheartedly. A particularly enthusiastic guy reckoned it was the best stadium he had ever been to. 'It puts the Emirates in the shade. It puts Wembley in the shade. It's got perfect views all over the place. The viewing experience is really, really good.' Is it? He had paid £289 for his season ticket. I was clearly sitting in the wrong place.

A mum obviously liked it too. 'As a woman, there are much better facilities for us,' she said. And she wasn't just talking about the toilets. 'You always get served and the guys are really friendly. So, yes, I'm quite happy with the ground. Some of the diehard fans will moan, but we've got to move on. There are 10,000 kids coming – they've got to grow up and start believing in this ground now.'

The 'move on' attitude seemed to be the order of the day. One supporter, who had outlined both the pros and cons as he saw them, summed up the situation most succinctly. 'At the end of the day, Upton Park has gone. The Chicken Run has been knocked down. We're staying here. Deal with it. Enjoy it. I think people need to look at the positives rather than looking at the negatives all the time.'

Fair point, mate. You'll get no more moaning out of me. I am definitely going to look at the positives from now on.

*   *   *

Inside the stadium, I took my seat without a word of complaint. To be honest, it generally took me about five minutes of serious deep breathing before I could say anything at all, but it did at least mean my nearest and dearest didn't have to listen to any moaning from an old diehard like me. (Actually, dying didn't seem at all hard after I'd climbed those stairs – with my heart going at the rate it was, death felt like it could be all too easy.)

The dad and his two young children were back in the adjacent seats. They'd missed the Burnley game – that had been a school night. Youngsters like these were the future of the club apparently, but they hadn't seemed terribly interested in any of the games they had gone to. The elder lad was generally more concerned with what was happening on his iPad, and the younger boy – who didn't look old enough to go to school – seemed determined to set a new club record for the number of times he could be taken to the toilet. I don't know if his plan was to try all 995 (you don't ask young children to whom you are not related questions like that) – but judging by his performance in the first half of the season there was every chance he would make it by the end.

I felt sorry for the dad. Buying those tickets must have seemed like a great idea when he got them. I can just imagine the conversation he had with his wife. 'Yeah, I know my ticket's a bit pricey, but it's only 200 quid for the two of them. It'll get them out of your hair on a Saturday – give you a bit of peace and quiet. You deserve it, love.' And all the time he's thinking: 'Bloody great – I haven't been to see the Hammers for years. This is going to be fantastic!' Bet it didn't seem so fantastic traipsing up and down those stairs with a nipper whose bladder control was about as shaky as Sofiane Feghouli's ball control.

Not that the two ankle-biters noticed, but West Ham got off to an iffy start. The boys had stopped trying to kick one another, but were still squabbling over whose turn it was on the iPad. Perhaps they planned to follow the game via a live blog on the tablet. If so, they may have seen something like this (and there's a free tub of popcorn for the first one who can spot which event happened an improbable three times during the match)...

14:52 The teams are out. The West Ham line-up is: Randolph, Kouyaté, Reid, Ogbonna, Antonio, Noble, Obiang, Cresswell, Lanzini, Payet, Carroll. Subs: Nordtveit, Feghouli, Adrián, Ayew, Fletcher, Fernandes, Quina. I don't care about the Hull team, to be honest.

14:56 BUBBLES!

15:00 They're off!

15:03 It's a cagey start by both sides.

15:04 A long ball forward from Reid is flicked on by Carroll and falls to Lanzini, who shoots from twenty yards. The shot is blocked.

15:07 Carroll and Lanzini team up again. The midfielder looks for Antonio at the back post, but the Hull keeper comes out to collect.

15:08 West Ham win a free kick on the right, which Payet takes. It's cleared. Was that Huddlestone? It's hard to tell from up here.

15:09 The Hull keeper puts the ball straight out of play and grimaces in the direction of the touchline. It looks like he's hurt. Nothing trivial, I hope.

15:13 Hull are awarded a free kick. I wouldn't have given it if I was the ref. Carroll is back defending and the ball is cleared.

15:15 Payet dances into the penalty area and shoots left-footed. A defender does well to get in the way and turn it behind for a corner. Got to put that down as a chance.

15:16 Hull engineer a one-on-one with Randolph in our area. That was Snodgrass if I'm not much mistaken. He should have done better if you ask me.

15:18 Payet takes another corner. That was about as piss-poor as the rest of them he's sent over this season. What has happened to that bloke? He was brilliant last year.

15:19 Hull go close. Two of their fellas combine and one of them puts his shot wide.

15:21 OFF THE POST! Lucky! A terrible back pass from Cresswell comes up short. The bloke who's just missed picks up the ball and has another go. His shot beats Randolph, but comes back off the woodwork.

15:24 Hull come again. Now that's the way to take a corner. Number 10. Hang on, let me check the programme. As I thought – that is definitely Snodgrass. You need to look and learn, Dimi – that boy could teach you a thing or two. They could have scored from that. Good job Randolph had his two Weetabix this morning.

15:26 The West Ham supporters aren't happy.

15:27 West Ham go long once more, looking for the lone figure of Carroll. The West Ham fans are really not happy. And can you blame them?

15:29 Another Payet corner. That one's rubbish as well.

15:32 REFEREE! Did you see that? He just took out Carroll! If that challenge had been much higher he'd have been classed as a hazard to low-flying aircraft. Dead right, book the dirty so-and-so. Is that Livermore? Yeah, thought so. Didn't he used to play for Spurs? Says it all.

15:33 In your own time, Payet! We haven't got all day. Bloody hell. What sort of free kick do you call that? My Mum could have saved it.

15:35 Obiang booked. Isn't that his fifth of the season? Hmmm, I think that means he'll miss the Boxing Day game. We could do with him. At least he puts in a shift every week. Unlike some I could name.

15:39 Right. I'm off for a pint. This is dreadful.

16:07 Did I miss anything? The queues downstairs were unbelievable. I thought they were going to sort all that out when we moved here. Blimey, it's a long way up those stairs. Give me a minute while I catch my breath.

16:10 Looks like West Ham have gone 4–4–2. Ayew and Fernandes are on. So who's he taken off? Lanzini and Obiang? You're kidding me!

16:11 Bilić has got the hump. No wonder, the way we're playing. Look at him down there: hands on knees, screaming at the players. He wants to be out on the park himself. Great player in his day. Probably still better than half of them now.

16:13 That's better West Ham! Sounds like the crowd has finally woken up. Not before time. Right, let's see what Payet can do with this corner. Seventh time lucky and all that. I like it! Handball!! Come on ref, are you blind or wot? Did you not see that? It was blatant. How much do they pay these refs?

16:14 Now they've got a corner. We should be taking a penalty, not defending.

16:16 OFF THE POST! What are you playing at, Noble? That nearly went in! If you're going to head it that way, make sure it goes over the bar. That's the second time the post has saved us.

16:18 OFF THE POST! I can't believe what I'm watching! Another one has come back off the woodwork. Randolph beaten all ends up. How did that fella get the chance to shoot anyway? The defence is all over the place. Good job the posts know what they're doing.

16:19 Noble is booked. Come on ref, give him a break. He tried to pull out of that challenge.

16:20 Carroll finally does something useful. Noble crosses and Big Andy heads it back across goal towards the unmarked Antonio. Shame the keeper was on his toes.

16:22 OFF THE LINE! Corner to West Ham. Ayew gets on the end of Payet's cross, only to see his header cleared.

16:23 OFF THE LINE! A great tackle by Kouyaté gives Hull a corner. Reckon he prevented a goal there. One of their blokes gets his head on it, but Antonio leaps to keep it out. Or was that Fernandes? You really can't see anything from up here.

16:27 That was close. Snodgrass with a side-foot volley. Eighteen inches lower and it was in.

16:31 Can't see West Ham winning this.

16:33 PENALTY TO WEST HAM! Great decision, ref. That was a foul on Ayew all day long. I've always rated that Lee Mason.

16:34 GOAL! Mark Noble gives West Ham the lead. Cool as you like. Get in!

16:40 Payet lines up a free kick from outside the area. Over the bar. He'd have scored that last year.

16:43 Payet with another free kick. That's his best effort all afternoon. Good save by their keeper. Shame. That would have sealed it.

16:46 Brilliant ball by Payet puts Antonio through on goal. It takes a decent tackle to stop him. Keep playing like that and we'll win this.

16:48 What are you trying to do to me West Ham? They could have scored there. Randolph did well to save that!

16:49 Four minutes added on! Where did they get four minutes from?

16:54 FULL TIME. Phew, I don't think I could have taken much more of that. Got to feel sorry for Hull. They must be gutted. Fancy a pint? Under the big screen or in St Pancras? You choose...

For reasons I still don't fully understand, the *Guardian* never invited me to write a live blog in all the time I worked there.

* * *

As we left the stadium I told Di and Geoff that I'd be voting for the post when the time came to elect the Hammer of the Year. I'm guessing I wasn't the only one to crack that joke. Unbeknown to us, however, the incumbent HOTY was brooding in the dressing room – making plans of his own to leave.

You didn't need to be a highly paid *Match of the Day* pundit to predict that Dimitri Payet was destined to be crowned the fans' favourite in his first season at the club. When the normally reserved ladies and gentlemen of the East Stand Upper begin to sing to someone's name it's a fair bet he is pretty special.

It wasn't long before Payet was being spoken of in the same breath as Paolo Di Canio, who is undoubtedly one of the best players we've ever had. Anyone who has ever seen PDC's jaw-dropping goal against Wimbledon when he defied gravity to volley home Trevor Sinclair's cross will know instantly what I'm talking about. Goal of the season? That was the goal of a lifetime.

It is no secret that Di Canio came with some pretty heavy baggage. But while the Italian maestro specialised in falling out with referees – not least Paul Alcock, who did fall over after that infamous push – Payet had public disagreements with teammates. While playing for Saint-Étienne in 2010 he was berated on the pitch by his captain for not getting stuck in. So he lamped the skipper. Rather than being thanked for showing the extra aggression required, his manager promptly substituted him and the club president imposed a heavy fine. There's no pleasing some people.

Football didn't always come easy to Payet. When he returned home to the Indian Ocean island of Réunion as a sixteen-year-old, after failing to make the grade at Le Havre in the French second division, it seemed his career was over before it had begun. Two years later, after starring in his local league, he was given the opportunity to return to France with Nantes – and nearly turned it down. He told the *Daily Mail*:

I didn't even want to hear talk about me ever going back to France. I was traumatised by the experience and the decision by Le Havre not to keep me. I felt I hadn't been seen in my best light. So when a second chance came along I argued about it with my dad and my uncle. They convinced me I should try my luck again, and they were right. But I didn't want to go.

Hardened both physically and mentally by his experience of playing as a boy against men on Réunion, he went from strength to strength – first earning himself a transfer to Saint-Étienne and then on to Lille, where he played with Joe Cole, before ending up in Marseille.

By the time he joined West Ham it looked like his stint as an international player had come and gone, but his performances in claret and blue clearly did not go unnoticed and French manager Didier Deschamps recalled him for friendlies against the Netherlands – hailing him as man of the match – and then Russia, in which he scored a trademark free kick from so far out he and the keeper were in different time zones.

Payet brought a sense of joy back to Upton Park. His touch was exquisite; his passing sublime and some of his goals were breathtaking. Yet he has ended up in the metaphorical 'Treacherous Bastards Sticker Book' alongside the likes of Jermaine Defoe, Paul Ince and the junior, but heavier, Frank Lampard. So how did that happen?

Saying au revoir to all of us at West Ham United, we learned later, was what Payet had wanted for some time. He was miserable, and the game we had just witnessed was the straw that broke the camel's back. Some months later he told French sports newspaper *L'Équipe:* 'Against Hull, we won 1–0 and they hit the post four times.'

It was three, actually Dimi. Sorry, you were saying?

'In the changing room everyone was happy, but the man of the match that day was the post. I thought that I would not have room for improvement. On the contrary, I risked regressing. I needed another challenge.'

His immediate challenge, though, was to convince the club to let him go. And the way he went about it was to turn his once adoring fans against him on an industrial scale.

Boleyn Ground
Monday 28 December 2015
Kick-off: 5.30
Final Score: West Ham 2–1 Southampton

If 2016 was the year of two halves, the last match of 2015 at Upton Park was the ultimate game of two halves. Another 'last' for the Boleyn Ground: I could picture the undertakers lining up with their tape measures. But, for me, the day also featured a 'first'.

I'd never been on the Woolwich Ferry. Not once. All those years of travelling to E13 from various directions and never, in all that time, had I gone by boat. I didn't plan to use it that particular Monday either, but life does have a habit of serving up some diverting surprises when you least expect them.

Only Geoff and I made the trip up from Brighton. Katie, my daughter, was back with us for Christmas, so Di stayed home with her. Katie doesn't like football. We tried, honestly! But it's not for her. The last game she went to was Gianfranco Zola's first match as manager – a lively affair against Newcastle which we won 3–1. It didn't do it for her. All I can say is, she should think herself lucky we didn't take her to see some of Zola's final games in charge – an evening encounter with Wolves in particular springs to mind. Even I had to think long and hard about ever going back to Upton Park after that one.

Being Christmas, the trains were all over the place so we decided to go by car. Geoff volunteered to do the driving, and I readily accepted his offer. To be frank, I'm not the world's greatest passenger. But I'm perfectly happy with Geoff at the wheel. Rarely will you see my right foot involuntarily searching for a non-existent brake pedal when he's in the driving seat.

We planned to take the tried and tested route through the Blackwall Tunnel, but while we were still on the M25 Geoff's satnav started to warn of long delays. It even enquired if we'd like an alternative route. Geoff asked me what I thought. I pondered for a while and decided that I was perfectly happy to put my trust in new technology, as I knew he was. I think you will have gathered by now, I've always been one to embrace change and modernity.

I really shouldn't have been as surprised as I was when I realised this new route included a ferry trip. If you are journeying from the south coast to the East End you have to cross the River Thames somewhere, and the choices are limited. You can either go on to Dartford; come off the motorway earlier and use the Blackwall Tunnel; go via Rotherhithe if you don't mind entering

Millwall territory (which I do); or crawl through south London on the A23 and take one of the capital's more central bridges such as Blackfriars. Eliminate all of those options, as Sherlock Holmes would have deduced, and you are left with the Woolwich Ferry.

When it became apparent we were headed for the ferry we could have ignored the satnav and resumed our original course, but for once I wanted to be on top of the river rather than underneath it. Di had told me how, when she was a kid, she and her mates would sometimes ride the ferry back and forth across the river for the sheer fun of it (or, more truthfully, to kill time when they couldn't think of anything better to do). This will sound silly, I know, but I felt that by taking the crossing I was tipping my hat in the direction of the family connections with east London, of which I am unduly proud. I fully understand that a proper Eastender would never have such a romanticised view of the Woolwich Ferry, especially when queuing up for more than half an hour to get on it, but the impending move from Upton Park was doing funny things to my mind. Besides, unlike the Dartford crossing, it was free.

Much as I enjoyed contemplating the lights on the other side of the river as we waited for the Ernest Bevin to carry us to the opposite shore, it has to be admitted that we did have to tarry for a fair amount of time before we got on it. The delay meant we cut it fine getting to East Ham and after we'd deposited Geoff's car in the parking space he had arranged for it we faced a brisk walk along the Barking Road to be in the ground in time for kick-off. Did I say brisk walk? To be truthful, it was a brisk walk for Geoff, but more of a jog for me. Had we been playing walking football, I would have been pinged more than once for infringing the rules. But Geoff is younger, fitter and has longer legs.

Had I known how the first half was going to turn out, I wouldn't have bothered trying to keep up. Instead, I'd have stopped off at the Central, had a pint and waited for the second forty-five.

Southampton murdered us in that opening period. With a number of first-choice players still missing due to injury, Bilić opted to play Carl Jenkinson out of position at left back. The whole team looked disjointed as a result. Shane Long, Steven Davis and Sadio Mané tore us apart time and again, creating a sleigh-load of chances. It was a Christmas miracle that they only took one of them. That happened in the thirteenth minute when Dušan Tadić put the finishing touch to a very classy move involving Long and Mané. West Ham were so bad they got booed off at the interval.

The second half, however, was a different story. Bilić identified the problem and switched Jenkinson to his more accustomed position at right back, with the ever dependable James Tomkins moving to left back. Alex Song and Mauro Zárate, who both looked like they had hangovers, were replaced by Andy Carroll and Manuel Lanzini. Carroll had clearly spent his Christmas bonus on a trip to the hairdressers. After contemplating the extravagant braids our big striker was now sporting, the reporter from the *Independent* who was covering the game suggested it looked like he had an armadillo on his head.

With West Ham revitalised, the crowd forgot that we were cross with them and got behind the team. Not for the first time did the Upton Park floodlights work their magic. The equaliser came after sixty-nine minutes, and it was one for the scrapbooks.

(Does anyone still keep a scrapbook? I wonder.) José Fonte appeared to bring down Michail Antonio in the box. While referee Michael Oliver was weighing up whether or not to give a penalty, Victor Wanyama's attempted clearance cannoned off the prone Antonio's bonce and into the net. It may have been an unusual way to score, but it was his first goal for the club. Can someone fetch the glue and scissors for Michail's mum, please?

The winner arrived ten minutes later – a cross from Enner Valencia was directed on to the underside of the bar by Antonio, leaving Carroll's pet armadillo to deal with the rebound. It made no mistake.

It was a cheery drive back to Brighton. But, looking back, I feel we should have been more sympathetic towards the visiting fans. 'One-nil, and you fucked it up', followed by 'Oh when the Saints, go two-one down'. Now that hardly demonstrates the spirit of Christmas, does it?

12

It's all about you, ref

London Stadium
Monday 2 January 2017
Kick-off: 5.15
Final score: West Ham 0–2 Man Utd

I'M SURE MIKE Dean is a very nice man. It's just that my heart sinks whenever I see that he is to referee a West Ham game. He certainly got my 2017 off to the worst possible start.

The decision to dismiss Sofiane Feghouli with just a quarter of an hour of the game against Manchester United gone was jaw-dropping. Yes, I watch every West Ham game through claret and blue tinted spectacles. And no, the view from row seventy-three is not the best. But a blind man could see that the decision would be overturned on appeal – which it duly was two days later. By then, however, the damage had already been done.

I'm not saying we would have necessarily beaten Man U if Feghouli had stayed on the pitch. But going down to ten men with seventy-five minutes of the match remaining seriously damaged any hopes we had of winning one of the big games of the season.

There was genuine fury all around the ground when Mr Dean reached for his pocket and produced a red card after Feghouli's entanglement with Phil Jones. Yellow, possibly. But red? Never. Still, don't just take my word for it.

This is what the *Guardian*'s Barney Ronay had to say about it.

With 15 minutes gone the key moment in the match arrived. Michail Antonio chested the ball back towards Feghouli, who stretched to reach the ball, as did Jones. No studs were raised. It looked like a hard but fair challenge, although Jones came off worse. The referee took his time and then flourished – the word is apt – a straight red card.

It was a poor decision in many ways, a needless intervention that skewed the entire night for players, TV viewers and the near 57,000 people inside the stadium. As mistakes go it was at least on a fittingly Olympian scale, in keeping with the hauteur of a referee whose sweeping gestures suggest each match he attends is a spectacle made up of three interlocking forces, Team A, Team B and Mike D.

In the *Telegraph*, Jason Burt was also critical. He wrote:

Jones's reaction may also have made up Dean's mind, and the referee was well-placed, but it appeared a harsh dismissal – the quickest, also, of the Premier League season so far and one which obviously affected the contest and incensed West Ham. The referee has to officiate as he sees fit and to the safety of the players – but could Dean be certain Feghouli's action absolutely warranted a sending off? It did not appear so clear cut and was an even greater shame given West Ham had started promisingly.

The *Independent's* Jack Pitt-Brooke saw it much the same way.

Feghouli reached for the ball with both feet, clattering into Phil Jones, himself over-reaching for the loose ball. It was a 50-50 situation but Jones's pained reaction made Feghouli's tackle look far worse than it was. Dean brought the red card straight out, a decision that looked worse with every replay.

The *Mirror* said:

At first look – what the referee gets – it looked a bad challenge but this was no knee-jerk decision. Dean didn't rush to show a red, instead taking his time to think about it and possibly consult with his fellow officials, before going to his pocket so he must have been convinced. He seemed to be one of few inside the London Stadium who was. ,

Perhaps what helped to make his mind up was the way that Jones, immediately after the challenge, rolled around more times than a man going over Niagara Falls in a barrel while Man Utd players swarmed all around him. Whatever the reason, it was a terrible decision. No wonder the crowd let the ref know what they thought: 'Mike Dean, it's all about you,' thundered around the stadium.

The BBC, which generally sits on the fence to such an extent it has splinters in its corporate bottom, didn't think the challenge was worthy of a red card. 'Replays showed it was more of a coming together between two players committed to winning the ball than a reckless tackle meant to cause harm.' Sky Sports thought it was a yellow-card offence. Even Man Utd's official website thought the call 'may have been harsh'.

Sam Cunningham of the *Daily Mail* gave Mr Dean two out of ten for his performance, commenting: 'Awful decision to send off Feghouli so early in the game. He had to be right to make that call; he was wrong. Ruined the match. Got decisions wrong all evening.'

He didn't mark the linos – sorry, assistant referees – but they wouldn't have got any gold stars either. Especially Simon Long, who failed to spot that two Man Utd players were offside when the visitors scored their second goal and ended any hope that justice might actually be done.

The goal came after Pedro Obiang's clearance rebounded off Ander Herrera. The ball fell to Zlatan Ibrahimović, who stabbed it past Darren Randolph. Not only was Ibrahimović offside – so was Paul Pogba, who might also have been penalised for obstruction. What made it even harder to take was that Ibrahimović didn't run offside from an onside position, making it harder for the lino to spot – he was standing two yards offside when the ball came to him. It's things like that which make you wonder why you bother going to football matches sometimes.

For the record, Man Utd's first goal came from Juan Mata after sixty-three minutes. And (unlike some referees I can think of) it was legitimate.

West Ham were terrific in the first half. As so often happens, going down to ten men fired up the rest of the team – and that fire was stoked by a sense of injustice. Not only did the Hammers defend resolutely, we could have scored more than once. Early on, Manuel Lanzini was thwarted when David de Gea turned away his shot for a corner. Then, with half time approaching, the keeper denied Lanzini a second time.

At the other end Randolph did brilliantly to save Antonio Valencia's side-foot effort from point blank range. Jesse Lingard, following up, should have scored from two yards out, but his shot hit the post and bounced back into Randolph's arms.

After the break Antonio had a couple of very decent chances. First he was unfortunate not to get on the end of Dimitri Payet's dangerous free kick. Then he should have scored after Lanzini put him through on goal. He had too much time to think about his shot, though, and de Gea blocked his overly cautious attempt. Sixty seconds later Mata got his goal, and the resistance faltered. Ibrahimović and the missing offside flag killed it off completely.

There were many other questionable decisions during the game. A Cheikhou Kouyaté challenge on Henrikh Mkhitaryan that might have warranted a card went unpunished, as did a foul by Lingard on Kouyaté. Winston Reid probably should have been booked for a deliberate handball. But it pays not to question Mr Dean. When Obiang had the temerity to raise an eyebrow after another decision had gone against the Hammers he was told: 'Don't look at me again, otherwise you won't be playing again.'

Had the red card stood, Feghouli wouldn't have been playing again for three matches. But of course it was rescinded – and by doing so the authorities effectively admitted that it never should have been issued in the first place. Why oh why does football still refuse to use modern technology to prevent this sort of mistake being made when the stakes are so high?

I simply don't accept the argument that taking a brief pause to discover what had actually happened rather than relying on the instant (and too often incorrect) assessment of a referee and his assistants will ruin the enjoyment of the supporters. They're fine with it in rugby.

Besides, Phil Jones was horizontal for so long there was enough time to have screened the first four episodes of *Star Wars*, let alone allow an off-field official time to adjudicate on whether or not Feghouli's challenge was dangerous.

Rugby also uses the sin bin – which again is something football should introduce in my opinion. A caution does nothing to help the side that has just been wronged – and in certain circumstances may actually be to its detriment.

Imagine you are in a relegation scrap (which, let's face it, is not difficult if you're a Hammer). You're one-nil down with ten minutes to go and the one striker you've got who's actually capable of scoring occasionally is just about to burst into the penalty area and shoot when their international defender unceremoniously takes him out.

It's outside the box, so no penalty. And there are other defenders between the action and the goal, so it's not a sending off. Instead, as the jeers turn to cheers, the ref awards a free kick and sternly produces the yellow card that demonstrates he is firmly in control of the situation.

Sadly, when the uproar has finally died down, the free kick comes to nothing, you don't get another sniff and consequently lose the game.

That's bad enough, but to make matters considerably worse that booking has resulted in the international defender being suspended for the next game – which is against your main relegation rivals. He committed the foul against you, yet they benefit. That's double jeopardy and it's inherently unfair.

If, on the other hand, association football had finally taken its head out of its rectal passage and looked at what other sports do, the villain of this piece could have spent the final ten minutes of that game in the sin bin, maybe allowing your team to equalise, and possibly even then go on to win in time added on.

The International Football Association Board, the sport's rule maker, is asking the four UK associations and FIFA to trial the idea in grassroots football, with a view to eventually considering whether or not it should be introduced into the professional game. Sadly, I can't see it ever happening in a sport whose governing body gives the impression it would still have jumpers for goalposts if it could.

*   *   *

Back in the London Stadium, I was astonished at how flat it all felt. Where was the passion? Where was the anger? I was still puzzled on the train home, and posted something to that effect in my favourite West Ham Facebook group. It got quite a response, which I believe is worth reproducing here because it gives such a vivid picture of how fellow Hammers were feeling and how the level of support varied around the ground. I've edited it slightly and changed the names, because people were posting in a closed group and had no idea their thoughts would be published in a book. But this is essentially what was said. Be warned, there is some language in there that you may find offensive.

Me: Last year at UP the Mancs had a pop at us with the chant of 'Where's your famous atmosphere?' in the cup game. Now we're in the new stadium I'd actually like an answer to that question. A game under lights against the hated Man U; a diabolical referee;

a fantastic performance by the ten on the pitch and *that's* the best we can manage in the stands? Really?

David: Yep. Gold and Sullivan have killed this club. Stone. Fucking. Dead.

Mark: Our atmosphere died with the Boleyn. Let's not sugar-coat it, the place is a fucking library. Can't see it ever changing to be honest. No noise, zero banter, it's just shit over there. Twenty per cent of the fans are under ten. I feel bad swearing where I am, because there are kids everywhere. That's why I let rip in this group so often. You can't express yourself any more.

Flora: People do realise that it's the fans that sing, right? Don't remember Gold and Sullivan being choirmasters. And let's not kid ourselves by thinking UP was this incredible atmosphere hub.

Mark: That match at the Boleyn would have been immense Flora. The big games were always good, especially when the team turns up like it did today. That decision would have made the place a boiling pot. No comparison.

Me: My point entirely Mark. Of course, not every game at UP was a cauldron, but that would have been. Can we ever get that back? If so, how?

Mark: The crowd has been diluted with tourists and kids. My mate has a bloke sitting in front of him that has three season tickets because they were so cheap and he likes to watch a few Premier League games. Turns out they are Leicester fans!

Graham: You can't say kids shouldn't be there to be fair. My son is five and on his third season ticket. But I do believe they should have a family section. Too many people have bought tickets to 'cash in' on them. Hence why I see so many different faces in seats time and time again

Mark: I'm not saying they shouldn't be there, I take my kids. But they don't cry when someone swears. Don't moan when someone stands in front of them, they just stand on their seats. There should be a family section for these people.

Graham: Yeah – acceptance works both ways I agree.

Patrick: I couldn't make it today so one of my oldest mates took my seats for him and his son. He's been before with me (v Chelsea) which was OK but just speaking to him now, as a sort of neutral, he said he was shocked how flat and quiet the home support was, especially considering it was such a big game during the hols. I personally thought it would improve over time, but it's not happening is it?

David: Not even close.

Shaun: It won't improve mate. In the same way if you put an Audi badge on your fridge, it won't become more of a car over time. It will remain a fridge, decorated as something it's not. I can't stand the place – at Upton Park or any away ground the atmosphere and footballing principles were/are there regardless of the result. This place is every bit as soulless and unfit for purpose as I dreaded it would be.

Me: Not once, in my hearing, did we remind the Mancs they only live round the corner. I'm sorry, but that's just not acceptable from a West Ham crowd.

Luke: Just walk round and stand with me and the fellow standees in the Bobby Moore Lower. Empty seats near me every game. Always standing. It's better.

Laura: It's very vocal where I am. We don't stop singing/chanting and abusing. What I'm guessing is, it's lost in that stadium and you can't hear a word. A real shame because we kept the referee's a wanker going for a good five minutes.

Me: Good to know there are pockets of resistance Laura. I was told by friends who went to the Rugby World Cup games there that the roof 'catches' the sound of the crowd and amplifies it. Perhaps it does when you've got 9,000 people singing Swing Low Sweet Chariot, but speaking as someone who can practically touch the roof without getting out of my seat, there's no atmosphere where I am. (Not much oxygen either, but on the plus side the top of the stand would be good for altitude training if we ever get drawn against a side from Peru.)

Laura: I shouldn't laugh... You really need to move your seats Brian. We don't stop singing, bring out all the old ones too. It at least gives the impression that the whole stadium is doing the same.

Patrick: The support around the away end is terrible. The Trevor Brooking Lower as it is now is mainly sitting. Mainly members

I think, who usually only get their tickets via ballots. You then have block 113 on the other side which seems to be over 'policed' for standing. I hope to god that next season those areas can be sorted. Doubt it though, no one in our club seems to have a clue any more.

Richard: I'm in the upper tier and it's too far away to create an atmosphere. The game was ruined by the ref and most people couldn't be bothered. The place is sterile.

Gavin: I was there for the Paralympics super Thursday. I wasn't expecting much to be honest and felt it was a consolation prize for not having got any tickets for the Olympics. How wrong I was. The place was so loud it was deafening. My ears were ringing and it was one of the best nights of my life. I'm not into athletics but was euphoric and went as crazy as everyone around me. So don't tell me it's a library. The stadium will be a fortress. If you'd been there that summer night in 2012, you'd agree that it's up to us to make it rock again. COYI.

Roger: I think there is a lot of truth in your point Gavin. The stumbling block is that unlike the Paralympics our support has a preconceived ideal based on a match-day experience over many seasons and completely different type of venue and that is everything to many supporters.

I fear that this is a debate that will carry on for some time yet.

Still, there was one bright spot in what had otherwise been a miserable evening. On the mooch back to the station we got the usual nonsense from the jokers with the stop-go signs. As we waited grumpily to be allowed through, a bloke turned to me and said: 'Reminds me of the toll booth scene in *Blazing Saddles*.' If you haven't seen it, check it out online. Then you'll understand why I was still smiling ten minutes later.

Boleyn Ground
Saturday 2 January 2016
Kick-off: 12.45
Final score: West Ham 2–0 Liverpool

If 2017 began badly, 2016 had got off to a flyer. We did the double over Liverpool for only the second time in all the many years I have supported West Ham. A 12.45 p.m. kick-off meant an early start. But the good news was that Payet was on the bench with every prospect of making an appearance. Bonne année, as they say in France.

The Southampton game had proved we could actually win a football match without our Gallic talisman, but the eight-game winless streak that had preceded it showed just how important Payet was to West Ham. Not that his absence seemed to hold us back in the first half.

Despite the rotten weather and the early kick-off, the West Ham support was in fine voice from the first peep of Bobby Madley's whistle. An early Liverpool chance brought a few gasps of concern, but after ten minutes the stadium erupted as Michail Antonio celebrated a goal he had started and finished. He had tracked back and dispossessed Alberto Moreno on the edge of the West Ham penalty area. In the swift counter-attack that followed, Kouyaté found Enner Valencia, whose cross from the right was headed home by Antonio who had bombed upfield in the hope of just such a chance. *To the Cockney Boys, one-nil!*

The early goal did wonders for everyone's spirits. The mighty Liverpool looked distinctly rattled, and were fortunate not to go two down after sixteen minutes. Manuel Lanzini let fly with a shot that swerved viciously and smashed into the upright with Simon Mignolet nowhere near it. *Come On You Irons!*

Five minutes later Valencia latched on to a through ball from Antonio and it called for a desperate tackle from Moreno to prevent him scoring. Shortly afterwards it was West Ham's turn for some last-ditch defence as Christian Benteke found himself through on goal. But his first touch was poor and James Tomkins cleared the danger. Emre Can almost equalised for Liverpool on the stroke of half time, but his shot came back off the crossbar. It would have been a major injustice if it had gone in. Mark Noble was dominant in midfield, the hard-working Antonio was terrorising the Liverpool defence down the flanks and, at the back, James Collins was outstanding. *There's only one Ginger Pele!*

We braved the scrum in the bar and grabbed ourselves a beer at the interval. As usual when trying to get a drink at Upton Park, Di, Geoff and I separated and joined the back of the melee in different places (you couldn't dignify it by calling it a queue). As I shuffled forward in the hope of getting a drink some time before the final whistle I dreamt of the next-level catering I would be enjoying at our new home in a few months' time. Perhaps there was something to be said for the move to Stratford after all. As always, Di got to the front first – I really don't know how she does that. Geoff reached over the throng that surrounded her and rescued the newly bought beer, which we then necked in record time to ensure we were back in our seats for the start of the second half.

Liverpool looked like they had been given a word of encouragement by Jürgen Klopp and started with rather more menace. Perhaps he had reminded them that the transfer window was now open and if they didn't buck up their ideas they might just find themselves on their way to Tranmere Rovers. Philippe Coutinho tried to create something for Benteke, but Collins put a stop to that. Then Coutinho tried a shot, which sailed over the bar. A Jordan Ibe cross came to nothing, and Liverpool's short period of domination petered out. *Sign on, with a pen in your hand!*

The second goal came after fifty-five minutes. Noble served up the sort of cross that Andy Carroll must dream about and the man for whom Liverpool had once paid a record fee of £35 million towered above Nathaniel Clyne to power an unstoppable header past Mignolet. *He left because you're...* Well, you know the rest.

With an hour gone Liverpool proved that the famed Scouse sense of humour was still alive and well, despite the fact they were losing 2–0 in the pouring rain. Dejan Lovren lined up a dangerous free kick thirty yards out from the West Ham goal – and blasted the ball straight into Lucas, who had tried to infiltrate our defensive wall. A comedy gem.

Barely five minutes later a buzz of excitement went round the ground as the supporters got the substitution everyone had been hoping for. Off went Valencia and on came West Ham's No 27. *We've got Payet – Dimitri Payet!*

It took him no time to get involved. Some brilliant combination work on the left almost set up another goal for Carroll. His powerful header from the edge of the six-yard box was too close to Mignolet, who managed to push the ball away, presenting Antonio with a half-chance he couldn't take. The cross that sparked this particular spell of mayhem was provided by West Ham's left back and reigning Hammer of the Year. *His name is Aaron Cresswell, he wears a magic hat.*

Payet strolled around the Boleyn Ground like he owned the place, Carroll continued to make a thorough nuisance of himself up front and Collins was calm personified at the back. Liverpool had a couple of half-hearted shouts for penalties, and Noble had to block an effort by Lucas on the line. But, in truth, the final twenty minutes was party time for the supporters – most of whom weren't even born the last time West Ham beat Liverpool at Anfield and followed it up with a victory at Upton Park in the same season. It was a fantastic performance by West Ham and Liverpool were second best all afternoon. *Can we play you every week?*

There was, however, an issue that niggled away at me towards the end of the game. The torrential rain finally found its way through the roof immediately above me and I was splashed by several large drips. I didn't mind getting wet – you could have thrown a bucket of water over me if it meant beating Liverpool. But it was a stark reminder that the Boleyn Ground was being allowed to fall apart. No one was going to repair a roof when the bulldozers would be tearing the whole place down in a few short months. This was the year that would see the end of my dear old friend. 2016. The final countdown had begun.

13

We haven't got Payet

London Stadium
Saturday 14 January 2017
Kick-off: 3.00
Final score: West Ham 3–0 Crystal Palace

FEW PEOPLE, LOOKING at the fixture list at the beginning of the season, would have picked out the Palace game as the most important of the year. But that is precisely what it had become.

A lot had happened since we'd last occupied our seats in row seventy-three. We'd been knocked out of the FA Cup in another humiliating defeat at home. And our star player had gone on strike. Life is rarely dull when you support West Ham.

Let's deal with the cup exit first. Like the vast majority of West Ham fans, I love the FA Cup, but we'd decided as a family we were going to give the game against Man City a miss. Di and I couldn't face another trip to Stratford, especially on a Friday night, and I suspect Geoff couldn't face listening to us moan about going to Stratford on a Friday night. Dutifully, he attributed his willingness to miss the game to work commitments in the Midlands, but that's not something which has ever stopped him in the past.

Season tickets do not cover FA Cup games, but we were offered the chance to buy our regular seats for the oh-so-reasonable price of £30. There were other, better, seats that we could have got for the same price, but even if we'd decided to go I think we would have passed up the chance of those. Sitting somewhere other than the back row would have only made us more brassed off when we had to return. For the same reason, earlier on in the season, I had turned down an incredibly generous offer from a Facebook friend who offered to swap seats for a week in the hope it might make me feel better about the London Stadium. We had never met face-to-face, but he was still prepared to make a gesture like that. West Ham supporters are, in the main, a fantastic bunch of people – and in my eyes they don't come much more fantastic than Colin (only don't tell him I said so).

We kept a close eye on our seats when they went on general sale. For a club that supposedly had zillions of fans on a waiting list desperate to get into the ground, they didn't get snapped up with quite the alacrity one might expect. If I remember correctly, they were eventually sold the day before the game as part of a hastily expanded kids-for-a-quid initiative.

What can you say about the way West Ham played that night? Woeful? Dismal? Awful? I think 'shameful' comes closest. Did those players out there have any idea what the FA Cup means to West Ham supporters? Getting beaten is one thing – we can all cope with that. But rolling over is unforgivable. It was a disgrace.

The bare bones of the game are that Yaya Touré scored from

the penalty spot in the thirty-third minute, Håvard Nordtveit put through his own net after forty-three minutes and David Silva got City's third two minutes later. After the break Sergio Agüero added a fourth on fifty minutes and John Stones got the fifth and final goal with six minutes left.

Would it have made a difference if Sofiane Feghouli had taken a gilt-edged chance to level the scores immediately after Touré's penalty? Should referee Michael Oliver have given the spot kick in the first place after Angelo Ogbonna and Pablo Zabaleta collided in the box? Did the fact that this was West Ham's third game in seven days have a bearing on the outcome? Might have events panned out differently if Dimitri Payet and Mark Noble had been on from the start rather than being introduced when the game was already lost?

These are the sort of things supporters will debate all night long in the pub after a defeat. There was no point trying to use the immortal 'the big clubs always get the close calls' defence after the drubbing City handed out. The answer to each and every question above is 'no'. Arguably, the one thing that might have made a difference was if the red card that Feghouli was shown in the Man Utd game earlier in the week hadn't been rescinded, but perhaps I'm being unfairly harsh on the fella.

In a funny sort of way, watching the game on TV was even more painful than being in the stadium. At least if you're in the ground you only have to put up with the taunts of the opposition fans and groans of the fellow West Ham supporters sitting around you. On TV you get Martin Keown telling the world that the team you love with all your heart and soul is rubbish, only to be followed by the incisive analysis of Alan Shearer. 'West Ham could not live with their passing, their movement, their one-touch football,' he informed us. Thanks Al. It was helpful of you to point that out. I never would have guessed from the 5–0 scoreline.

And in a demonstration of the utmost insensitivity the BBC used the half-time interval to look back on the 1991 FA Cup final – the one in which Tottenham beat Nottingham Forest. Not only do most West Ham fans find it unpalatable to watch Spurs win anything, this of course was a game that the Hammers may well have featured in if, during the semi-final, a referee by the name of Keith Hackett hadn't taken it upon himself to send off Tony Gale in what is to this day the worst decision I have ever witnessed. At least, I hope it was merely thoughtlessness. Either that, or someone at the Corporation really was taking the piss.

In case you're wondering if we stuck it out for the duration: yep, we did. While thousands of diehards, newcomers and tourists were pouring out of the London Stadium, the Williams family was taking rope-a-dope punishment right to the death on our settee in Brighton. How daft are we?

And if that's not enough gloom and doom for you, here's a little footnote: that game was to be the last time a certain Frenchman who we had all taken to our hearts turned out for West Ham. It probably shouldn't have come as so much of a surprise as it did.

No one was unduly worried when Dimitri Payet made himself unavailable for our early season European campaign in the Europa League. He'd had a demanding summer, taking France to the finals of the European Championship. He had been brilliant, especially in the early part of the tournament, and it was clear that he and Slaven Bilić had an unbreakable bond when the West Ham manager celebrated the Frenchman's goal against Albania by jubilantly climbing on to a table in front of the ITV cameras.

Ian Wright, a pundit on the same broadcast, had the temerity to suggest that Payet was playing so well West Ham would struggle to keep him. Bilić was having none of it. 'He knows what he is going to do. I see it every day in training. He has got a plan.'

It was music to our ears. Bilić had brought the almost unknown Payet to West Ham from Marseille for a paltry £15 million – it was generally agreed to have been the signing of the 2015–16 season. Payet had repaid him with some sensational performances and had himself been rewarded with a recall from an international wilderness to the French side in time for the Euros. These two men were made for each other. What's more, our playmaker had a plan.

Unfortunately, as we were to learn later, Payet's plan was to leave West Ham at the earliest possible opportunity. He told the club of his desire to go even before the showpiece fixture against Juventus.

The owners turned him down. Given the number of season tickets that had been sold on the back of his performances at Upton Park, it was impossible to do anything else. Maybe, just maybe, if it had been a normal season they could have cashed in their prize asset and used the money to rebuild. There would have been complaints from many supporters (me included), but it could have been done if we were staying in E13. The move to Stratford, complete with promises about the next level, meant that selling Payet was never an option.

Payet's disenchantment with all things claret and blue had dominated the first half of the season. There were flashes of brilliance, of course – that goal against Middlesbrough was a stunner. But it was clear that he wasn't anything like the player he had been the previous season. And his performance in the League Cup defeat at Old Trafford was, quite simply, a disgrace. One particularly perceptive column on the Knees Up Mother Brown website likened it to that of Paul Ince when he was after a move to Man Utd and in regular contact with Alex Ferguson. Ince (a dead cert for the Treacherous Bastards sticker book if ever there was one) had missed a few games through a questionable 'injury'. It has been suggested that when he returned to action (which is hardly the right word in this case) it was with a request from the Man Utd boss to stay out of trouble and not get injured. Whatever the truth of that, Ince probably didn't move more than twenty yards in the whole match. Payet may have shifted himself a tad more than that, but it was blatantly obvious he wasn't trying. The club would have been within their rights to withhold his salary that night.

As we discovered later, the Hull game was the straw which broke this particular camel's back. When the transfer window opened he again asked for a move and was again turned down. So he went on strike.

The official line was that he wanted to return to France because his family had failed to settle in the UK. That, it emerged later, was not the full story. Payet has since been quoted in the French press as saying (in French, naturally): 'I had no desire to play in the lower reaches of the Premier League. The defensive system that we put in place did not give me any pleasure.'

He was also concerned about losing his place in the French national side – forgetting to mention that if he'd not been given his chance at Upton Park he probably wouldn't have been in the

French side in the first place. On French TV channel Canal+ he said: 'No, it was not difficult to leave the Premier League. There was urgency to leave West Ham. Given my level of play and the way it went, I was afraid of losing my place in Team France and being selected less.'

The interview in *L'Équipe* also quoted Payet as saying:

> Bilić knew that I wanted to go elsewhere. We discussed it at the start of the season when I returned from Euro 2016, but the club closed the door and I respected their choice. When a club announces that you're worth €100 million, negotiations never get far. I could have gone to war last summer. August was badly managed. In January, I told them I wanted to go to Marseille and nowhere else. The day they told me no, and that it was definitive, I responded to them by saying I would no longer play for West Ham.

Bilić broke the news on 12 January. Apparently, the West Ham media team was unaware that the manager was about to spill the beans until minutes before the press conference. It is said to have caused all sorts of 'internal discussions' at the highest level.

Journalist Pierre-Étienne Minonzio, who writes for *L'Équipe*, told me that his paper knew Payet wanted to return to France several days before it was made official in the UK and ran a story that Marseille were ready to sign him on 2 January.

Minonzio was at Anfield when West Ham played Liverpool and tried to interview him after the game. He says: 'I spoke to him in French but he politely refused to answer. He looked a bit depressed at this time, although he had just scored a beautiful free kick.'

Were there domestic issues as well? 'His wife Ludivine and his three kids were not really happy with their life in London – they all missed the sunshine of Marseille.'

Apparently, according to rumours in France, Mrs Payet was also concerned that her husband might be playing away, and not in the 'I'm off to Anfield, see you later love,' sort of way. But whoever heard of a Frenchman taking a mistress? That's about as likely as a club's star player turning up at training looking like he'd just staggered out of the Black Lion to hint that he was not happy about having his transfer request turned down.

West Ham remained adamant that they didn't want to sell Payet. But here was a man on a five-year contract worth £125,000 a week refusing to play for the club. It was, in Payet's native tongue, a fait accompli – the owners had to let him go. Before January was out Payet was on his way to Marseille for a reported fee of £25 million. It would be an interesting encounter if West Ham were to ever find themselves drawn against the French side in a European competition. Payet, at least, understands the reception he would get. He said on TV: 'I have regrets, in so much as I'll never forget all the love the club and the people gave me. I think they hate me as much as they loved me.' Treacherous Bastards sticker book, here we come.

Payet's departure could have been the moment at which our season disintegrated altogether. Instead, in true West Ham fashion, adversity became a turning point.

For the first game without him, against Palace, the atmosphere in the ground was the best it had been for weeks – displaying utter contempt for our former No 27 and loyal support for Bilić. It was proof, if proof were needed, that no player is bigger than our magnificent club.

After 'Bubbles' the songs varied between Anglo-Saxon abuse for Payet and repeated choruses of 'Super Slaven Bilić'. And on this occasion the crowd didn't pipe down after fifteen minutes. There was an attempt at some synchronised booing on twenty-seven minutes, but that confused more people than it enticed. However, such was the concentration of fury, the fact that Sam Allardyce was managing Palace barely registered with the supporters who didn't much care for his way of doing things when he was in charge at Upton Park.

Despite the heightened level of support, West Ham were lacklustre in the first half. James Tomkins, like Allardyce returning to his former club, could well have given the visitors the lead. We weren't too clever for the opening fifteen minutes of the second half either. Then Palace keeper Wayne Hennessey rushed out of his area in an attempt to close down Michail Antonio, who calmly rounded him and passed to Feghouli. The tap-in was the Algerian's first goal for the club.

The second goal was really special. Lanzini played the ball to Antonio, who flighted a great cross to Andy Carroll. The big striker, who had been terrific all afternoon, steadied himself before taking off and catching the ball with the sweetest of overhead kicks. There was simply no stopping it. I think the ground shook as Carroll came back to earth. Or maybe that was the thunderous roar that greeted the goal.

Although not quite in that class, the third goal wasn't too shabby either. It came in the eighty-sixth minute after Antonio had set off on a lung-bursting counter-attack before he gave the ball to Lanzini, who continued the run before chipping the ball over an advancing Hennessey. Who needs Dimitri Payet?

With goals like that it's easy to forget the dross that had gone before it, and we did. For once, waiting at the top of the stairs to begin the long descent didn't seem quite so bad.

Not that we knew it then, but this was the last time we would experience the delights of row seventy-three. By the time the next home game rolled round, the Williams family would be at a different level.

Boleyn Ground
Saturday 23 January 2016
Kick-off: 5.30
Final score: West Ham 2–2 Man City

The Upton Park encounter with Man City was one of the best games of the season. Di and I weren't there to see it, though. The trains were all over the place so we decided to go by car for once. In need of fuel, we pulled into a filling station just outside Brighton – and couldn't get the cap off the petrol tank.

The key simply wouldn't turn in the lock. We bought some WD40 from the garage shop, but even the greatest miracle-worker of our age couldn't do the trick on this occasion. (If the makers of WD40 are reading this and would like to offer me a lifetime's supply on the back of that endorsement you can contact me via my publisher.) What trains there were wouldn't have got us to the game in time so, without enough petrol to make it to London and back, we had no choice other than to go home and watch it on the telly.

Very entertaining it was, too. Enner Valencia scored after just fifty-three seconds. Eight minutes later Sergio Agüero went down in the penalty area and equalised from the spot. The scoring pattern repeated itself in the second half – Valencia restoring the lead after fifty-six minutes and Agüero levelling it late on. Yet my everlasting memory of that game is a Payet free kick which, unusually in that season, didn't end up in the back of the net. It was only prevented from doing so by Joe Hart's stunning save. Payet's reaction? At half time he waited by the tunnel with a broad smile for the Man City keeper and congratulated him as if he were a teammate. He may be a Treacherous Bastard, but that's classy.

We had no way of knowing it then of course, but the next time we watched West Ham play Man City on TV it would be nowhere near as pleasurable.

In the league, there had been two away games before we entertained 'Citeh'. In the second of those, West Ham had gone to Newcastle and got beaten 2–1. In a midweek fixture preceding that, the Hammers went to Bournemouth and won after going a goal behind. Inspired by Payet, making his first start since being personally mauled by Everton, they chalked up a 3–1 victory. What Bournemouth would have given to have had Joe Hart in goal as first Payet and then Valencia smashed world-class free kicks past poor old Artur Boruc. The West Ham goal that was the filling in this delicious sandwich was scored by Valencia who had been set up by... guess who?

Two weeks before the City game we played Wolves at Upton Park in the third round of the FA Cup. Before the match Di and I looked in at the Newham Bookshop on the corner of Green Street and the Barking Road and while we were there we bumped into Pete May, the author of several fantastic books about West Ham.

Pete has been something of a journalistic hero of mine for

thirty years – ever since I read a piece by him in *Midweek* magazine in which he recounted one of the funniest lines ever to come out of the Chicken Run (and that really is saying something). The story goes that the West Ham side of the mid-1980s that had gone from being title contenders to relegation fodder within two short seasons was struggling against a particularly robust team of northern heavyweights – with a back four composed of giants who towered over Tony Cottee, who had been left to play on his own up front. The frustration in the stands was on the point of turning ugly when the cry went up: 'Never mind Cottee – Snow White and the other six will be along to help you out soon!'

The guy who came up with this particular gem went on to launch the ground-breaking *Fortune's Always Hiding* fanzine with Pete and Phill Jupitus among others.

Shortly after we bumped into Pete, he bumped into one of the myriad piles of tomes that make up the Newham Bookshop and sent them flying. Not that something like that would ever faze the awesome proprietor Vivian Archer. Between them, she and Pete had everything stacked up again to her satisfaction in no time. It really is a remarkable place – there are books piled high everywhere. It's estimated there are more than 50,000 scattered around the shop. Even getting through the door successfully involves some careful navigation around Viv's unorthodox method of display. Once inside, the first impression is that no one could find anything among the chaos – but Viv knows exactly what she's got and where it is. Chances are, she's probably talked the author into signing a copy as well.

While we were there I bought Pete's *Flying So High: West Ham's Cup Finals*. He is also the author of – among other things

– *Hammers in the Heart* and *Irons in the Soul*, both of which are essential reading for anyone who bleeds claret and blue. I first met him in the Newham Bookshop when I was invited there to sign copies of *Nearly Reach the Sky* in February 2015.

Never having written a book before, I'd never done a book signing – so I had absolutely no idea what to expect. I was nervous to begin with and my concern turned into full-on trepidation when Viv suggested I park myself outside to attract passing custom. Did I say 'suggested'? When Viv suggests something, there's not much point in arguing.

I've done some strange things in my time, but sitting behind a desk in the Barking Road on a match day with nothing more than my deluxe West Ham book-signing pen and a bemused expression that is trying to convey the message 'please don't hurt me,' has to be right up there with the strangest. And scariest. Not that I had any reason to be concerned as it turned out. In fact it was a wonderful experience – not least because it gave me a chance to meet a lot of delightful West Ham supporters.

That day coincided with the finale of yet another astonishing fundraising exercise on behalf of the Bobby Moore Fund for Cancer Research by Kent teenager Jonjo Heuerman. On this occasion he had walked and cycled between every Premier League football club, covering 800 miles in just over two weeks.

Prompted by the death of his Nan from bowel cancer when he was just seven, he set out to raise money in honour of both her and his footballing idol who, as every West Ham supporter will know, had died of the same condition. Jonjo has now raised more than £300,000 for the Bobby Moore fund and has been honoured himself with the British Empire Medal.

His odyssey – he calls them 'challenges' – ended at the

Champions statue, directly opposite the bookshop. I was lucky enough to be able to have a brief chat with Jonjo's mother, Donna. At one point I heaped praise on her remarkable son and all he has achieved, at which point she looked me straight in the eye and said: 'He is up for adoption, you know.' I must have looked quizzical for a brief moment, because Donna gave me a very wicked grin and added: 'I hope you like walking!' Trust me, that boy is in good hands.

I'm proud to say that I was able to help with Jonjo's fundraising on that occasion. Viv had persuaded Russell Brand to autograph a copy of *Nearly Reach the Sky*, which was then auctioned. In all, it helped to swell the cancer fund by £500. What intrigued me was the winning bid was made on the understanding that the individual concerned *didn't* get the book signed by Russell Brand. I think this opens up a whole new line in fundraising. So, what am I bid for a freshly printed copy of these musings – which I can guarantee has not been inscribed by Vlad the Impaler? All proceeds to the Bobby Moore fund via Jonjo.

It would have been a real pleasure to have accepted the family's invitation to join them for a pre-match cuppa in the East Ham Working Men's Club, but I was unable to abandon my post in the Barking Road, where I found myself not only signing copies of my book but also a petition that was part of the 'Keep the Rich Off the Pitch' campaign. They were trying to ensure that when developers Galliard finally got their hands on the Upton Park site it was not given over entirely to luxury flats and that there would be some social housing as well. I was more than happy to put my name to that.

Now the ground has been demolished I fear for the future of Newham. Independent traders such as the Newham Bookshop are bound to suffer as a result. They simply must not be allowed to go under – not that I could ever picture the indomitable Viv being beaten by something as minor as the football club that has been the heart and soul of the area for more than 100 years clearing off to another postal district.

In fact the Newham Bookshop, which has been in existence since 1978, has become something of a heartbeat in its own right. Poet Benjamin Zephaniah can certainly put it more eloquently than I could ever hope to. 'This bookshop has helped local people pass exams, fall in love, meet authors, become authors, get work experience, learn to read, understand Britain, understand the world and understand themselves,' he says.

The FA Cup game against Wolves wasn't exactly a classic. Chances were few and far between, and we had to wait until the eighty-fourth minute for the only goal of the game. Mind you, it was a goal worth waiting for. With the Wolves fans starting to think they'd got themselves a replay back at Molineux, Andy Carroll – on as a substitute – laid the ball off to Nikica Jelavić, whose sweetly hit shot from just inside the penalty area left the keeper clutching nothing more than fistfuls of thin air as the ball whistled past him.

Other than that, there wasn't much else to report. Mauro Zárate had seen a tame shot saved; Pedro Obiang's deflected effort was kept out by the keeper; and Carl Jenkinson had a fierce drive tipped over the bar on the stroke of half time. As I say, this was no classic.

The Wolves fans made most of the noise, but the West Ham supporters – a good number of whom had used the chance of a cup game to get a reasonably priced ticket to Upton Park for possibly the last time ever – went home happy.

With a victory under our belts and a copy of Pete May's book of West Ham cup finals in my pocket, I allowed myself to dream as we left the Boleyn Ground. Wembley. Now that, I thought, would be a fitting way to round off this historic year.

14

Going down, going down, going down…

London Stadium
Wednesday 1 February 2017
Kick-off: 7.45
Final score: West Ham 0–4 Man City

Farewell row seventy-three, hello row fifty-four. Our complaints about sitting in the stratosphere had finally got a hearing and the Williams family was moving closer to ground level.

The offer of new seats had followed a meeting between Karren Brady and West Ham's alternative media. David Blackmore asked me to represent *Blowing Bubbles*, and I was more than happy to do so. I nearly didn't make it, though.

As a rule, David's organisational skills are second to none – but on this occasion there was a small glitch. 'Did I say that meeting was tomorrow?' he asked in a text. I replied that he had.

You can guess how the conversation went from there. It was less than an hour before the conflab was due to begin, so I handed over the reins to my ever-understanding deputy and headed for the station. Working near St Pancras, as I did then, getting to Stratford International was no problem. The difficulty I had was finding the main entrance to the stadium. Having always approached the ground on the same level as the turnstiles, I didn't know it was on a lower tier.

It was dark and the area around the stadium was deserted when I got there. It was quite spooky, actually. I assumed the entrance would be somewhere near the club store. I also assumed it would be easy to spot. Right on the first count, wrong on the second. There had to be a sign somewhere: Entrance; Press; Anything. By the time I had done a complete circuit I realised there was nothing. No problem, I thought: I would simply call the contact number David had given me and someone would rescue me. I hit the link – and the battery in my phone went dead. The expletive that involuntarily passed my lips is one I usually reserve for Mr Michael Dean.

The only sign of life was in the club shop, which had just locked up for the evening, so I banged on the door. At first, the assistant who was closest indicated that they were closed. I mouthed through the glass door I knew that, but I needed to talk to them. Warily, he opened the door a crack and asked what I wanted. He reminded me of the days, long ago, when I had a morning paper round and at Christmas would visit my clients in the evening to wish them season's greetings in the hope of a getting a tip. They used to look at me in much the same way when they finally answered my persistent knocking.

He looked doubtful when I explained that I was there for a

meeting with Baroness Brady, but directed me to the front entrance anyway. When I got there I encountered an extremely disgruntled security guard sitting in a tented area protecting the entrance itself. When he finally completed his mobile phone call, I explained why I was there. He asked if I had a contact number he could call. I resisted the temptation to enquire whether or not someone guarding the entrance to the London Stadium needed a visitor to provide him with the number of the press office and instead told him that I did have a number but it was in my phone, which was dead. I saw that he had a charger which would have sparked my mobile into life and asked him if I could use it. I couldn't. Instead, he instructed me to sit down and wait. As I did so I tried to position myself in such a way I could benefit slightly from his hot air blower while he tried to locate someone who was prepared to come and get me. It was a chilly night. In more ways than one.

The atmosphere was a good deal more convivial in the meeting room when I eventually got there. I made my apologies for arriving late and looked around for a spare seat. There was only one – directly next to Lady Brady herself. I settled myself in, exchanged smiles with Karren and tried to tune in to the conversation. (She asked me to call her Karren – honestly. It was all very informal. First-name terms, don't you know.)

Karren was accompanied at the top table by Tara Warren, the club's marketing and communications executive director. There were some big hitters among the West Ham independent media gathered around the other three sides of the conference table. Sean Whetstone from the news site Claret and Hugh was there, as were Kris Gonzo from the forum Hammers Chat and S. J. Chandos from the West Ham Till I Die blog. The West Ham Way, West Ham Fan TV, West Ham World and Sex, Drugs and

Carlton Cole were also present. Last, but in no way least, also at the table was Knees Up Mother Brown founder and editor Graeme Howlett – the biggest of the lot if you ask me. If this had been a gathering of mafia rather than media, Graeme would most certainly have been the godfather. Oh, and sitting quietly in a corner, like Little Jack Horner, was young Jack Sullivan, who may have spoken before I arrived but said nothing while I was there. Perhaps he was checking his Twitter account.

It became apparent that stewarding had been discussed, although it was a subject we would return to. The resale of tickets had, seemingly, also got a good gallop but – unlike the stewarding – it was not an issue that appeared to overly trouble *Blowing Bubbles* readers. They, like me, were more concerned about the pricing of season tickets, but I chose to bide my time before wading in with that.

Someone mentioned that the quality of stewarding had improved and cited an incident which he had witnessed involving an elderly supporter being helped to his seat. In an effort to inject some humour into what was clearly a pretty serious gathering I asked if he was sure that the old boy was actually being shown to his seat, and not getting chucked out for trying to stand up. Karren forced a smile.

It was a fast-moving conversation. There was no formal agenda. Everything and anything, big or small, was up for discussion. We spent some time on the issue of how long it took to get served in the bars, and there was a suggestion that beer should be poured before half time so the glasses would be filled by the time they were required. Then it was mentioned that, once you got a pint, there was nowhere to put it. Karren agreed that the club would try to put in some shelving asap. A small item maybe, but something that would make the experience of going to the London Stadium marginally more palatable.

There was a request for more betting outlets around the concourse, and a call for a stall selling pie and mash. The Rib Man got a mention, as did the Supporters' Club, which understandably wants to be based nearer to the new ground. And we talked about flags. It was agreed that, in an effort to make the London Stadium feel more like home, the club would store supporters' banners and put them up in appropriate places around the ground before kick-off. Tactfully, no one asked if a flag calling for Baroness Brady to be sacked, which had seen its irate owner thrown out of the ground the previous month, would be gracing the stadium.

Naturally, we all wanted to know whether or not there was any chance of resolving the Dimitri Payet issue. We were told the club was standing firm and didn't want to let him go. Despite the bullish stance, I don't think any of us envisaged No 27 wearing claret and blue again.

There was disquiet about the fact supporters had been filmed by the stadium operators LS185. We were assured this would stop if there was no repetition of the trouble that marred the League Cup tie against Chelsea. And there was another hangover from that game that had upset some of the supporters represented by those around the table. In the aftermath of the trouble, highly respected journalist and self-confessed West Ham fan Martin Samuel had written an impassioned piece in defence of Stratford. He wrote in the *Daily Mail*:

Stadiums do not riot. Stadiums do not smash seats. Stadiums do not throw bottles and coins. Stadiums do not shout abuse or punch you on the nose. Stadiums just stand there, unseeing, unfeeling. So let us turn from the preposterous notion that recent events at West Ham are the work of an unsatisfactory new arena.

People. That is the problem here. People who fight, people who destroy, people who taunt and abuse; uncivilised, violent, horrible people. That is what West Ham must be rid of, not the new stadium.

The club had run the piece in full on its website, with all the implications of official sanction that brings, and many law-abiding, upstanding, peaceable citizens who support West Ham had taken offence. The press office, we were told, would be more careful about what it published in future.

Unsurprisingly, perhaps, the biggest bone of contention with the stadium itself was the running track. Could there not be more retractable seating which would allow some supporters to be closer to the pitch? No, we were told. The technical difficulties were insurmountable. And even if they weren't, the cost would be prohibitive. Get used to it folks, players may come and go but the running track's here to stay.

And while we're at it you can forget about the idea of safe standing as well. I reminded Karren that *Blowing Bubbles* editor David Blackmore had once been told by David Gold in an interview that there was every possibility there would be areas where supporters would be allowed to stand at the London Stadium. In turn, she reminded me of the Premier League rules, which make sitting mandatory. I asked whether the club was prepared to ask for those rules to be changed in any way, and again drew a blank. Despite Mr Gold's optimistic view while we were still at Upton Park, there really is no appetite for standing of any sort among the powers-that-be at West Ham United FC.

Attention then turned to what happens outside the stadium – much of which is beyond the club's control, of course. It was recognised that supporters with mobility problems can find it difficult to get from the various stations on match days, and the number of shuttle buses for people with disabilities was being increased. Karren confessed that she gets a taxi from Stratford International to the stadium most days, because it's a tricky walk in high heels. I told her, tongue in cheek, it was a problem with which I was all too familiar – which earned me an ooh-you-are-awful slap on the thigh. That's the price you pay for being the last one to arrive at a meeting when the only seat left is the one next to the boss.

I took the opportunity to have a gentle moan about the stop-go boards on the way back to Stratford International. There were some helpful suggestions from my own side of the table – such as avoid Stratford International altogether. Had I tried Stratford Underground station, for example? Well, yes, I had actually. Once, for the Watford game. It was not an experience I planned to repeat. So how about Pudding Mill Lane? Thanks for asking. And yes, I've used that, too.

I didn't go into details at the meeting but the one time we did try to get away from the ground using Pudding Mill Lane it was not a great success. First we found ourselves scrambling up a muddy bank and, if I remember correctly, there was a wire fence involved as well. Then we had a long schlepp through the sort of terrain that you wouldn't want to find yourself alone in late at night before arriving at the fabled Pudding Mill Lane station.

You're probably not all that bothered why we had deviated from our normal Stratford International route, but I will tell you anyway. Geoff was coming back to Brighton for the weekend and had driven down from Leamington Spa. Rather than leave his car at Westfield, he had found a last-minute parking space in Bow. Don't ask. It gave Di the chance to relive her musical youth as we emerged at Bow Church DLR station and strolled down Bow Road past the Little Driver, but other than that, Pudding Mill Lane didn't have much to recommend it in my eyes.

My first instinct when I heard the name was that it had been concocted by the Dick Van Dyke Institute For London Affairs. 'Lor, luv a duck Mary Poppins, I'm just orf to Pudding Mill Lane for a right old knees-up wiv me china plates.' It sounds as if someone has taken what I always thought of as the seat of the Great Fire of London and stuck the word 'mill' in the middle of it. (Did you know that the latest research reckons the fire actually started in Monument Street and that what we've been taught all these years is, in fact, a fallacy? Neither did I until very recently. Please, have that one on me.) But no, there was once a real life Pudding Mill in Stratford. Its proper name was St Thomas Mill, but it was shaped like – you guessed it – a pudding bowl. Hence the nickname, which it generously lent to the nearby lane, the river and later the station.

If you're ever tempted to choose the geography of Stratford as your specialist subject on *Mastermind*, here's some information that might come in handy. Pudding Mill River, a minor tributary of the River Lea, was pretty unremarkable as rivers go. It did actually contain water until the 1960s but was later relegated to ditch status after part of it was filled in and what was left became clogged with weeds and contributions from local flytippers. That was back in the bad old days when the area was a polluted industrial wasteland. There was even a small nuclear reactor nearby. (Don't worry, the Trevor Brooking Lower isn't going to start glowing in the dark all by itself – the area has been declared perfectly safe.) When the millennium dawned, Pudding Mill River enjoyed a new lease of life as trees were planted and swans, fish and eels (no, not the jellied ones) made the river their home. However, the wildlife was relocated – something we happy Hammers can sympathise with – when the river was filled in and the stadium we all know and love was built over the top.

Anyway, back to that meeting. Karren could see no problem with the stop-go boards and it seems that they are here to stay along with the running track and a total ban on standing.

Stewarding, on the other hand, was an issue on the club's to-do list. In fact it was top priority, we were told. It was generally agreed that the quickest and easiest way to improve matters was to hire people who had worked as stewards at the Boleyn Ground. The problem was, not many of them wanted to work for the sort of money LS185 was offering them. West Ham, to their credit, were pressing the operators to pay all stewards the London Living Wage. There was also a plan to increase the number of match-day supporter liaison officers from ten to fifty. I didn't want to ask what the difference is between a steward and a supporter liaison officer. However, I was pleased to hear that the club recognised it made sense to regularly put the same stewards in the same places so they and the fans could get to know each other's funny little ways.

Part of the new stewarding initiative was to no longer search children on the way into the ground – and not before time. There was also a commitment to buy more security 'wands' to hasten the checks carried out on adults. Perhaps the next consignment will include the deluxe model that can detect drums being brought into the stadium by Crystal Palace supporters. Again, that was a thought I kept to myself.

I was not so coy about the issue of season ticket pricing though. At *Blowing Bubbles* we thought many of the band one and two seats had been wrongly designated, and I was keen to make the case for reclassification.

The sale of tickets in general got quite an airing. The plus-two policy was controversial, and the members of West Ham's independent media rightly conveyed the feelings of their viewers and readers to Baroness Brady. She put up a stout defence, arguing that being able to buy two extra tickets had enabled parents to take their children to games regularly. The club wanted to attract younger fans, and this was the best way to do it.

The exchange system, whereby supporters who can't get to a game can resell their ticket, was also proving unpopular in some quarters – mainly because the refund amounted to 90 per cent of the price with 10 per cent going to Ticketmaster as an admin fee. A review was promised.

And then I got my chance to hold forth about the season ticket prices. The promise, before we moved from Upton Park, had always been that anyone who renewed would get like-for-like. Only row seventy-three at the London Stadium was nothing like row K at the Boleyn Ground. Neither were rows seventy-two, seventy-one, seventy – or anything in the sixties come to that. They were, quite simply, overpriced.

The problem lay in the fact that the bands had been calculated on the same basis as they had in E13 – namely their proximity to the half-way line. No one had factored in the distance from the pitch, which in a stadium designed the way ours was is quite considerable. Sit at the top of a stand which rises steeply and chances are you will get a decent view. Sit at the back of a bowl and you are a long way from the action.

The stadium, clearly, was not going to be rebuilt. The alternative, therefore, was to reduce the price of seats towards the back. I proposed the top twenty rows, but would have settled for fifteen. I also suggested to Karren that she joined me and my family in row seventy-three for the next game so she could see (or not see) for herself. Clearly my negotiating skills are not what they once were – both proposals were politely declined.

I was asked why I hadn't made my feelings known sooner. I pointed out that I had raised the issue immediately after the Juventus game at the start of the season. On investigation, it seems my emails had got lost in the system. Still, least said soonest mended as my old granny used to say (this is the other granny – not the one with piss on her plate). Within forty-eight hours I had been offered some alternative seats on a trial basis. They were a trifle more expensive than the ones we were in, but they were ours if we wanted them. It would have been churlish to have turned them down.

So, for the game against Manchester City we had a vastly improved view from row fifty-four. The previous owners, I was told, had some mobility issues and found it difficult to climb that many stairs. I savoured the irony and hoped the new seats would bring a change of fortune. They didn't. City scored four. We didn't score any. It was a bloodbath, pure and simple. That's it. Move along now. There's nothing to see here.

Boleyn Ground
Tuesday 2 February 2016
Kick-off: 7.45
West Ham 2–0 Aston Villa

For the game against Villa we arranged to meet Geoff outside
the Boleyn Ground by the burger stall in Priory Road. Di made
contact with him while he was on a Tube held up between Plaistow and Upton Park stations, and as the two of them worked
out the optimum moment for us to start queuing for the Mad
Dogs so his would be ready and waiting for him when he arrived
I turned my attention to the people around me.

It was a crisp winter's evening, illuminated by the stadium lights,
and came with all the hustle and bustle you would expect outside a
Premier League football ground. 'Not many evening kick-offs left,'
I heard one guy say to his mate as they passed me. Then, without
another word exchanged between them, they both stopped and
briefly took in their surroundings. The queue for the hot dogs; the
scrum outside the Priory Road ticket office; the fella trying to flog
OLAS; the stall selling flags and scarves; supporters chatting to one
another as they headed for the turnstiles; the brightly lit corner of
the East Stand, dwarfed by its newer and larger neighbour at the
southern end of the ground. Clearly I wasn't the only one trying to
relish every last minute of what little time we had left.

These blokes were probably half my age, yet they obviously
loved evening fixtures every bit as much as I did. And why not?
The knowledge that games under the Upton Park lights are
special is ingrained in every West Ham supporter. Nights such
as the Cup Winners' Cup semi-final against Eintracht Frank-
furt; the play-off against Ipswich; the League Cup thrashing of

Liverpool are more than just folklore. It's as if games like those have become part of our collective DNA. You didn't have to be there to share the joy and the glory – it is your heritage. And, as part of the deal, every time you stepped into the floodlit stadium you could make that connection. I doubted this invisible thread would survive the move to Stratford.

I checked the programme to see how many more evening encounters there would be. In the league we were scheduled to play just two other midweek fixtures after the one we were about to watch – Spurs in March and Watford at the end of April. But a 0–0 draw at Anfield in the fourth round of the FA Cup three days before we were due to play Villa had set up a bonus night game in a week's time.

Liverpool under the lights in a cup game – that should be enough to make any West Ham supporter's mouth water. If nothing else, it would give us the chance to avenge the oh-so-painful FA Cup final defeat of 2006. And maybe, just maybe, the way in which we had got Liverpool back to our place meant our name was on the trophy this time. Darren Randolph had played a blinder in goal, denying Liverpool several times. When he wasn't saving what the Scousers had to throw at him, they were wasting chances all by themselves. From what I saw on TV we did well to get away with a draw. But, as any supporter who's been lucky enough to go to a Wembley final will tell you, in the FA Cup you have to ride your luck sometimes.

Geoff finally having made it to Upton Park station and then the ground itself, we made short work of what were always generously long hotdogs (although my one criticism is that I would have preferred the onions to be cooked) and headed for our seats.

West Ham didn't always play well under lights at the Boleyn, and they weren't very good in the first half against Villa. Perhaps the Sunday cup game at Anfield had taken its toll. It certainly took its toll on James Tomkins, whose head had more stitches than the Bayeux Tapestry as a result of his trip north. Not that he was going to let a little thing like that put him off playing.

Villa thought they should have had a penalty after ten minutes when Michail Antonio jumped to block a cross and the ball hit his arm. Despite a mass protest by the Villains, referee Jonathan Moss was having none of it. Their frustration boiled over seven minutes later at a throw-in. There were some shirt-pulling shenanigans and then – bam! Jordan Ayew lost it completely and elbowed Aaron Cresswell in the face. Mr Moss didn't think twice before producing the red card.

West Ham generally don't play very well against ten men. I'll be perfectly honest here and admit that I have not gone back and checked the records for the exact win/loss percentage figures when playing a team after one of the opposition has been sent off, but it is my contention – based on more than fifty years of empirical evidence – that we generally cock it up when we have a man advantage. I had no reason to change that view at half time after the league's bottom side had successfully rebuffed West Ham's rather feeble attempts to break the deadlock.

The second half was more productive. The signs were good when a Mark Noble volley required a terrific save from Villa keeper Mark Bunn, then Payet hit the post from a free kick. The breakthrough came just before the hour, when Noble's deep cross found Antonio, whose looped header back across goal fooled Mr Bunn the Goalkeeper into thinking it was going wide. He had to revise that opinion as he picked the ball out of his net.

The goal forced Villa to abandon their siege mentality and they looked to attack when they could. That gave Payet more room in which to operate and the game as a whole improved as a result. The killer blow came in the eighty-fourth minute, immediately after a Villa corner. The ball was cleared and fell to Enner Valencia, who set off towards the other end at a rate of knots. Kouyaté, despite carrying an injury from the Liverpool game, kept pace and his exquisite finish was the perfect complement to Valencia's perfect pass.

It was hard not to feel sorry for the Villa fans. It's a proud old club but everyone could see it was destined for relegation. Still, if a side wearing claret and blue has to go down, I would rather it was them than us. Not that we looked like being relegated – we were sixth in the table with our eyes on a European spot. And, of course, there was always the FA Cup. Roll on that replay!

15

The Super Furry Coat Boys

London Stadium
Saturday 11 February 2017
Kick-off: 3.00
Final score: West Ham 2–2 WBA

AFTER A BRIEF family conference it was unanimously agreed that the new seats in row fifty-four were a big improvement and we decided to take them for the rest of the season. It meant forking out an extra £135 between us because they were classed as band one, but sometimes you just have to pay up and shut up. I did suggest to the club that, as a gesture of goodwill, they waived the money on the understanding I would give it to the Bobby Moore fund, but they didn't seem very keen on that idea. I guess they were saving up to buy a replacement for Dimitri Payet.

We were settled in our new seats in good time for the game

against West Brom. It was cheering to think that for the first time at the new ground I now had sufficient reserves of oxygen to sing 'Bubbles' without fearing that my complexion might go from an alarming shade of claret to deathly blue before I'd got to 'Then like my dreams'.

Row fifty-four felt much more like the East Stand at Upton Park. In many ways, the new seats were equivalent to the ones we had at the Boleyn Ground. You can hardly say it's like-for-like when you have to get a band one seat to replicate what had previously cost 100 quid a head less, but we weren't going back.

Before we leave row seventy-three for the last time, though, let me try to give you a flavour of what it was like up there. You've met the dad with the incontinent son. He seemed like a really nice bloke – I felt his pain every time he headed for the stairs. I just hope he lives long enough to pay the boy back forty years from now by repeatedly asking to be taken to the toilet at the most inconvenient times. (I'm hanging on just so that whenever one of our kids drives us anywhere Di and I can sit in the back of their car, squabbling endlessly and enquiring every five minutes if we're there yet.) The people on the other side were friendly, too. But you never really got the sense that we were all watching a football match together: no singing, no chanting, no abusing the referee – we could have been at the theatre.

It didn't help that the seats directly in front of us were frequently empty. And when they were taken, the occupants generally arrived late and left early. I never actually saw one of them wearing a half-and-half scarf (I would have cheerfully garotted them with it if I had) but they often had the demeanour of someone who would.

A few rows further forward there was, on match days at least, what may well have been the single largest pool of testosterone on the planet. There were about a dozen guys in all and they came in varying ages, from schoolboy to senior citizen. They would arrive in dribs and drabs, which was when the fun began. Each member of this tribe had to greet all the others – without exception – in what an anthropologist could only describe as a ritual manner. Old and young would all shake hands using the alpha male thumb grip, while hugging and patting their counterpart with their spare hand. No one was excused. The last time I saw that much man-love in one place was at a Chas and Dave concert in Brighton. (What a night that was – a room full of square, bald men staring into one another's eyes and singing 'There Ain't No Pleasing You'. I swear you could have thrown a brick in any direction and hit a scaffolder.)

What made the London Stadium group even more remarkable, apart from a striking similarity of hairstyles among those who actually had some hair, was the fact they all wore exactly the same sort of coat. I don't know if a lorry-load of fur-trimmed, army-green, three-quarter length parkas went missing in Billericay shortly before the start of the football season, but if it did this firm might be able to help the police with their inquiries. Di dubbed them the 'Super Furry Coat Boys'. They will live with me for ever.

Still, there was one good thing about being in the back row – there was no one sitting behind us. Normally it isn't a problem, but once in a while you get an 'expert'. You know the bloke I'm talking about. He's the fella who turns up once a season and imparts the wisdom he has gleaned from watching an array of TV pundits for the other fifty-one weeks a year to all those around him – whether they want to hear it or not. He is so knowledgeable it makes you wonder why he never became the manager of a Premier League side.

Every moment of the game is subject to his forensic scrutiny. Unlike the players, he knows the exact moment to cross the ball, the precise instant to lay it off, when to give and when to go. Not a clearance is allowed to pass without it going under the electron microscope. Playing it out from the back is invariably wrong – your own penalty area is not the place to be taking risks. But any attempt to get the ball forward more rapidly is dismissed with a cry of 'hoooof!' – followed by a chuckle as if he's the only one who's ever said it.

I'm not a fan of the long ball game myself. In fact, I've always rather prided myself on my unwavering support for what I believe to be Ron Greenwood's West Ham Way in the face of some stiff opposition in recent years. But I am clearly a dinosaur compared with the purist who once sat behind me at Upton Park. The moment I realised how out of touch with modern football I had become was when a James Collins clearance was ridiculed as a 'hoooof!' What made this different was that it was a header.

A cross-field pass to a better placed teammate doesn't always fit the bill either. Chances are, there's no 'second ball'. It's about then that the expert in the seat behind conducts his own investigation. 'Who's helping? Who's moving? Who's looking?' Good questions, my friend. 'To feet, to feet,' is another constant refrain.

As a rule, he's a man who sees no point in going aerial. When it comes to winning a ball in the air, your main striker either can't because he's inept, or won't because he is too idle. And he doesn't just save his tactical nous for the front men: the rest of the team can expect to have the rule run over them as well.

Criticisms will be based on a player's refusal to shoot at every opportunity; a reluctance to overlap; eccentric decision-making; an inability to cross a ball accurately and positional sense.

Of course, you may have been luckier than most and never had the 'expert' sitting behind you. If so, count your blessings. One suggestion though: maybe ask yourself if the bloke in front can say the same thing.

Right – that's enough of row seventy-three. We're in row fifty-four now and all that is behind us. (Did you see what I did there?)

I started to have my doubts about how the West Brom game was going to pan out when the referee and his two assistants took to the field wearing blue and white scarves. Well, maybe not literally. But they might just as well have been.

The pattern for the rest of the afternoon was set as early as the sixth minute, when Nacer Chadli put the visitors ahead. From my new, improved vantage point it looked very much like Sofiane Feghouli had been fouled in the build-up. Referee Michael Oliver had other ideas, unfortunately.

I couldn't see why he disallowed what looked like an equaliser by Feghouli ten minutes later, however. The Algerian put the ball in the net during a goalmouth scramble which left defender Craig Dawson flat out, having been cleaned up by his own keeper. Again Mr Oliver ruled against the Hammers – although no one quite knew why. Was it for offside (which Feghouli clearly wasn't) or a foul by Michail Antonio on Ben Foster (which was nowhere near as clear cut as Foster's foul on Antonio which caused him to miss the ball entirely when the goal was at his mercy)? West Ham's assistant coach Nikola Jurčević strode down the touchline in an effort to find out from the linesman, and was promptly sent to the stand for his trouble.

Slaven Bilić was ticking like a clock in his technical area. And his mood wasn't improved when the ref rejected Robert Snodgrass's appeal for a penalty after he went down following a challenge by Jake Livermore in first-half injury time. The manager was so angry he waited in the mouth of the tunnel to confront the referee at the interval.

West Ham did get the equaliser they deserved shortly after the hour. A stinging shot by Manuel Lanzini was tipped on to the bar by Foster, but Feghouli was first to the rebound. And with only four minutes left of normal time, the Hammers looked to have won it when Lanzini ran at the West Brom defence and let fly with a long-range effort that beat Foster allends up.

That was not the end of the scoring though. In the fourth minute of time added on Jonny Evans got his head on a corner, steering the ball beyond Darren Randolph. The equaliser tipped Bilić over the edge – not least because it looked as if the goalkeeper had been impeded as he attempted to punch the ball clear before it reached Evans. In his rage he threw a television microphone to the ground, and was immediately sent to join his assistant in the stand.

He had barely calmed down when he gave his post-match interview. 'The decisions were big time against us, every one of them,' he said. 'It is hard for referees but when you are on the wrong side of all decisions it makes you very, very angry. The referee was very bad today.'

My friend Nick is a Baggie – and he was in the away end that day. I wanted to know how a visiting supporter viewed our new home, so I asked him.

I know you've been to Upton Park to support West Brom on numerous occasions. What did you think of the London Stadium?
The overriding impression was that it's a nice stadium but it's not a real football ground. It feels too impersonal, too distant, like watching a performance rather than a battle for victory. With the gap between the crowd (or should that be audience?) and the pitch, it feels as if you're less involved – certainly less than at Upton Park which could be intimidating at times. The only thing intimidating at the London Stadium was Bilić prowling the touchline and kicking the corner flag. That was pure panto!

As an away supporter, how does the new stadium compare with the Boleyn Ground?
Even outside the ground before the match, the difference was marked. Heading towards Upton Park the streets were always thronged with noisy supporters chanting, drinking, eating: the shops were all open selling everything you could want and it felt like the heart of a community. At the London Stadium it all felt formal, regimented, like an international friendly where you could take it or leave it.

What did you think of the atmosphere?
Inside the ground it was better than I had expected. Our lot were quite noisy – especially with a last-minute equaliser – and so were the West Ham fans, particularly the ones near us. So it was not quite the library I had feared. But it was nowhere near as intense as Upton Park.

What was the view like?

Our seats were relatively low down – by choice – so we were not too far away from the action, but further back would have made it even more difficult to get properly involved. The running track really emphasises the gap between the crowd and the match.

What about the facilities?

They were good, like a modern stadium should be. But the point is it could have been any modern stadium anywhere.

How about getting away at the end?

That was fine; the segregation at the end seemed to work OK as far as we could tell although we did manage to lose our way a bit looking for the Tube. I have no idea how!

It's a bit different to the Hawthorns, right?

I guess the fact that the West Ham insignia were removed from the stadium over the summer says it all. It feels like a temporary stadium the club is renting while something else is being built, not a real home. Maybe things will feel different once the new place has gained a bit of history of its own, and it will start to feel more like it should. But at the moment I know I'd be disappointed if it was the Albion's home ground, that's for sure.

Thanks mate. All I can say is, cross your fingers and hope that Birmingham never gets the Olympics!

Boleyn Ground
Saturday 27 February 2016
Kick-off: 12.45
West Ham 1–0 Sunderland

A lot had happened since we'd last been inside the Boleyn Ground. Following the victory against Aston Villa the Hammers had lost at Southampton, beaten Liverpool in a pulsating FA Cup replay, come from two goals behind to earn a draw at Carrow Road and then gone to Blackburn where they thrashed Rovers 5–1 to set up a sixth-round tie with Manchester United. All that, and it was the shortest month of the year!

We turned up for the Sunderland game in a buoyant mood. West Ham were seventh in the Premier League, with Southampton above us on the most slender of goal differences and Man Utd, who were fifth, only one point better off. A European place of some sort was looking distinctly possible. Better still, though, we were now on a serious cup run.

These were exciting times, reminiscent for those of us old enough to have been there of the heady days we'd enjoyed thirty years beforehand. Could Bilić and his team emulate the achievements of John Lyall and his Boys of '86? There were certainly some similarities.

The players who so nearly won the league title in 1986 have gone down in West Ham folklore. There were eighteen in all, and every single one of them deserves a place in any Hammers Heroes sticker book. Several of them made it into the publication that was produced when we went to Stratford: Phil Parkes; Tony Cottee; Alvin Martin; Steve Potts; Tony Gale; Alan Devonshire and Frank McAvennie. But I'd like to take this opportunity to honour the rest of them: Ray Stewart; Alan Dickens; Neil Orr; Paul Goddard; Geoff Pike; Mark Ward; George Parris; Steve Walford; Paul Hilton; Greg Campbell and Bobby Barnes. Gentlemen, we salute you.

As with Bilić's squad, this was a group of players who appeared to actually like one another. You got the impression that they were mates off the field as well as comrades-in-arms on it. What's more, as a supporter, you felt that every one of the Boys of '86 wanted to do it for *you*. The spirit of unity was infectious and increasingly that year we walked away from Upton Park after yet another victory feeling as if we were part of something special. That was precisely how I felt after we'd beaten Liverpool in the replay.

The Boleyn Ground excelled herself that night. Think of her as an East End matriarch whose kids have all left home but periodically come back for Sunday lunch – giving her the chance to prove that while she may not be all she once was, she can still come up trumps when called upon. On this occasion, the old girl served up a banquet.

As a rule, any meal at Upton Park normally started with a first course of 'Bubbles'. On this occasion we began by honouring Ron Greenwood with a minute's applause to mark the tenth anniversary of his death in February 2006. What can you say about Greenwood that hasn't been said before? West Ham may, in future, have managers who win more trophies, but it's hard to imagine there will ever be one who lays down an everlasting template in the way he did.

When we got round to the anthem that sums up a club more than any other song, we dished it out loud and proud – knowing all too well that it could be the last time we ever had a chance to witness an FA Cup game at our old home. As we sang, the West

Ham players hugged and cajoled and urged one another on in preparation for the action that was about to follow. But despite the bonding and display of camaraderie, the Boys of '16 started uncertainly – as they had so often in home games that season. The early enthusiasm in the stands began to falter slightly.

An inexperienced Liverpool side had all the best moments in the opening quarter of an hour. West Ham's first serious attack ended with Joey O'Brien hitting the post from the edge of the box. It was his first start in six months – now that would have been some comeback!

Ten minutes later Liverpool created a decent chance which Jordon Ibe made a hash of. Next, João Teixeira had a shot which went just wide of Darren Randolph's right-hand post. Then Philippe Coutinho rattled the same piece of woodwork. This wasn't supposed to be on the menu.

The atmosphere inside the ground changed dramatically moments later when Payet hit the post with a signature free kick from the edge of the D and Antonio nearly converted the rebound. Our appetites were whetted – and we were given something to really get our teeth into on the stroke of half time when Antonio volleyed home a sweet cross from Enner Valencia. He marked the goal by hugging Joey O'Brien. The Williams family hugged one another.

The second half didn't start anywhere near as well as the first period finished. Within four minutes of the restart Liverpool were level. Jürgen Klopp had sent his side out early and it seemed to work when Christian Benteke won a free kick just outside the penalty area. Coutinho gambled on the defensive wall jumping – which it did, allowing his daisy-cutter shot to find its way past a surprised Randolph and into the net.

After that, it was cut and thrust from both sides. Daniel Sturridge came on for Coutinho and looked dangerous. Benteke stayed on and looked toothless. West Ham should have had a penalty when Valencia found himself the victim of some serious shirt-tugging. Andy Carroll replaced Kouyaté and looked to put Simon Mignolet under pressure, but still the winner wouldn't come. Not even the eight minutes of time added on could produce the decisive goal.

West Ham started extra time much better than they had the match itself, but it was Liverpool who should have taken the lead. Benteke saw a shot go inches wide then, thirty seconds later, he found himself one-on-one with Randolph, who was able to block the weak effort with his legs. They were worrying moments.

In the second half of extra time both sides looked weary. Randolph was the busier of the two keepers, but a goal appeared hard to come by. We steeled ourselves for penalties and part of me wished that it was Adrián, rather than his understudy, who had got the job of trying to save them. And then, with time added on in extra time, Angelo Ogbonna decided enough was enough. As Payet stood over a free kick sizing up his options, Ogbonna attached himself to a queue of players on the edge of Liverpool's penalty area. White shirts outnumbered claret and blue by two to one. Defenders looked anxiously at Carroll and the Ginger Pele. But Payet wasn't interested in home cooking – he wanted Italian. The ball came over, Ogbonna climbed above everyone around him and his delicious header looped over a helpless Mignolet. It was his first goal for the club – and the first time West Ham had ever beaten Liverpool in the FA Cup. But nobody cared about that right then. All we wanted to do was celebrate our momentous victory. Slaven Bilić hailed it as one of the greatest nights in West Ham's history, and I wasn't going to argue with him.

Had I been an argumentative sort of individual I might have had words with the bloke sitting behind me, though. He was the dreaded once-a-season 'expert' who had taken advantage of the fact that regular season ticket holders can't always get to mid-week cup games and had bagged the seat for the night. We got all the usual pearls of wisdom, plus a couple of bonus offerings. 'Run him' was the preferred option. But he also liked 'drive, drive, drive!' He had nearly driven me to distraction. However, I consoled myself with the thought that our season tickets for Stratford, purchased the month before, meant I would never again have to endure this sort of nonsense because our new seats were in the back row. Smart move, eh?

The game against Sunderland was televised, which resulted in a 12.45 kick-off. There should be laws against that sort of thing. What sort of time is quarter to one to start a game of football? If God had meant kick-offs to be that early he/she wouldn't have invented the pre-match pint.

All the talk before the game was about the reception Sam Allardyce would get on his return to the Boleyn Ground. As it turned out, no one seemed all that bothered. What little hostility that could be mustered was mainly directed at Jermain Defoe for old times' sake.

The programme cover was a replica of the one which had been printed in 1968 when West Ham thrashed the Mackems 8–0 at Upton Park. Sadly, the score wasn't replicated. The one and only goal came after thirty minutes when Michail Antonio cut in from the right touchline, played an impromptu one-two with a Sunderland defender and then slid a precision left-foot shot past Vito Mannone. It was the sort of effort that often prompts TV pundits to talk about slide-rules. Goodness only knows why: slide-rules were used to do complicated sums, you didn't measure things with them. But let's not go there.

Antonio marked the goal with a replica of his own: this one a recreation of a horizontal circular dance Homer Simpson once performed after he had outwitted Mr Burns. Chav Corner loved it, although one or two of Antonio's teammates looked a bit bemused as he turned himself into a human helicopter – albeit one that never left the ground.

West Ham hit the woodwork a couple of times: a Mark Noble shot produced a fantastic reflex save by Mannone in which he palmed the ball on to the bar, and Andy Carroll had a close-range effort ricochet off the goal-frame. In the second half Defoe tried a couple of volleys, but his once-deadly accuracy had, happily, deserted him. The Bobby Moore Stand tried to lighten what was a pretty humdrum affair by suggesting to our friends from the north that their team was going down with Adam Johnson, one of their former players who was on trial accused of unlawful sexual activity with an underage girl. As it turned out, they were right about Johnson's porridge, but Sunderland themselves got a stay of execution at the end of the season.

The one saving grace about an early kick-off is that, if you win, you get the points on the board while your rivals can only sit and watch. The win took us above both Southampton and Man Utd.

One of the day's talking points had been Sir Geoff Hurst accidentally using the F-word over the PA system at half time while reminiscing about the six goals he had scored in the 8–0 thrashing of Sunderland. He was there as one of the 'Sixties Legends' who were part of the last-season celebrations. Some months before, in the game against Newcastle, several of the Boys of '86 had been paraded as part of the same jollifications. Back then I had applauded loudly for the wonderful memories they had given me, but never for one moment thought the final year at Upton Park could be as special in terms of results. Having beaten the Geordies' deadliest enemies to go fifth in the table I was beginning to wonder if Noble & Co could replicate the success of Alvin Martin and his legendary teammates. Not that I was going to get carried away you understand. We are talking about West Ham, after all.

16

Are we Chelsea in disguise?

London Stadium
Monday 6 March 2017
Kick-off: 8.00
Final score: West Ham 1–2 Chelsea

SKY WANTED TO see if West Ham could put a dent in Chelsea's title aspirations and decreed the game should be their first *Monday Night Football* offering in March. I didn't have to work that day, but switching the fixture from Saturday meant I had to drag myself up from the south coast to London on Britain's ramshackle rail network anyway. Thanks guys.

Brighton, St Pancras, a pre-match pint, Stratford International – that had become the match-day routine for Di and me. However, the monotony of the Thameslink train journey was lightened somewhat by the driver, who couldn't quite get to grips with the name of London's finest Victorian railway station. He insisted on calling it St Pancreas.

Everyone was hoping there would be no repetition of the violence that had marred the League Cup encounter earlier in the season, although a similar scoreline wouldn't have gone amiss. Sadly, it was not to be.

West Ham started well enough, trying to utilise Andy Carroll's aerial power whenever possible, but Chelsea were well organised and in defensive midfielder N'Golo Kanté they had the most influential player on the pitch. He had been named the Premier League Player of the Year at the London Football Awards the previous week, and it wasn't hard to see why. From a West Ham perspective it was good to see Carroll back, but we missed Michail Antonio, who had got himself sent off at Watford in the previous game.

In an effort to blunt Chelsea's attacking threat Bilić went for a back four, with Cheikhou Kouyaté at right back. I, like many others in the stands, would have preferred to have seen him in a more advanced midfield role. Nevertheless, with Robert Snodgrass and Sofiane Feghouli looking to get down the flanks and cross at every opportunity, West Ham were on the front foot with Chelsea forced to concede several corners and free kicks in the first twenty-five minutes. Unfortunately, one of those free kicks led to their first goal.

Eden Hazard fouled Mark Noble twenty-five yards from the Chelsea goal. Manuel Lanzini lined up the free kick, but could only smash it into the defensive wall. A blink of an eye later, Darren Randolph was picking the ball out of the West Ham net. Chelsea countered through Kanté, who found Hazard on the half-way line. The Belgian swapped passes with Pedro before skipping round Randolph and slipping the ball into an open goal. I began to get a very uncomfortable feeling in my unsaintly pancreas.

For the rest of the half West Ham continued to press forward, and Chelsea continued to counter. It pains me to say it, but they looked far more dangerous. They put the game to bed five minutes after the break, when Diego Costa scored from a corner. West Ham pulled one back through Lanzini in time added on, but by then the stadium was half empty.

What really hurt, as we walked away from the ground, was the feeling that not only had Chelsea won on the pitch, they'd also won in the stands. Sure, we advised their fans what to do with their blue flag in the early stages when the scores were level. However in the second half, with their team clearly on top and the London Stadium feeling anything but a fortress, they came back at us with a chant of 'You're not West Ham any more' – which was a bit rich coming from a club that sold its soul many years ago but, I'll admit, it did set me thinking. Were they right?

I suppose the answer depends on what your idea of West Ham United is, and what it should be. Do we now have a new identity? To understand the present and possibly predict the future, it helps to know what happened in the past. So, sit up straight and put your mobiles away while we have a quick history lesson. And it's automatic detention for anyone I catch sticking their chewing gum to the bottom of the desk.

For most of us, the club's history is primarily about the games played, the trophies won, the relegations, the promotions and the players who have turned out in claret and blue over the years – good and bad. But how the club is run underpins everything that happens on the pitch.

In the beginning, there was Thames Ironworks FC, a factory team formed in 1895 by industrialist Arnold Hills. The original home ground was in Hermit Road, Canning Town, less than a mile from the Thames Ironworks and Shipbuilding Company, which was situated at the mouth of Bow Creek. They played there for two years before being given notice to quit.

Next stop was Browning Road in East Ham, which became home in March 1897. Thames Ironworks FC didn't stay there long, however – moving in the summer of the same year to the massive Memorial Grounds, funded by Hills himself. The name commemorates Queen Victoria's diamond jubilee – hence 'Memorial'.

The capacity was said to be well over 100,000 – although the side never attracted anything like that sort of a crowd. Author John Powles, who has studied West Ham's history extensively over the years, told me that the record attendance was 17,000 for a game against Tottenham – and that required a temporary stand. The grounds included tennis courts and a swimming pool. And, just to prove that history has a tendency to repeat itself, the football pitch was circled by a running track. In fact, John says, there was a banked cycle track outside the athletics lanes, which meant football supporters were a mighty long way from the action. Sound familiar?

Thames Ironworks FC continued to prosper, joining the Southern League in 1898 and immediately winning promotion to the first division. But success on the pitch was not matched by support on the terraces. This was essentially a works side and those who weren't employed by Hills failed to take it to their hearts.

Hills himself had his doubts about hiring professional players – he wanted a team bearing the company's name to be made up of his employees, although he was prepared to stretch a point on occasions. Those handling the day-to-day running of the football club thought differently. They tried to attract the best footballers of their day.

By 1900 Hills was increasingly disillusioned by what he had created. Furthermore, he wanted to raise money to enlarge his business interests, which involved turning his firm into a limited company to attract capital. With shareholders to answer to, he felt unable to plough other people's money into his football team. Instead, he chose to wind up Thames Ironworks FC. But, rather than walk away completely, he proposed a new club, which would be a limited company with him as the major shareholder. This, of course, was West Ham United. Apart from putting his own money into the new venture, he allowed the fledgling club to continue to use the Memorial Grounds. However, his relationship with the new directors became increasingly fractious and at the start of the 1904 season the club was told, in no uncertain terms, to find a new home. The directors opted for the Boleyn Castle site in Green Street.

Historian Charles Korr believes the enforced move was the best thing that could have happened to West Ham. For one thing, it was easier for supporters to get to the new ground – there was a railway station and a tram stop nearby. But there was more to it than ease of access. He says: 'The setting was radically different from the docklands location of the Memorial Grounds. Boleyn Castle was the site of a Catholic school in a neighbourhood surrounded by small shops and residential streets. It was very different from the squalid conditions that outsiders usually assumed to be typical of east London, and was much closer to the support upon which the future of the club would be based.'

This was the move that defined West Ham – it put the club at the heart of a football-loving community that was prepared to turn out and cheer it on in a way that had not happened previously. Profits from the increased gate money went up by 50 per cent, enabling the club to clear its debts and buy better players.

Although Hills showed no interest in how the club was run, he remained the largest shareholder. He was actually the majority shareholder until 1910 – if anyone could be described as the owner it was him. When he died in 1927 the directors were concerned that his heirs may not take such a hands-off view and tried to buy the family's shares. The attempt came to nothing, but there were assurances that there would be no interference and things would go on as before.

More than twenty years later, in 1949, there was a second attempt to buy the Hills family shares. The chairman of the board at this time was W. J. Cearns, whose own family had been involved with the club since its formation. Again, there was no sale. But the fact that the board did not own anything like a majority of the equity between them didn't prevent them running the club pretty much as they saw fit. There were annual shareholder meetings, but the real power lay with the chairman and his fellow directors.

The overriding characteristic of West Ham United for years to come was that of a conservative organisation run by a board of directors who looked to improve the ground and the team when they could, without taking massive risks. There were times when this approach wasn't popular with some supporters, who criticised the directors for lack of ambition. But there was never any question of the club going bust.

That all changed towards the end of 2006 when an Icelandic

consortium headed by a businessman named Björgólfur Guðmundsson bought the club for £85 million. Outgoing chairman
Terence Brown collected £33.4 million from the sale of his
shares while the Cearns family received £7.7 million for their
stake. The sale truly marked the end of an era. Jimmy Cearns
was one of the founding fathers. Martin Cearns, who was on
the board when the club was sold, was the third member of the
family to have been chairman at one time or another. One of
the directors who approved the sale to Guðmundsson was the
great-grandson of Arnold Hills, without whom there would be
no West Ham United.

Those who believed the previous regime had been too cautious
for too long saw the takeover as the start of a bright new period
in West Ham's history. Incoming chairman Eggert Magnússon
made all the right noises and we sat back in expectation of
more trophies than you could haul in with an Icelandic trawler.
All appeared to be going reasonably well for a couple of years
until, shortly after the start of the 2008–09 season, club sponsor
XL Airlines went bust – a collapse that was said to have cost
Guðmundsson £200 million.

The airline's failure came at the start of the Icelandic financial
crisis, which lasted three years and saw Guðmundsson's personal
wealth go from $1.1 billion to zero.

When he sold the club to the present owners he had debts of
almost £500 million and was declared bankrupt shortly afterwards. As a result, West Ham United was facing ruin.

In January 2010, David Sullivan bought 50 per cent of the
club's shares for £52.5 million from the holding company, rather
unimaginatively named CB Holdings, which owned the club
on behalf of Guðmundsson's consortium. A few days he later he

sold some of these shares to David Gold, and they became joint owners.

Right from the start Sullivan said their vision for the future was based on relocating to Stratford. 'It is the natural home for West Ham,' he told the *Guardian*. 'We hope to persuade the government to let us move into the new Olympic Stadium and I believe the people of east London would support that move.'

Later in 2010 Sullivan and Gold shelled out a further £8 million to take their combined stake to 60 per cent. Then, in 2014, Sullivan bought a further 25 per cent of the shares for £25.5 million. In all, they bought £86 million worth of equity.

In an ideal world, the day-to-day cost of running any club would be financed entirely by ticket sales, television money and merchandising profits. This rarely happens, certainly not at West Ham. To bolster this revenue, Sullivan and Gold (or, more accurately, companies they control) have lent West Ham almost £50 million in the form of shareholder loans.

Leading West Ham blogger Sean Whetstone keeps a close eye on the club's finances. He says:

These are loans dating back to 2011 but they continue to attract accrued interest of between 6 per cent and 7 per cent. This debt grew to £61.5 million up to May 2016 before the owners cashed out £4.2 million. The remainder of the debt is not due to be paid back until 1 January 2020 but with compound interest, the remaining shareholder loans could reach around £71 million in just under three years time – meaning that around £75 million could be paid back for £49 million originally loaned to the club by the owners.

If anyone could tell me where I can earn 6 per cent interest on my savings I'd be very grateful. But this is about the club's finances, not mine. So what happened to the money from the sale of Upton Park?

The Boleyn Ground land was sold to developers for £38 million, with £15 million going to pay off all external bank debts that were mortgaged against it and a further £15 million going to stadium owners LLDC to contribute towards the £323 million transition costs of the former Olympic Stadium. The remaining £8 million was used for the WestHamification of the London Stadium including fitting out the club shop, the seats and the claret and blue branding, so the Boleyn Ground money has all been spent.

Is the club still in trouble financially?

If you ask the West Ham board about the state of the finances of the club they will say the club is still over £100 million in debt. While this is technically true, closer inspection will show that £60 million of this debt is owed to the owners in shareholder loans and £41 million owed to other clubs in staged transfer payments which are the norm nowadays. A further £30 million is a short-term loan borrowed against future TV money.

Moving to Stratford must mean there's more money coming in – otherwise, what was the point?

Ticket sales and match-day activities at the London Stadium are expected to rise by £12 million from the record £27 million received from the last season at the Boleyn Ground to £39 million at the London Stadium. Retail shop and commercial sponsorship income are also expected to increase by around 30 per cent from £29 million in 2015/2016.

Karren Brady has said the club is worth around £800 million. How much of that would the owners receive if they sold up?
Sullivan would receive £400 million plus £35 million for his loans. Gold would get £280 million plus £35 million for his loans. However, both would need to pay a windfall tax to the government if they sold the club before August 2027. If the club was sold for £800 million before August 2022 they would pay the government £207 million in a windfall tax. After August 2022 and before August 2027 that would reduce to £135 million on a £800 million sale. After August 2027 they pay the government nothing if they sell.

The big question that divides opinion among West Ham fans like no other is would West Ham have really gone under without Sullivan and Gold?
Sean has no doubt: 'Yes, they saved the club from financial Armageddon in my opinion.'

Whether or not the present owners really are the saviours of the club is something that historians of the future will no doubt debate endlessly in years to come. And that is the beauty of history: while it may be open to interpretation it is nevertheless a constant timeline that can be added to but not altered. As supporters, depending on our age, we all board that timeline at a different stop, but the history belongs to all of us. I began supporting West Ham when Bobby Moore was in his pomp. Geoff first came to the party when Paulo Di Canio was king of the castle. But my son is every bit as entitled as I am to his share of the pride that comes with being part of a club that was once home to such a giant of the game. It's part of his legacy as a supporter. Similarly, I never saw Vic Watson in his playing days, but I am able to take a huge sense of gratification from his achievements in a way I never could from those of, say, Sir Stanley Matthews.

A club's culture, on the other hand, can and does change. The people in charge can alter it – just as the directors did when they moved to the Boleyn Ground in 1904. But the supporters have a huge part to play as well. Charles Korr believes our role is pivotal. He calls us 'the real owners' and goes on to say: 'It is absurd to think of the business of football without taking into account the emotional link between supporters and the club.'

In short, without us there is no club. We may not have had a real say in the move to Stratford – forget the consultation process, the decision had already been made. But we can shape our destiny now we're there. 'You're not West Ham any more'? I beg to differ. But we have to understand exactly what sort of West Ham we want to be.

Me? I know what sort of club I want. In the boardroom, I want honesty, integrity and a recognition that supporters must be involved in the decision-making process. On the pitch, I want attractive, attacking football played by a team that understands it is an honour to wear the claret and blue shirt. And in the stands I want to be surrounded by those who share my ridiculous passion – people who care deeply about what they are witnessing rather than merely a passive audience which sits in silence as events unfold in front of us.

I most certainly do not want West Ham United to become

another Chelsea, no matter how many trophies they win. If the
move to Stratford brings that about the owners who took us
there won't have saved the club – they will have destroyed it.

Boleyn Ground
Wednesday 2 March 2016
Kick-off: 7.45
Final score: West Ham 1–0 Tottenham

As America was weighing up the results of the election-fest they
call Super Tuesday, we were having a jolly super Wednesday in
east London. The weather was shocking – Storm Jake had seen
to. that – but West Ham's very own ray of sunshine who goes by
the name of Michail Antonio meant that by the end of a fantastic game the only cloud in E13 was the one hanging over the
Tottenham fans in the Trevor Brooking Stand. (All right, that's
enough dodgy meteorological similes. Promise.)

The sense of anticipation was palpable as we took our seats.
The Clash were setting the scene with *London Calling* on the PA
system. The top of the table was calling for our opponents – as
the teams emerged from the tunnel both sets of supporters knew
that a victory would send Spurs to the summit of the Premier
League. They wanted the points desperately; we were equally
desperate to deny them.

The wet pitch glistened under the lights. Mass-produced bubbles from the battery of machines located around the ground
hung in the air. We filled our lungs with the damp air and roared
West Ham's famous old anthem. Was I the only one trying to
remind fortune that this was not a night for hiding?

West Ham started well. There was a real sense of urgency. It was as if everyone understood that we simply couldn't lose the last ever game against Spurs at the Boleyn Ground. The expectation level went up a notch as Dimitri Payet set himself to take our first corner. Seconds later Upton Park erupted as Michail Antonio beat Hugo Lloris with a near-post header that put the Hammers in front. Just seven minutes gone and we were 1–0 up. Antonio danced in celebration as Geoff embraced Di and me in a massive family bear hug. It was a joyous moment.

The West Ham faithful savoured it to the full and taunted the away supporters. 'Who are you?' we enquired none too politely. The Bobby Moore Stand had already reminded them of a game played ten years beforehand when West Ham had wrecked Spurs' hopes of getting into Europe after several of their players had complained of food poisoning. It only took one word to get the message across: lasagne.

On the pitch, the boys in claret and blue were dominant. Barely ten minutes after the goal, Mark Noble nearly doubled the lead with a shot from outside the area. Lloris had to be at his best to keep it out. The keeper was in the thick of it again a few minutes later. First he looked clumsy in dealing with a back pass and almost gifted Emmanuel Emenike a goal. Then he was forced to save a Payet free kick after the Frenchman had been felled by Toby Alderweireld, who got a yellow card for his trouble. With the interval approaching, Kevin Wimmer joined his teammate in the book after the Spurs defender pulled back Emenike. Then Antonio put the ball in the Spurs net, but was clearly offside. Only one team wanted the half-time whistle, and it wasn't West Ham.

As the second half started I feared that Tottenham could only get better, but West Ham continued to press. Noble was everywhere in midfield; Antonio was tireless; Cresswell looked dangerous going forward and the back three of Kouyaté, Ogbonna and Collins were solid as a rock.

The one and only heart-in-the-mouth moment came just after the hour mark, when Adrián pushed a long-range shot by Alderweireld into the path of Harry Kane. The England striker should have scored, but for once he fluffed the chance. Did the fact he was wearing a face mask to protect a broken nose explain the miss? Perhaps, given the teeming rain, he should have fitted some windscreen wipers.

Tottenham were lucky not to be reduced to ten men when Wimmer escaped a second booking after bringing down Emenike again. To everyone's astonishment, referee Andre Marriner gave the free kick to Spurs. Maybe he would have benefited from some windscreen wipers as well. Or specs to put them on.

With twenty minutes remaining the Ginger Pele hobbled off to a standing ovation. He was replaced by teenager Reece Oxford, who looked composed from the instant he came on. The same could not be said of Tottenham, who became increasingly frantic as the time ticked by. We revelled in their discomfort, reminding them they were going to win sweet Fanny Adams (although that was expressed as two other words beginning with F and A). The final whistle was greeted with delirium by every West Ham supporter in the ground. We'd won, and Spurs were not going to be top of the league. 'Tottenham Hotspur, it's happened again,' we sang gleefully as the visiting fans contemplated the title they thought they were going to win slipping from their grasp.

For us, however, the table made wonderful reading. West Ham were just one point behind fourth-placed Manchester City. The Champions League? Surely not.

Di and I had followed West Ham for too long to be carried away by thoughts like that as we dawdled home on the Thameslink train from St Pancras, toasting our triumph with a four-pack of Marks & Sparks cider.

We tried to work out the significance of Antonio's goal celebration. In the end we had to refer the matter to Professor Google, who informed us that it was a dance move from the TV programme *The Fresh Prince of Bel-Air*. Some weeks later it emerged that it should have been something rather different. Antonio told one of the tabloids: 'As soon as the ball was played over I was thinking this ball is heading right for me and I didn't even see it go in. I completely forgot my celebration that I had planned. I had planned it so much and it was going to be The Worm, but the emotion of scoring in a derby got to me and I ended up doing the Carlton dance!'

On the table that separated Di and me, next to the empty tins of cider, was the match-day programme. Smiling up at us was Vic Watson, West Ham's all-time leading scorer – a man who would have celebrated every one of his 326 goals for the club with nothing more than a handshake. I wondered what he would have made of it all.

17

East, east, east London

London Stadium
Saturday 18 March 2017
Kick-off: 3.00
Final score: West Ham 2–3 Leicester

AS A RULE, going 2–0 down in the opening seven minutes of a game is not to be recommended. And it's certainly not a good idea if you do it against the defending champions just as they are rediscovering some decent form after sacking their manager. For once, I almost envied the people still waiting patiently outside the ground for a steward to give them the once-over with a security wand.

The way West Ham started against Leicester, Slaven Bilić could have done with a magic wand to conjure up a defence. The first goal was laughable. Aaron Cresswell gave Riyad Mahrez all the time and space he needed to assess his options. As his harmless-looking cross from the right sailed into the penalty area, Winston Reid jumped and missed it. Behind him, José Fonte didn't even attempt to levitate. Darren Randolph looked on in bewilderment as the ball rolled in, untouched, at his far post.

It got worse two minutes later. Marc Albrighton, left to his own devices on the edge of the West Ham penalty area, was allowed to slip a free kick to Mahrez, saunter a few unimpeded paces to collect the return pass and then chip the ball to the far post, where Robert Huth was being ostracised by those who were employed to mark him. If I'd had a magic wand right then, a few highly paid athletes in claret and blue shirts might well have got the old Harry Potter Twatterarmus spell and disappeared before your very eyes.

Without wishing to stretch this too far, there was a touch of magic about the Manuel Lanzini goal that put us back in the game. It was a free kick from twenty yards that left Kasper Schmeichel rooted to the spot as it flew into his top right-hand corner.

Reid had hobbled off a few moments before that, which may well have contributed to Leicester's third goal six minutes before the interval. No one seemed to want to take responsibility as a Leicester corner came into the West Ham box and, while defenders dithered, Jamie Vardy smashed the loose ball into the net. Football's answer to Albert Steptoe chose to celebrate his goal ostentatiously in front of the Bobby Moore Stand, which lacked a certain amount of class. 'Arold needs to have a word with his old man about that sort of thing.

The second half was a different story entirely, especially after André Ayew scored with an hour gone. The final thirty minutes was all West Ham – Bilić later described that last half-hour as the best performance his team had produced all season. He then wondered out loud why the players felt they couldn't play like that until they were behind in a game. Good question, Slav. We were wondering the same thing.

Schmeichel had already pulled off a fantastic save to push a Lanzini free kick round the post before Ayew's goal. He produced another to deny an Andy Carroll header that would have been the equaliser.

Ayew should have levelled moments later when Michail Antonio drove into the heart of the Leicester defence and set him up with a sitter – which he blazed over the bar from twelve yards out with only Schmeichel to beat. Incredulously, I asked Geoff precisely why we'd paid £20.5 million for this man, to which he replied that Ayew is not naturally right-footed. He has a very generous nature, my son.

Schmeichel, who had been outstanding all afternoon, saved his best until the second minute of injury time, when he somehow managed to block a shot from point-blank range by Carroll. A Robert Snodgrass free kick found its way through the defensive wall and on to the left foot of Big Andy. It had 'goal' written all over it. Carroll was so astonished that his effort didn't go in he actually face-palmed.

There was a time, not so long ago, when you looked at the fixture list, saw Leicester and knew there were three points ripe for the picking. That is clearly not the case now. I know we're all supposed to love them for winning the Premier League in 2016, but I don't. Take those stupid plastic clappers they use to make some noise – that's pathetic. Worse still is: 'aaaaaaah, you're shit' at every opposition goal kick. Please, Leicester fans, that ceased to be even faintly amusing in 1971 – grow up, will you?

Boleyn Ground
Saturday 2 April 2016
Kick-off: 3.00
Final score: West Ham 2–2 Crystal Palace

Since beating Tottenham a month beforehand, West Ham had been busy bunnies. On the Saturday following that game the Hammers had gone to Everton, which has never been a happy hunting ground. It appeared to be a case of same old, same old with the home side 2–0 up and only twelve minutes to go – then the mighty Irons scored three to rekindle memories of the great Sid Waddell and his fabulous line: 'That was the greatest comeback since Lazarus.'

Next on the agenda, the following Sunday, was a televised FA Cup sixth-round game at Old Trafford, which will always be remembered for a brilliant free kick from thirty yards by Payet to give us the lead, and a rotten refereeing decision that gave them a totally undeserved equaliser in the eighty-third minute. Had Martin Atkinson, who is certainly not the worst ref I've ever seen, spotted Bastian Schweinsteiger's foul on Darren Randolph we'd have been looking at a semi-final rather than a replay.

Just to show how far the club had come under Bilić, the next league game was a 2–2 draw at Stamford Bridge. Not so many years ago that would have been hailed as a triumph. On this occasion, there was a real sense of disappointment we didn't come away with all three points and fourth place in the table. Another dodgy refereeing decision? How did you guess? This time it was Bobby Madley awarding Chelsea an eighty-ninth minute penalty that (a) wasn't a foul and (b) happened outside the area. Still, who wants to play in the Champions League anyway?

For the game against Crystal Palace we had the pleasure of Mark Clattenburg's company. Did he affect the game at all? I hear you ask. Hardly at all – apart, that is, from the straight red card he showed Cheikhou Kouyaté with twenty-three minutes left on the clock. Clattenburg was lucky he didn't have his clock cleaned by Bilić, who was incensed by the decision. 'It is simply never a red card,' the manager said afterwards. 'For me personally it is not even a yellow card. In England maybe it's not even a foul – it's a 50-50 challenge!'

West Ham were 2–1 up at the time, thanks to another brilliant free kick from Payet and a goal from Lanzini. Payet's effort was truly spectacular, even by his standards. Keeper Wayne Hennessey demanded a seven-man wall to defend the right-hand side of his goal, but couldn't resist the temptation to edge that way himself. Payet spotted him, so rather than lift the ball over the wall he curled it into the corner that Hennessey had left unguarded. He had an area about the size of a handkerchief to aim at. Palace manager Alan Pardew, himself no stranger to Upton Park, was philosophical afterwards. 'I think that's just unsavable,' he said.

The visitors got their equaliser eight minutes after the sending-off, and then hung on like grim death for a draw that it was hard to see them getting against eleven men. Referees, eh?

The Palace game may have ended disappointingly, but the day had a wonderful surprise in store in the unlikely shape of the Overdraft Tavern. It was the first time we went to that pub. Another 'first' in a season of 'lasts' – and a thoroughly enjoyable one at that.

We had Eddy and Barry to thank for the introduction. We'd got to know each other over the course of the season. Initially, we struck up a conversation because, on the way out, we would always reach the gangway at the same time. Having been brought up properly, Di, Geoff and I would always let them out first. They appreciated the minor courtesy, and said so. Funny what little things such as that can lead to. Some people you like, some you don't. We really liked Eddy and Barry.

We'd told them that, generally, we went for a drink after the game in the Denmark. They expressed surprise, partly because the Denmark had seen better days but also because they knew we had to go back into central London to get home, which meant we were going out of our way. But, to borrow a line from a bloke who knew a bit about Stratford, there was method in our madness (ah, sorry – wrong Stratford). We used the Denmark because it was on the way to East Ham station, enabling us to get on a Tube going west before the crowds piled on at Upton Park and Plaistow. That was Di's idea. You can't beat a bit of local knowledge.

Anyway, to cut a long story short, they suggested that we joined them for a pint in the Overdraft – which was even closer to East Ham station. It was an invitation the Williams family was more than happy to accept. Mind you, we only planned to have a quick one. We spilled out of there about half-past ten. Don't look at me like that! You're all grown-ups. You know how these things happen sometimes…

Five days before the Palace game, on Easter Monday, Upton Park had staged Mark Noble's testimonial game. We should have gone, but I'm ashamed to say we didn't. It's a decision I still regret.

However, my friend Jacqui did go. What's more, unlike me, she's proper East End – and for that reason alone it's more fitting she tells the story of that day. This wasn't just a game of football –

this was the embodiment of what West Ham United means to the people who grew up in the shadow of the Boleyn Ground. So, if you'll excuse me, I'm going to put my feet up and have a cup of tea while Jacqui takes it from here. Trust me, you're going to enjoy this:

This was always going to be a special day. Not because it was Mark Noble's testimonial, to mark his twelve years and 352 appearances for the club, but because I was going to watch it with three generations of my family, including the head of that family – my 83-year-old father, William Watts, better known to most as Bill or Billy.

This was also to be the last game Dad would ever watch at our beloved Upton Park, the ground that held so many of our collective and personal memories. We all knew this would be the end of an era, not just for the club, but for our family. It was going to be bitter-sweet.

There were eight of us there that day: Dad, five of his grand-children and two of his children – that's me and my brother. Each and every one of us was born a Hammer. Dad's father – my grandfather – William Watts Senior was born in 1890 in the workhouse infirmary, St George in the East, following the death of his father. His mother also died far too young, leaving William, aged five years old, and his two brothers dependent on charity for survival. They all became inmates in the East Ham Industrial School for Pauper Children in Green Street. There is a story, passed down through generations, that my grandad and his brothers watched West Ham play their earliest games at the Boleyn Ground. I like to imagine that it was the one shining light in their tragic, impoverished lives. I know, for me, that when life hasn't been so kind, those home games were vital. Leave your worries on the doorstep, and all that.

Dad has given every baby born into the family their first teddy – claret and blue of course. I've rocked my children and grandchildren to sleep many times with a lullaby of 'Bubbles'. Rumour has it that those little bands that were placed on our wrists at birth had WHU written next to the bit that asks for religion. From cradle to grave, that's us.

We had so much more planned for the day than just the match. We intended to have a mooch around the area, soak up the atmosphere, reminisce, perhaps try to join the long queue to get into Nathan's for pie and mash, or Ken's caff, for a last supper of a full English. What we, and 35,000 other fans, hadn't banked on was the Underground being out for planned engineering works (shouldn't that be planned maximum disruption?).

We stepped out of Barking Tube station and were met with chaos. Thousands of fans were trying to find a way to the ground. Dad may just as well have stepped from the Tardis. His head was visibly spinning with the changes to the streets of Barking as he tried to get his bearings. His suggestion that we take a bus to the ground was soon scuppered when we broke the news that we couldn't pay the bus fare with actual, real, money any more. Eventually we boarded a replacement bus and took our place in the queue that crawled its way down the Barking Road. The bus was gridlocked inside too with passengers, and the family were split up for the journey. I stayed with Dad, who was immediately offered a seat by a fellow supporter.

And so began a beautiful conversation between Dad and other supporters crammed inside the bus. They addressed Dad as Sir throughout. 'Do you mind me asking how old you are

Sir?' I watched and listened as they asked – and he told – of his earliest memories; of his East End roots; his earliest games; the time when, as a boy, he watched West Ham play, lost among a crowd of men in uniform, ready for war.

I'd heard his stories many times, but this time I heard them differently. They treated Dad with a reverence and respect be-fitting a lifelong supporter. I beamed as Dad held court, and glowed with the warmth of love for this man and our club. Handshakes, doffed caps and thanks and best wishes given, we joined the throng making their way up Green Street to the game, only just making it to our seats in time for the first of many renditions of 'Bubbles' that day. We'd arrived home.

Our seats that day were in the Bobby Moore Lower, the best I could muster to accommodate us all. I loved the BM Stand because they did exactly that – they stood, for the duration of the game. And they sung their hearts out. It was where my season ticket was too. It was also the stand that was obliterated in 1944 by a doodlebug, so quite fitting in terms of Dad's wartime sto-ries, told not half an hour since. It wasn't the place my family memories were made of though, and I'd have loved to have recreated our routines and rituals, one last time, by taking up our old place next to the tunnel.

From the mid-1960s, for a period that spanned ten years, this was 'our' spot. We'd always get to the games early, settle Grandad in his seat and make our way to the terrace, next to the tunnel. My brother and I carried our little stools, which doubled up as shields when we had to work our way through the crowds. We greeted familiar faces with hugs and kisses – these were our friends, they'd taken us children to their bosoms, always a card and a treat for us at Christmas or birthdays. Other familiar faces were the St John's Ambulance men who took up their places in the tunnel for every home game and a young lad with cerebral palsy who sat in the disabled section in front of us. He had every WHU badge ever made pinned to his scarf, much to my envy, and he was an enthusiastic supporter. His joy was catching.

Dad would hold a 'pot' for a group of us; a few pennies each to guess the crowd capacity that day. We'd wait eagerly for the half-time announcement and congratulate the winner, who duly took all.

My place was near the top of the tunnel perfect for reaching over and tousling the players' hair as they walked out on to the pitch. 'Good luck Bobby... Geoff... Billy... Frank... Trev... Harry... Ticker... Patsy...' I'd repeat the ritual with a 'Well played...' as they came off at half time and again when they came out for the second half, and finally, when the game had ended. If I wasn't quick enough and missed a player's head the likelihood was they would have a bad game. In retrospect I must have been a right pain in the arse.

Mark Noble's testimonial was never going to be about just the game for me, perhaps going to Upton Park never was. It's always been about the whole experience – my brother might remind me of a spectacular goal from forty years back, and I'm likely to ask if it was the game where 'that big bloke got slung out for swearing'.

Waiting for the kick-off, others may have been remembering a particular game, or goal, or victory. I was remembering my childhood, when life was simple and good. I remembered Grandad and his brothers. I remembered the roasted chestnut man, and the badge man, and the old club shop where pocket money was regularly handed over. I remembered rosettes and home-made rattles, too big and heavy to turn. I remembered squeezing through the turnstiles, and cups of Bovril when the terraces were blanketed in snow. I remembered Boxing Day matches and reserve games on Sundays. I remembered the young women in the crowd and how envious I was of their age and beauty (what hope did a child have of catching Bonzo's eye?). I remembered my fascination with the accents of visiting fans. I remembered being thrown in the air by Dad as we celebrated a particularly fine goal or victory. I remembered love and warmth and laughter and happiness. I remembered halcyon days.

Not surprisingly, I also remembered my favourite game of all time: another testimonial, some forty-six years earlier, for the legendary West Ham and England captain Bobby Moore. Nowadays, given how highly paid footballers are, the 'gate' for testimonials is given to charity, but back in the day it was a means of honouring and rewarding a player for services to the club and football.

In 1970, on the back of the Mexico World Cup plus nominations for the BBC Sports Personality and European Footballer of the Year, Moore was able to attract fitting opponents for this memorable game: Celtic – arguably Europe's best club side at the time – gave Bobby the honour of fielding a very strong team.

The game was under the floodlights, which always brought something magical to the occasion. We were known for our attacking football then, but so too were Celtic. This match was, from the first whistle, fiercely competitive. Celtic took the lead three times, only for us to equalise on each occasion. Both teams played their hearts out.

What did I remember of that night? I remember a spectacular cross from Moore to Hurst, who headed home our opening goal (or perhaps my brother reminded me of it). I remember Billy

Bonds wasn't playing that night, due to injury – however, there was a new kid on the block: little Johnny Ayris. At seventeen years old, and small in stature, surely here was a player who might look twice at me. He scored our second goal. John McDowell (good hair for tousling) and Tommy Taylor played that night too; both were virtual newcomers to the side. I remember we couldn't stand in our usual place: we were further along and down the terrace, pitchside almost. This added to my memory of Clyde Best pounding the wing, and literally the ground beneath my feet vibrating. He was a big old lump. Clyde scored our final goal. I adored big Clyde.

It was a magnificent game by any standards but my overriding memory is of the atmosphere. I stood tucked in among the big Scotsmen who made up the 3,000-strong visiting support that night. Their accents were so broad I didn't understand a word they said, but I laughed along with them anyway. It was a cold November night but I was warmed through to the cockles of my heart by the body heat of 25,000 supporters and the fumes on the breath of these merry Celt men. It was glorious. We were there to enjoy ourselves; to watch a cracking good game and to honour a great man. And *that* is what I remember of my favourite West Ham game of all time – belonging.

Mark Noble's testimonial couldn't have been more different. A match between the current first team and a team of West Ham All Stars. This game was Fun with a capital F, and it had everything to offer. Mark took to the field through a guard of honour, made up of his current and past teammates, and the crowd belted out 'Stand up if you love West Ham!' We rose to our feet; lips quivered, tears fell, throats closed… we all stood up because we love West Ham.

And so began a game that gave Mark 'Mr West Ham' Noble the respect and love he has earned from players and fans alike. They took us on a trip down memory lane and in return, we gave them our adoration.

The return of some of our most celebrated players ensured we sang every song and chant in our repertoire that day. I can still feel the goosebumps from the wave of noise we produced when 'Paulo Di Canio!' took to the field. And for once, Ludo was there to hear us sing that he '...Comes from near Moscow!' 'Twist and Shout'; 'Carlton Carlton Cole'; 'Come On You Irons'; 'We've Got Payet' (although not for long...); 'Ain't Nobody Like Lanzini'; 'We All Follow The West Ham Over Land And Sea'; 'We Are The West Ham Claret And Blue Army'; 'One Man Couldn't Carry, Couldn't Carry Lampard'; 'Andy Carroll's Having A Party'. We gave it everything we had, and the laughter and the cheers grew louder as the game wore on. And the players applauded and bowed down, paying homage to us, their fans.

For some, it would be the last time playing on that hallowed turf. And it was hallowed: grown from the scattered ashes of a thousand West Ham 'til they died' fans. Watered with the blood and the sweat and the tears of our heroes, who pounded across that ground in a bid for glory in our name. For more than 100 years they did it for us. And we were the light that shone down on them. With every victory, every celebration, every cheer and chant, sunshine beamed down on that turf, from thousands of faces.

When it was over and we parted company in Green Street we all looked slightly dazed. It was agreed, repeatedly, that a brilliant day had been had by all, but we could find no words for what was clearly an overwhelming moment in time. So much was left unsaid. No more would those surrounding streets see us make our way, as a family, to our ancestral home.

I took the long walk to the Black Lion, Plaistow, deep in thought, carried along by the crowds and my inner satnav. This was my routine now. Meeting up with good friends, pre-game, to discuss our hopes and expectations, washed down with a pint of Guinness. Taking that same long walk back, post-game, to commiserate or celebrate. That ritual too would soon be gone.

But for today, at least, we talked of Dean Ashton's incredible scissor kick, of Adrián dribbling the ball the entire length of the pitch to score, the highly entertaining penalty shoot-out, which eleven from each side took part in; there were some hilarious misses, including Harewood's – they couldn't have tried harder to help him score. And we laughed at Sakho's 'selfie' with teammates. And we swallowed hard when we recalled the standing ovation for Taylor Tombides's goal, in the name of his brother Dylan. That was perhaps the most poignant moment of the game for me. The promising youth player, Dylan Tombides, taken by testicular cancer. He was just twenty years old. It had hit us all hard. But in that moment, when his brother saluted the heavens, it was a cathartic act which allowed us all to cry for Dylan, for the loss of our own loved ones, for the passing of time, for the loss of our home, for forgotten memories.

Speak to any diehard West Ham fan and they will all tell you we were never there for the glory. Or to chase the silverware. Disappointment and acceptance, week in week out, relegation and celebration, come rain or shine, we are still here. We are West Ham and West Ham is us. It is our past and it is our future. Try to work out why and you will fail. It defies analysis.

I will always hold Upton Park in my heart and memory. And to my Grandad and my Dad: thank you, for so very much.

See, I said you'd enjoy it.

18

A view from the away end

London Stadium
Saturday 8 April 2017
Kick-off: 3.00
Final score: West Ham 1–0 Swansea

THERE WAS A real sense of tension around the London Stadium as we awaited the encounter with Swansea. West Ham had lost their previous five league games. The two before that were draws. Yes, we were marginally higher in the table than our opponents, but two points from a possible twenty-one had dragged us into a genuine relegation battle. The move to Stratford had come with hints of the Champions League, not the Championship. I silently pondered whether or not the Super Furry Coat Boys would keep coming if the unthinkable happened. Burton Albion on a wet Wednesday night – now that would be a test of their loyalty. And their parkas.

Happily for the Hammers, relegation looked rather less likely come the final whistle. We had won 1–0. The solitary goal was scored by Cheikhou Kouyaté who, just before half time, fired home a bullet of a shot from twenty-five yards after Robert Snodgrass had provided the ammunition. The victory could have been more emphatic, but Swansea goalkeeper Lukasz Fabianski was in fine form. I counted five top-drawer saves.

The win pushed West Ham up to fourteenth, eight points above eighteenth-placed Swansea, who appeared to be in serious danger of going down. Mark Noble, making his 400th appearance for the club, was a relieved man at the end. 'That's our biggest win in a few years,' he said. 'I thought we played well under pressure. Swansea were only a few points behind us. It was so important and it's a fantastic win for the club. One more win should see us safe.'

There was a problem, though. Michail Antonio – who had been terrific all year and was destined to be voted Hammer of the Year – pulled a hamstring as he sprinted down the left touchline in the first half. He didn't play again for the rest of the season.

While we left the ground reasonably contented, the same could not be said of the Swansea supporters. My friend Seonaid was among them. 'Leaving the stadium at full time is a nightmare for away fans,' she told me.

We were led around the west part of the Queen Elizabeth Park and it felt like we walked miles. There were people starting to panic over missing trains as after twenty minutes we didn't seem to be any nearer to public transport. I even doubted myself, despite living in London. When we asked for reassurance that we were going in the right direction we got no help at all from the security staff. One of them actually refused to speak to a Swans fan who asked if the Tube station was nearby. The Upton Park stewards appear to have been replaced by nightclub bouncers.

It is worth pointing out here that Seonaid is a serious sports fan, who has travelled all over the world watching football, rugby, tennis and plenty more besides. She's been inside some of the most famous stadiums on the planet. She also visited the Boleyn Ground whenever Swansea were playing there.

What was it like as an away supporter at Upton Park, Seonaid?
It was intimidating! As soon as we left the Tube we were funnelled into a sea of claret and light blue, the small streets with their shops, cafes and pop-up merchandise stalls heaved with singing fans. The area was proper working class London and the Hammers fans reminded you of that at every turn. The Boleyn Ground was the same – it was a proper ground. You could hear the tackles being made, feel the home fans' anger when the referee gave a decision against West Ham. You were part of the match and, like it or not, connected for ninety minutes. You couldn't let go until the final whistle. But one thing you learn at Upton Park is, despite the feeling of intimidation, West Ham fans are generally the nicest people you could possibly meet – no moaners like they have at Arsenal or stuck-up glory hunters at Chelsea. These are genuine fans who love their club.

What did you make of the London Stadium?
Compared with Upton Park it was a total shock. Leaving Stratford station there was no sense of the intimidation you used to encounter. The route to the stadium felt nothing like Upton Park – have the home supporters been ordered not to sing or chant until you get into the stadium? I know it was Swansea visiting that day and

not Manchester United, but it was quiet and this was never the case at Upton Park. Gone, too, is the pre-match trip to a greasy spoon for a tea, bacon roll and a football chat between both sets of fans. That was replaced by a condensed natter at the self-service checkout at Waitrose with a meal deal. How has it come to this?

What about when you were inside the ground?
Once through the turnstiles the space for fans to mingle was great. My pack of Haribo was confiscated on the way in but, funnily enough, they had smaller and more expensive Haribo packets to buy in the stadium. I'm sure this wouldn't have happened at Upton Park. The pre-match socialising for away fans was quite relaxed until you met one of the jobsworth security staff. And the hotdogs were crap.

You didn't like our wonderful stewards?
They seem to have had all their personality trained out of them and don't appear to have any link to the club or like West Ham at all. There is a London Stadium script and they refuse to deviate from this, which is impersonal and just plain daft. If you're not really enthusiastic about stewarding at a football match then why are you doing it? The security staff on a match day are representing West Ham but give the impression they actually hate the club. Maybe they hated Swansea. The staff at Upton Park did care and took some pride in what they were doing and that always came across.

Did you get a decent view?
As I took my seat my first thoughts were that it was a great place to watch rugby union, not football. You are too far away from the pitch and the only saving grace is the big screens which show

replays and the broadcast feed when the match is being played at the opposite end.

What about the atmosphere?
The stadium doesn't feel intimidating at all and the atmosphere doesn't pick up until the bubble machines are turned on. The best staff member on the day was Hammerhead, the mascot who engaged with away fans better than the stewarding staff. Even though we lost there was something not quite right in the stadium, the home fans were missing that spark and then I twigged what it was. When I walked in I immediately thought, this is a great place for a neutral fan and I think this is the issue. It felt that West Ham are being rebranded in the new stadium and so are the fans. How many in the home section during the match were actually West Ham supporters or just London-based neutrals who'd never have gone to Upton Park? You can spot some of them on the big screen – arms folded or just sitting down, showing no great emotion when anything happens.

So you weren't impressed?
The stadium is impressive and it's a wonderful venue but it's not a football stadium. It's similar to the Etihad in that respect. West Ham is not a club the Piers Morgans of this world would support, but it feels the scarf-sellers, greasy spoons and proper pubs have been abandoned in order to attract these people.

You, of course, know all about what it's like to move home, having gone from the Vetch Field to the Liberty Stadium just over ten years ago. Do you miss your old ground?
When I walk into Craven Cottage, Vicarage Road or Carrow

Road as an away supporter I get a flutter of nostalgia for the Vetch and my childhood. I felt the same way at Upton Park.

We've been told that moving is about going to the 'next level'. What prompted Swansea to relocate?
The Swans moving from the Vetch Field had been discussed since the early '80s but the only place to go without a new stadium being built was St Helens – the home of Swansea RFC and Glamorgan CC. Sport is tribal in Wales and if the ground share had gone ahead it would have been less popular than naming a coal mine after Margaret Thatcher. Fast forward twenty-three years and Glamorgan CC had departed for Sophia Gardens and regional rugby was coming which meant that, despite a glorious history, Swansea RFC were joining the Ospreys regional outfit (that was a bitter pill). On top of all that, the city was fighting to keep the Swans afloat and in the football league.

So you weren't opposed to the move?
We needed a new home for both football and rugby. When the council finally gave the go-ahead to build the new stadium it came as a real shock. I don't think anyone believed it until they saw the JCBs. Our council had a terrible track record when it came to wasting opportunities, so the Liberty Stadium being built seemed too good to be true.

There must have been some opposition to the new stadium?
There was from people who wanted to hold on and modernise the two grounds we had, but that option had passed in the early '80s. The thought of sharing a new ground with the 'other' team was a main source of fear. Some thought the new home for the

Swans and Ospreys would actually force them out of the closet and they would have to admit they supported the Swans but strayed on Saturdays to watch the All Whites at St Helens.

Did you find it difficult to say goodbye?

The last season at the Vetch was emotional as the Swans were chasing promotion from League Two. Dad and I wouldn't mention the new stadium as it felt like we were cheating on the Vetch and in the short term we needed promotion. We both said goodbye to the Vetch on 28 March 2005 with a 2–0 win against Macclesfield on our own terms. We just wanted to watch the football, but the hype of promotion and the new stadium had started in full and this sadly brought a new influx of part-time supporters. The club shop asked for ID due to ticketing demand despite the ladies who ran it knowing me since the age of six and Dad a lot longer! We wanted promotion as it was hugely important and thought the new stadium could wait, but it was getting too much. We were being asked questions by the part-timers on the lines of what colour do the Swans wear? Or 'I can't wait for us to play Cardiff in the league next season'. My response was that Cardiff were in the Championship while League One was the next step up for us, so this may prove tricky!

Did you warm to the Liberty Stadium straight away?

The first game was a pre-season against Fulham and the opening party had Bonnie Tyler, Max Boyce and just about anyone other than season ticket holders who wanted to claim they were there for the opening game. We cheerfully skipped this and went to the next pre-season friendly against Blackburn Rovers. Dad and I were both excited and really tried not to let it show, but we failed and annoyed Mum so much she drove us to the Liberty Stadium two hours early! We walked around the outside of the stadium so we could suss out how our match-day routine would now fit into this new area and then we went through the turnstiles. Walking up the stairs to our seats and seeing the pitch for the first time was incredible and I thought we've done it, it's perfect – we've only gone and bloody done it! We sat in the Lower West Stand and within minutes decided that we had found our home in the new stadium. To this day we sit in the West Stand, seven rows from the pitch. The new stadium wasn't too big and the pitch wasn't miles away, you could still hear the players and the sound of a crunching tackle, but the clincher was you knew you were going to enjoy watching football there. Watching the match, we forgot about the Vetch. The general conversation between fans was that we'd got it right and this was our new home. After years of watching football in a stadium that Jack built it was a marvel to have working taps in the toilets, an electronic scoreboard and sprinklers on the pitch.

Do you think there are any lessons we could learn at West Ham?
The stadium was marketed as belonging to the people of Swansea and not just the Swans or the Ospreys. It was built in the heartlands of Swansea's industrial past and the marketing team wasted no time in selling this link to the wider city. Football and rugby have both come home. At the Liberty Stadium you are part of the match, whether it be eighty or ninety minutes. The planners did their homework and built a stadium that fitted the city – an oval design with a 30,000 capacity would have been a disaster. We lost some staff from the Vetch Field but offered the opportunity for others to carry on working as part of the club in the new stadium. When the private security firm took over

the stewarding there was still a sense that the staff were fans, or still had that Vetch Field link. Finally, we just got on with it. After the Fulham match the party was over and it was business as usual. The Liberty Stadium is a reminder of how we almost lost everything and how it was turned around. That gives me a great sense of pride once I go through the turnstiles.

I'm really worried about what will happen to the area around Upton Park now West Ham no longer play there. What happened in Swansea?

The Vetch was central and easy to get to with an array of pubs and cafes en route. Once the final match at the Vetch had been played the seafront pubs started to close and then the buildings fell into disrepair. The council stood by and let it happen. I can count on one hand the places you can eat and drink and the escape routes out of the Liberty Stadium. The ticket prices didn't go up dramatically but the cost of getting to and from the stadium and all the other things that go with a football match did. Following the Swans became more expensive overnight and match day had to be pre-planned in order to get to and from the stadium, which was never the case at the Vetch. However we accepted this as we have an amazing stadium which, win or lose, I feel at home in and love every visit.

Many thanks for that Seonaid. By the way, I'm really pleased that the Swans stayed up in the end – I hope I'll see you at the London Stadium. Only hide your Haribo better next time. A Palace fan managed to get a drum into the ground, so it should be possible to smuggle your sweets in!

Boleyn Ground
Saturday 9 April 2016
Kick-off: 12.45
Final score: West Ham 3–3 Arsenal

The last time we would play Arsenal at the Boleyn Ground. I could barely get my head round the idea. In four days' time we were due to play the last ever FA Cup tie at Upton Park. That was unthinkable. I checked the programme for the remaining home fixtures, even though I knew them off by heart. Arsenal, Man Utd in the cup, Watford, Swansea, Man Utd in the league. And then that would be that. The sense of loss was almost too much to cope with.

I forced myself to concentrate on the here and now. The good news was that Kouyaté was in the side – the ridiculous red card he had been shown by Mark Clattenburg had been overturned. That was the third time in the season that a West Ham sending-off had been rescinded. Shame you don't get the points that are dropped as a result of refereeing blunders. What you do get is a sense of righteous indignation, but that doesn't count towards qualification for the Champions League.

With thirty-one games played, West Ham had an impressive fifty-one points – only two behind Man Utd and three fewer than Citeh, who were fourth. If we could complete the double over the Arse that would put us on... No! You can't let yourself think like that! This is West Ham United: we all know that fortune is just waiting for the appropriate moment to pack its bags and clear off on an extended holiday in the Balearics.

The beach towel and suntan lotion appeared to be in the suitcase already when referee Craig Pawson joined Clattenburg &

Co in the campaign to keep West Ham out of Europe and disallowed a perfectly good goal. Manuel Lanzini got his head to an Andy Carroll overhead kick and put the ball past David Ospina, only to be ruled offside. The TV cameras that had prompted the early kick-off showed the decision was clearly wrong.

Four minutes later Arsenal went in front with the sort of goal that enrages opposition supporters. Nacho Monreal did a wonderful impersonation of Tom Daley in an effort to win a penalty and only when he realised his theatrics were being ignored did he get up and move from his offside position – allowing Mesut Özil to occupy the space and score. Some of the ruder elements in the crowd let Mr Pawson know precisely what they thought of him.

After thirty-five minutes West Ham found themselves 2–0 down, courtesy of a goal from Alexis Sánchez. It could have been three after Adrián dawdled when he should have cleared and Danny Welbeck nearly made him pay. Champions League? You're havin' a laugh. It certainly looked that way. But what we didn't know was that Andy Carroll was intent on having a party.

It started on forty-four minutes with a lovely cross from Aaron Cresswell. Carroll accepted the present by rising above the static Arsenal defence and thundering a header past Ospina. And in time added on he invited everyone to get up and dance with a left-foot volley from just outside the six-yard box that levelled the scores. We danced all right.

West Ham's defence had looked shaky in the first half so Slaven Bilić changed things at the start of the second period, replacing James Tomkins with Emmanuel Emenike and reverting to four at the back. The Hammers appeared more comfortable and attacked with confidence. It looked like we'd taken the lead when Dimitri Payet put the ball into an unguarded net, but Mr Pawson penalised Carroll for a foul on Laurent Koscielny and chalked it off. The neutrals reckoned he just about got that one right. But, I'll be perfectly honest here, I'm not neutral.

West Ham did go in front soon after. Michail Antonio muscled his way past Monreal on the right-hand side, then stood up the perfect ball for Carroll to convert at the far post. Big Andy celebrated his hat-trick in front of the Bobby Moore Stand. There wasn't a West Ham fan in the ground who didn't want to give him a hug at that moment.

Carroll nearly got a fourth when he latched on to a cross from Payet and put the ball just over the bar. It was a fantastic match. In case our friends from north London had forgotten, the West Ham support reminded them that they had been 2–0 up and rather made a mess of things. However, the Gooners went some way to making amends when Koscielny equalised with twenty minutes to go. Game on!

Payet tested Ospina with a right-foot effort; Cresswell did the same with his left foot. Winston Reid almost bundled the ball home after a Payet corner had been met with a Carroll header. But there was to be no winner – other than the crowd of just under 35,000 who had been fortunate enough to witness the encounter.

Some games live with you for ever. One of West Ham's greatest ever victories was against Arsenal in the 1980 FA Cup final, and I'm eternally grateful I was there to see it. Some of the wonderful players who had made me so proud that day were at the Boleyn Ground as part of the farewell celebrations.

Leading the parade were Billy Bonds and Sir Trevor Brooking – the captain and goalscorer on that historic day. Every football supporter has his or her heroes. These are mine. There was so much to admire about both of them – as players and as men. Sir Trevor oozed class like few others before or since. And Bonzo was the heartbeat of every team he played in. They had all the talent in the world, but that isn't the only reason West Ham supporters of my generation remember them with such affection. What we admire above all else is their loyalty.

West Ham were in the old second division when we beat Arsenal at Wembley. They had been out of the top tier for two seasons – and would remain in Division Two for another year. Bonds and Brooking were with the club when we went down. It is unthinkable nowadays that players of that stature would remain with a second division club for three minutes, let alone three years. But they did. Between them, they personify everything I would like West Ham to be.

Also presented to the crowd from the 1980 FA Cup winning team were Phil Parkes, Ray Stewart and Alvin Martin – and I roared my approval of every one of them. Big Phil simply has to be the best goalkeeper West Ham has ever had. No one took a penalty like Tonka. And Alvin, who went on to become club captain, was a rock in defence. Great players. Great days. Great memories. And only a handful of games left at the Boleyn Ground. I tried my hardest to soak it all up while I still had the chance.

After the game, it was off to the Overdraft. Eddy and Barry had repeated their invitation, and we didn't hesitate in accepting. Being an early kick-off meant we had plenty of time for a swift beer knowing we could still be back in Brighton in time for a leisurely supper and *Match of the Day*.

We chatted on the way to the pub. Then we chatted in the pub. We talked about football, of course. And then the conversation became more wide-ranging. Life, the Universe and Everything, in the classic words of Douglas Adams. Horse racing definitely cropped up. It was the day of the Grand National. I'd already had a flutter, basing my decision to back The Romford Pele on the fact the horse was named after a former Arsenal player and we were playing the Gooners that day. But Barry was convinced he knew the winner and persuaded me to invest another couple of bob. Turned out Barry's judgement was as flawed as mine. Still, why stick to just one loser in the National when you can have two?

Politics may have got a mention. I had come clean and admitted I worked on the *Guardian*. Generously, the regulars decided against burning me at the stake. I think Di's connections with the area had a large amount to do with that. She chatted with regulars in the pub about schooldays and teachers mutually remembered – and, without giving away too many personal details, it's fair to say it's a while since Di left school.

Oh, and the Brexit referendum. That definitely raised its ugly head. The real thing was still a couple of months away, but I thought I'd carry out a quick straw poll to judge the mood of the nation as represented by the lovely people who frequented the Overdraft. The result is as follows: to remain in the EU – two (Di and me), to leave the EU – the entire pub. Of course, this wasn't the most scientific of surveys and there is a built-in margin of error of plus or minus three percentage points, but I think it reflected the general mood of the hostelry's patrons at that time.

No matter, I thought. I would convince them of the benefits of staying in the single market and the customs union. With Di's help it would be a shoo-in. Did I say we planned to be home in time for *Match of the Day*? We only just made the last train back to Brighton. But I was convinced our combined persuasive powers would bear fruit when the nation went to the polls on 23 June.

19

There's only one Ginger Pele

London Stadium
Saturday 22 April 2017
Kick-off: 3.00
Final score: West Ham 0–0 Everton

EVERY WEST HAM supporter worthy of the name knows that any time Romelu Lukaku plays against us he scores at least once – it seems to be some kind of cosmic law. Only on this occasion he didn't. The Ginger Pele saw to that!

James Collins was immense that day. He excelled in a three-man defence alongside Winston Reid and José Fonte, making an impressive five interceptions and eight clearances. Lukaku didn't get a sniff all afternoon. Had he scored, it would have been the tenth game in succession he'd put the ball in West Ham's net while wearing an Everton shirt. As it was, he only touched the ball three times in the Hammers' penalty area throughout the game.

Everton had to wait until the seventieth minute before they could register a serious attempt on goal – a thirty-yard effort from substitute Ademola Lookman which was wide. The winger tried another long-range shot soon afterwards, but that went over the bar. The only other cause for concern at the back was self-inflicted. Adrián had been recalled to the side and almost gifted Everton a goal on fifteen minutes after failing to control an Edimilson Fernandes throw-in – it took a desperate scramble to prevent Kevin Mirallas capitalising on the error.

Not that chances were coming thick and fast at the other end. Maarten Stekelenburg was required to make just one save in the first half – keeping out a thirtieth-minute deflected effort by Håvard Nordtveit, who got a second chance to shoot after his initial attempt from thirty-five yards had been blocked.

Jonathan Calleri should have done better with a header after first Arthur Masuaku on the left and then André Ayew on the opposite flank did well to put the ball in a dangerous area. Kouyaté was just wide with a shot from outside the box, but it's fair to say the excitement was not exactly at fever pitch.

Ginge himself might have scored with a header towards the end of the first half. A Manuel Lanzini corner was only half cleared and the ball came back to the Argentinian, who hung up a cross for Collins to attack at the near post. He got the run on his Welsh international teammate Ashley Williams, but could not quite get his towering header on target. Collins beat the ground in frustration before picking himself up and returning to his defensive duties.

Perspicaciously (ooh, get him), the match-day programme featured the Ginger Pele, who was pictured on the cover wheeling away in celebration after scoring West Ham's second goal in a 2–2 draw at Sunderland the previous week. 'I should score more, really, with the amount of free kicks that we get and I go up for,' he said in an interview on page thirty-one. Don't beat yourself up, mate. You do more than enough for the team as it is.

West Ham continued to be the better side in the second half. Lanzini had a powerful effort blocked and then a rather tamer shot saved before nearly playing in Diafra Sakho. Right at the death Fonte might have won it from a corner, but he could only head the ball into the ground and watch it bounce up into Stekelenburg's arms.

After the game most of the players headed for the tunnel. Collins headed for the East Stand, where he threw his shirt into the crowd. Crossing the green tarpaulin that covered the hated running track – hated by me, anyway – struck me as symbolic. He was crossing the divide that modern football, epitomised by our swanky new stadium, had created between those who play the game and those who watch it. The waterways of the Olympic park form a moat around the stadium. Inside, the running track acts as an equally forbidding barrier.

Unlike my wife, I have never bumped into Bobby Moore in an East Ham shop, nor lived round the corner from Ronnie Boyce, but I still yearn for the days when players dwelt among the community they represented. I know it will never happen of course – not unless the weight of money that is continually heaped upon association football in ever increasing numbers brings the whole house of cards crashing down and we all go back to square one – but a man's allowed to dream.

With guys like James Collins, you get the feeling that if he did live next door he would be a top neighbour – the sort of bloke who wouldn't moan when you didn't give him back his lawnmower and never parked in front of your drive.

I was a fan of his when he first played for West Ham – I thought the club made a mistake letting him go while hanging on to Matthew Upson, who never seemed to be up for the fight in the way Ginge always was. Collins left to go to Aston Villa in 2009, having been at West Ham for four years. (I can only assume he has a predilection for all things claret and blue.) He returned to Upton Park three years later, much to my delight.

Coming back makes a Hammer a little bit special in my eyes, particularly if they didn't want to leave in the first place. It's a rarity, of course. Since the birth of West Ham United in 1900 more than 800 players have represented the club. Of those, if I counted correctly, only twenty have returned to play for the first team a second time.

The first man to do it was Billy Grassam, who played for West Ham from 1900–03, left for Manchester United and then returned for a second spell from 1905–08. He was an inside-forward (that's 'striker' if you're under forty) and clearly had an eye for goal, scoring four times on his debut, which was also West Ham's first game at the Memorial Grounds. Despite rumours to the contrary I am not quite as old as Methuselah, so I wasn't at that game and neither did I ever get to see Grassam play. But, thanks to the wonders of photography, I can reveal that he had a moustache-and-a-half. You could have attached a broom handle and swept the road with it.

Using the twenty players who have come back over the years, it is possible to select a pretty decent starting XI. Admittedly it's a bit light on defenders, but I'm old school. We'll play on the basis that if the opposition gets four we'll score five.

In goal, simply because he is the only keeper I can find who returned, is Shaka Hislop. Not that there was anything wrong with Shaka, of course. He may not quite have been in the Phil Parkes league (who is?) but he never let the Hammers down in his time with the club – which was 1998–2002 and again from 2005–06. In fact, in 2006 Shaka turned out for Trinidad and Tobago in the World Cup finals. In the group stages he got to face an England side with not a single West Ham player in it. I'll leave you to guess who I supported that day.

The back four is tricky. The Ginger Pele is an automatic pick, naturally, but central defenders are in short supply. Much against my better judgement I'm going to have to play Calum Davenport, who was with the Hammers on loan in 2004 and then returned permanently for a three-year spell in 2007. You'll forgive me if I draw a discreet veil over the events that led to his contract being terminated in 2010: this is neither the time nor the place to rake all that up again.

We're OK for full-backs, but the trouble is they are both left-backs. I'm sure George McCartney will forgive me if I give the nod to Julian Dicks. For one thing, Dicksie is a West Ham legend. For another, I'm scared of him. Having seen Linda play out of position at right-back, I think I'll go with a three-man defence and hope my wide men track back.

We have to find a slot in midfield for 'Deadly' Don Hutchison, who was at Upton Park from 1994–96 and came back for a second stint covering 2001–05. Not that the fans called him 'Deadly' – that was something the stadium announcer dreamt up. We called him 'Budweiser'. Before joining West Ham the first time he had appeared in the tabloids having thought it would be a good idea to decorate his Hampton with a label from a beer bottle while on holiday. As so often happens when you try this sort of thing, there is a helpful passer-by who is all too happy to photograph the event. The stunt hastened his departure from Anfield, where Liverpool manager Roy Evans was far from amused.

Given the players at my disposal, I've opted for three in midfield. Alongside Hutchison we've got Joe Cole and Yossi Benayoun – now there's class for you. It's true that both of them never reproduced their earlier brilliance when they came back, but we'll forgive them that. What they did first time round is more than enough to get them selected. I suppose I should find a spot for Lee Bowyer to add some much-needed bite, but I'm not going to. His return to the club in 2006 sent all the wrong messages to West Ham's many non-white supporters in my opinion, and he's not getting in any team of mine.

The good news is, we're spoilt for choice up front. Frank McAvennie, Tony Cottee, Iain Dowie, Carlton Cole are all in this squad – and there's plenty more where they came from. My first pick for a four-man forward line is Syd Puddefoot, who first played for West Ham from 1913–22 before being sold – much against his wishes – for a world record fee to Falkirk. This guy really must have been something special. He once scored five against Chesterfield in a cup game. The 8–1 thrashing we handed out that day still stands as West Ham's biggest win in the FA Cup. Many supporters were apoplectic when it was announced he was leaving to go to Scotland, making way for Vic Watson in the side. His return in 1932 was greeted with delight by those who remembered him, but as with so many who followed in his footsteps the second coming at the Boleyn Ground was nothing like as successful as his initial years.

Puddefoot makes the side primarily because of his undoubted goal-scoring prowess, but there is a personal reason too. His nephew was best man at my parents' wedding, having been responsible for introducing Dad to Mum in the first place. Blood is thicker than water, after all.

Tony Cottee has to get a place: he's West Ham through and through. We are talking about someone who supported the club as a boy and then scored against Spurs on his debut as a seventeen-year-old. If stories like that don't bring a lump to your throat, you probably shouldn't be a Hammers' fan.

I've also got a slot for Bryan 'Pop' Robson – who first played for West Ham from 1971–74 and then again from 1976–79. I loved that man with all my heart. He too scored on his debut, which is always a good way to win me over. And he kept on scoring – in fact he did it so often he was Hammer of the Year in 1973. I was devastated when he left to join Sunderland, and thrilled when he came back to us. Unlike so many others, he was just as good second time around.

Which leaves us one last place. If it were down to skill alone, it should probably go to Frank McAvennie. If it was based on a refusal to watch your waistline simply because you were a professional sportsman, it would have to be Brian Dear. For hairstyles, no one in this squad could live with Iain 'Bartman' Dowie in his heyday. But this team is all about the players who really understood what West Ham is all about – and for that reason alone I'm opting for Carlton Cole.

No one is saying he's the greatest to have ever turned out in claret and blue, but he cared. Really cared. Like Ginge cares. Carlton was with the club from 2006–13, and then released. He couldn't find another club, West Ham couldn't find another striker and so, fanfare trumpets please, let's hear it for the return of the conquering hero. Always believe in... Cole! The affection with which he was greeted when he said his final farewell to the Boleyn Ground following defeat by Everton at the end of the 2014/15 season was something to behold (and, yes, Lukaku scored that day as well).

If West Ham do ever make it to the next level, I have a word of advice for the owners. Make sure you take a few players like James Collins and Carlton Cole with you. You'll need them if the going gets tough.

Boleyn Ground
Wednesday 20 April 2016
Kick-off: 7.45
Final score: West Ham 3–1 Watford

Watford were our second midweek opponents under the Upton Park lights in a matter of just a few days. Exactly a week beforehand we'd lost to Man Utd in an FA Cup quarter-final replay. I'd have given my signed photo of Bobby Moore to have had the results reversed. Yes, beating Watford kept our hopes of European football alive. But going out of the FA Cup is always painful for me – more so when a trip to Wembley is within touching distance.

Let's start with Watford who, unlike us, had made it through to the FA Cup semi-finals. They were set to play Crystal Palace on the following Sunday and, with that in mind, put out an under-strength side against us. I wasn't complaining – I wish a few more opponents would field weakened teams when we face them.

It didn't take Andy Carroll long to make his presence felt. With just ten minutes gone he snuck in between Watford's two central defenders and applied his left shin-pad to a beautiful cross from Dimitri Payet, deftly guiding the ball past goalkeeper Heurelho Gomes. To the Cockney Boys, one-nil!

April was turning out be an interesting month for Carroll. His hat-trick against Arsenal had awoken media interest in his chances of being picked for England's European Championship squad. Then when West Ham went to title-chasing Leicester – a game that was the filling in the Watford/Man Utd sandwich – he made the headlines once more. After coming on as a second-half substitute he had scored from the penalty spot to equalise – Jamie Vardy had put the home side ahead before the interval. A brilliant Aaron Cresswell volley had given the Hammers an unlikely lead with just four minutes left – only for Carroll to concede a naïve penalty in time added on. That was West Ham's fourth Premier League draw in a row, and the lack of victories was not helping our chances of making the top four.

Penalties were all the rage that week. There were three in the game against Watford, who had also conceded two in their previous game against West Brom. Gomes had saved both of those, but he got nowhere near Mark Noble's spot kick, which gave West Ham a 2–0 advantage on the stroke of half time. The penalty was awarded after José Holebas attempted to go for an uninvited piggy-back ride on Cheikhou Kouyaté. Gomes went right. The ball went left. We went wild. Well, wild-ish: it was only Watford, after all. To be honest, there had been more noise during the thirty-eighth minute tribute to young Dylan Tombides on the second anniversary of his premature death.

Such was West Ham's superiority at that stage we could have gone 3–0 up in stoppage time when Diafra Sakho set up an unmarked Manuel Lanzini. His shot was wide, however.

Payet continued to run the show in the second half: his

movement and passing were different class. Watford created a rare chance, which José Manuel Jurado wasted. Then Almen Abdi pulled down Michail Antonio in the box to give away the second penalty of the evening. Up stepped Noble once more – and this time he put the spot kick straight down the middle. That did make it 3–0.

The visitors pulled one back through Sebastian Prödl after sixty-four minutes, but it never seemed like West Ham were in real danger. There was no tension in the stands – neither was it a joyous celebration. It felt more like a well-behaved party: the sort of thing you used to have as a teenager while your parents stayed upstairs.

Just to keep the penalty theme going a little longer, our old friend Mike Dean awarded Watford one in the last minute. Troy Deeney took it – and Adrián got in the way. Oh, and for the record, Watford's Nordin Amrabat was sent off in time added on for a second bookable offence. Like we cared.

What we did care about was getting home, so on this occasion we had to decline the invitation to join Eddy and Barry for a swift one in the Overdraft. I like to think of myself as a strong-willed, abstemious sort of chap. But I was starting to suspect those two reprobates could be a very bad influence.

It had been a very different atmosphere when we took our seats for the game against Man Utd the week beforehand. We all knew it was the last ever FA Cup tie at the Boleyn Ground. Win, lose or draw, there would never be another one. The pouring rain might have been the tears of history, but I kept the thought to myself. You sound like a real bellend if you say things like that in a football stadium.

As the players and officials trotted out I checked the back page of the programme. Was that Roger East with the whistle?

It was indeed. Fair enough – it could have been worse. The front cover worried me more: it featured a mock-up of Billy Bonds and Bobby Moore holding three FA Cups aloft. I'd been privileged to witness two of those victories, and the other one shaped the course of my life, but I didn't think this was the time to be quite so bullish about days gone by. If supporting West Ham all your life teaches you nothing else, you do get to learn that the Fates don't much care for hubris.

That's not to say I don't cherish my club's part in the FA Cup's illustrious history. I'm immensely proud of the fact we were the last team from outside the top flight to win the trophy, and despite all the talk about the big clubs not taking the competition as seriously as they once did I can't see that changing any time soon.

The first time West Ham played Man Utd was in the FA Cup at the Boleyn Ground. That was in 1911, and the Hammers were still in the Southern League. Guess what? We turned over the mighty Mancs of the old First Division 2–1. The winner was scored by a fella named Danny Shea – one of the twenty players to do a 'Ginge' and re-sign for the club after leaving.

Then, of course, there's the White Horse final of 1923 when West Ham lost to Bolton Wanderers. Some estimates put the number of people inside Wembley Stadium that day as high as 300,000. Thousands upon thousands of people had turned up without tickets, hoping to see the inaugural final at the new stadium. When they couldn't get in, many of them simply climbed over the walls. The Pathé News coverage is fascinating – it shows a good-natured crowd spilling on to the pitch before being calmly dispersed by mounted police: notably one bobby on a white horse named Billie. (For the avoidance of doubt here, the horse was called Billie, not the policeman. He was PC George

Scorey. Oh, and the horse was actually grey, but looked white in the newsreel footage.) Despite the huge numbers of people involved, the kick-off was only delayed by forty-five minutes. As a demonstration of crowd control it is a lesson that some stewards at the London Stadium would do well to learn.

It is strange for me to think that for anyone born after 2007, the 1964 Cup final predates their birth even more than the White Horse final does mine. For some young fans the likes of Bobby Moore and Geoff Hurst are more distant to them than Vic Watson, Jimmy Ruffell and the other monochrome heroes of 1923 are to me. It's a sobering thought.

The '64 final will always be remembered for Ronnie 'Ticker' Boyce's winning goal, just as 1975 will be remembered for the two scored by Alan 'Sparrer' Taylor. Perhaps we need to come up with some nicknames as good as those if we are ever going to repeat the success of 1980 and that historic win against Arsenal.

Where were we? Ah yes, Man Utd in the sixth-round replay. The 7.00 p.m. kick-off was a nuisance, particularly for Geoff who had to come from the Midlands. My first thought was that it had been arranged that way in case the game went to extra time and then penalties – as had so nearly happened in the previous round. Last trains to anywhere become touch and go when a game doesn't end until *Newsnight* has begun. Had the FA done this with the best interests of supporters in mind? Of course not! The game was being shown live on the BBC and this was all about its schedules. Give us a break will you? We pay the licence fee, you know.

Someone should have told Enner Valencia the game was an early kick-off. The way he strolled around in the first half it appeared that he thought it was the warm-up. And he wasn't the only West Ham player who looked sluggish. Had the importance of the occasion got to them? I wondered. The defence looked solid enough with James Tomkins playing alongside Angelo Ogbonna at the heart of it, but we struggled in midfield. Payet, Noble – even the powerhouse Kouyaté were strangely off the pace.

The noise from the stands that had been generated at the start lessened as the game went on. 'Where's your famous atmosphere?' asked the Mancs. The one row in the stadium where it didn't get any quieter was the one behind me. The racket was generated by an old dear, who was clearly being taken to Upton Park to say her final farewell. Every time the ball went anywhere near our goal there were shrieks of anguish, whenever the ball was up the other end there were high-pitched squeals of encouragement. She might have come straight from an audition for *EastEnders* – she could not have been more 'Cor blimey' if she'd tried. She took a particular dislike to Man Utd goalkeeper David de Gea, whom she repeatedly referred to as 'the big canary bastard' – based, we could only assume, on the fact he was wearing a yellow shirt. (The Williams family now, and will do for evermore, call de Gea 'the big canary bastard' whenever his name crops up in conversation. I hope it catches on elsewhere.)

Towards the end of the first half we gathered that she had brought with her a hard-boiled egg, which she planned to have for her tea. Luckily for us she decided to eat it on the concourse rather than remain in her seat during the interval. The sort of atmosphere generated by a hard-boiled egg in confined spaces is something you can live without.

The second half started badly. Very badly. Nine minutes after the interval Anthony Martial played the ball to Marcus Rashford, who stepped inside Tomkins and then curled his shot beyond Darren Randolph into the top corner. A quarter of an hour later we were two down – a Martial shot going in off Marouane Fellaini's thigh.

And then the penny dropped that, in Carroll, West Ham had an aerial threat that might cause the Man Utd defence some problems – and his teammates began to send over some crosses for him to attack. With just over ten minutes of normal time left, the tactic worked. Carroll got his head on a Payet corner, diverting the ball into the six-yard box – where Tomkins fearlessly put his bonce among the boots and scored. There was nothing questionable about the atmosphere from then on.

The place was rocking as West Ham surged forward. Carroll stoked the passion by heading just over the bar. It was frantic, but an equaliser was on the cards. It was Upton Park. It was under lights. It was where miracles were supposed to happen. With a minute left, it looked for all the world as if the divine intervention we had been praying for had been granted after all. First there was dismay as the big canary bastard pulled off a remarkable double save to deny Kouyaté and Carroll – and then Kouyaté put the ball in the net. Oh joy; oh radiant joy; oh climactic, orgasmic, nut-bustin' joy! We were level, and the momentum was with us. We would win this in extra time – the FA Cup dream was still alive. Then I saw the linesman's flag. And I knew the dream was over.

Much as I loved her, the Boleyn Ground could be a cruel mistress at times.

20

We'll always have Paris

London Stadium
Friday 5 May 2017
Kick-off: 8.00
Final score: West Ham 1–0 Tottenham

WE DON'T ASK much out of life at West Ham. Contrary
to public perception, we don't want to see tricks and flicks all
the time – that's not what the oft-quoted West Ham Way is
all about. We're not terribly bothered about consistency. Some
of us don't even care about going to the next level. But we do
like beating Tottenham. In fact, there's only one thing better
than beating Tottenham, and that's beating Tottenham when
they think they're about to win something. Oh, and if you can
do it under the lights, so much the better.

Of course, losing to Spurs is more painful than losing to
anyone else. The 2–3 setback at Upton Park in 2013 left many
of us with emotional wounds that may never heal entirely. Sure,

we appear to be OK on the outside, but inextricably lodged in our subconscious, ready to surface at any moment, is the horror of Gareth Bale's winner. For some it was a wonder goal. For us it is a nerve-racking time bomb that is liable to explode just when you think life, on the whole, is pretty good.

Life felt about as good as it gets when we spilled out of the London Stadium after our first game against the old enemy at our new ground on a blustery Friday night. Despite having to put out an under-strength side because of the growing injury list (which hadn't quite finished growing, as it turned out) we played as well as at any time in the entire season.

Everyone worked their socks off. Up front, Ayew and Calleri pressed like they'd never pressed before. In midfield, Kouyaté was immense; Noble was exemplary and Lanzini was a constant threat. In goal, Adrián started to look like the keeper we remembered from the previous season. In front of him, centre-backs Reid, Fonte and Ginge were an impenetrable barrier while fellow defenders Cresswell and Byram were up and down their respective flanks like men possessed. When substitutes Snodgrass, Fernandes and Fletcher came on, they too knew the order of the day was: 'they shall not pass'.

As I say, it is a myth that West Ham fans only want to see showboat football. The occasional bit of wizardry is always a delight when it comes off, but what we really want is some blood and sweat (we'll supply the tears). Like football supporters everywhere, all we ask is that the players look like they care as much as we do. Give us some effort when you pull on that claret and blue shirt and we will forgive you just about anything. That's why every one of those players who took on and defeated Tottenham that night deserves a mention. They may not be the greatest XI to turn out in the name of West Ham United FC, but they gave it everything they had, and we hail them for it.

Their achievement is not to be underestimated. Tottenham were second in the league, hard on the heels of Chelsea. Had they won, they would have been just a point behind the west London mob. Spurs had won nine matches on the bounce and looked like genuine title contenders. They had beaten Arsenal the previous week to guarantee finishing above the Gooners for the first time in more than twenty years. The bookies could only see one winner, quoting odds of 15–2 against a West Ham win. In a two-horse race, that borders on the insulting.

In the stands, the atmosphere was electrifying. There was an intensity about the support that was reminiscent of Upton Park at its best. The noise was concentrated. 'Bubbles' broke out regularly, punctuated with repeated cries of 'Come On You Ironnnnns'. Every time the visiting fans piped up with their ridiculous 'Yid Army' chant we shouted them down. 'When the Spurs go marching in' got equally short shrift. The only other time during the season we, the supporters, had put on a performance that came anywhere near it was against Chelsea in the League Cup. This most definitely surpassed that.

On the pitch, the players responded. With the support we were giving them it would have been hard not to. Lanzini could have scored as early as the fifth minute when Tottenham defender Kyle Walker failed to track back. Ayew spotted him in acres of space and played a decent pass, but our Argentinian No 10 failed to do it justice and dragged a weak left-foot shot wide. Minutes later the Tottenham goal was under threat again as Cresswell latched on to a clever back-heel by Calleri and crossed to the far post, where Byram was making a nuisance of himself. To the disappointment of everyone bar the Spurs fans, he was beaten to the ball and the resultant corner came to nothing.

The tackles were now flying in. Walker clattered Lanzini and got booked; moments later Noble took a piece of Eric Dier and got a yellow card of his own. From where I was sitting, he appeared lucky that it wasn't red. All that, and there was only a quarter of an hour gone.

Just as you could feel the confidence growing in the stands, we had a wobble in the twentieth minute. Adrián fumbled a long-range shot by Harry Kane. Fonte blocked Dele Alli's follow-up shot, then Kane had another dig from fifteen yards. This time Adrián, desperately trying to get back in position, threw out his left foot as he was going right and sent the ball over the bar. As if to prove the initial mistake was nothing more than an aberration, Adrián then comfortably dealt with Dier's header from the first of a succession of corners that followed.

On twenty-six minutes we were out of our seats howling for justice. Hugo Lloris had hurtled out of his penalty area as Lanzini was about to latch on to a through ball from Noble with only the keeper to beat. What followed was a knees-first lunge that would have resulted in serious trouble for any outfield player attempting something similar. Referee Anthony Taylor decided that even though Lanzini had been well and truly cleaned up there was nothing untoward about the challenge. Justice would have been done had Kouyaté controlled the lob that presented itself as the ball fell to him, but he seemed more focused on the collision than the precise whereabouts of the Spurs net.

A minute later Kouyaté was back challenging near the corner flag as Spurs broke clear. Walker hit the deck and won a free kick – our midfielder kept on going before being tripped by the green matting that covers the running track which the owners are so keen to disguise. Did I mention that the London Stadium has a running track? Ah. I thought I might have done.

After ten minutes of tit-for-tat exchanges Christian Eriksen unleashed a shot from twenty-five yards that went just wide. So surprised was he that his effort was off target his hair stood on end. Oh, sorry. It seems that's his usual hairstyle.

Not so surprising was the yellow card Reid found himself looking at following a challenge on Victor Wanyama as he tried to bring the ball out of defence and lost control in the centre circle.

Five minutes later (plus the customary two added on for nothing in particular) Mr Taylor called a halt to the first half. The players headed for the dressing rooms; thirsty supporters headed for the bars; and those who had been in the bars earlier headed for the toilets. I stayed put and silently wondered if we would end up paying the price for not scoring when we'd had the chances.

The second half kicked off to another cracking rendition of 'Bubbles' from all quarters. And the confidence that they had gained from the success of the first-half game plan clearly hadn't been left in the dressing room as Calleri and then Cresswell tested Spurs on the flanks.

Once again we were hunting in packs, chasing down Spurs at every opportunity, regularly winning the ball and then using it intelligently as we pushed forward.

The first chance of the half fell to Ayew after a precise cut-back from Byram, but the shot from the edge of the box posed more danger to the denizens of the Bobby Moore Stand than it did to Tottenham's goal. The battling Calleri then nearly put

Ayew through on goal, although had the pass not been overhit it is likely the striker would have been flagged for being offside.

Eriksen should have caused Adrián more trouble than he did with a tame side-foot effort from eight yards. The keeper faced a stiff test a couple of minutes later, but Son Heung-min's fierce drive was eased round the post with the minimum of alarm. A goalless draw was starting to look a distinct possibility, and in truth many of us would have been delighted with that had we been offered it at the start. But in the sixty-fourth minute we got so much more to celebrate.

Lanzini started the move on the left with a ball to Cresswell. The first attempt at a cross was blocked; the second found its way to the far post via Calleri's chest. Byram put it back into the danger area where Ayew was lurking. His stab at goal was kept out, but the ball found its way to Lanzini, who was now six yards from goal and untroubled by Tottenham defenders. He slammed it into the net before wheeling away to the north-west corner of the ground, where he accepted the acclaim to which he was duly entitled.

There was utter delight on the pitch and in the stands. We all wanted to savour the moment – none more so than our goalscorer, who got booked for supposedly delaying the restart.

No sooner had a minor disturbance that accompanied the celebrations been quelled, someone lit a flare in the opposite corner. It can often take fifteen minutes to get through the security checks at the turnstiles. You're not allowed in if your bottle of water has a top on it, but someone managed to get a flare in the ground. I wonder where he hid that.

'To the Cockney Boys, one-nil!' was the taunt. That should have become two-nil on seventy-five minutes when Calleri dispossessed a dithering Toby Alderweireld in the Spurs area, but Lloris produced a brilliant point-blank save to deny him.

Before that, Byram had joined those teammates already in Mr Taylor's little black book when he pulled back Son. Spurs threw on a bunch of subs. They huffed and puffed, but we played the more incisive football and genuinely looked more likely to get a second goal.

Two minutes after Calleri's effort, Spurs won a corner – and the Trevor Brooking Stand did its bit by hanging on to the ball. A new one was found eventually, which of course prompted the return of the original – causing a further hold-up because, as any supporter knows, you can't have two balls on the pitch at the same time.

When Dele Alli squared up to Kouyaté briefly it was clear that Spurs were rattled – and fast running out of time. Snodgrass came on for Ayew; Fletcher replaced Calleri; Fernandes relieved Lanzini. Five minutes were added on. And five minutes ticked by. Tottenham looked flattened at the final whistle. We were ecstatic. For the first time, for me at least, the London Stadium felt like home.

The victory left us on forty-two points, which is still the record number accrued by a team relegated from the Premier League. And who holds that record? Why, we do of course! But no one was thinking about league positions as we left the ground to the strains of 'Twist and Shout' and 'Hi Ho Silver Lining'. It reminded me of the play-off final in 2012. Winning promotion back to the top flight had been wonderful. This felt every bit as good.

It is true that Slaven Bilić deserves a good deal of credit for the victory – it was his tactics that enabled us to blunt a razor-sharp

Spurs attack that was to finish the season by scoring six at Leicester and then seven at Hull. But I would like history to record that the Williams family played its part thanks to a brilliant tactical shift by Di. It was she who suggested that Geoff should wear my 'lucky' scarf for the evening, and it did the trick. So will Geoff be wearing my scarf for all West Ham fixtures next season, thus ensuring Champions League football at the London Stadium? I'm afraid not: voodoo that strong is not to be messed with. We'll save repeating that particular masterstroke for a cup final or something similar.

Immediately after the game had finished both Geoff and Di said they thought it would end 1–0 to us but didn't dare say anything beforehand in case they jinxed the result. Not that my family are a superstitious bunch of simpletons, you understand. It's just that years of supporting West Ham teaches you not to tempt fate more often than you have to. Di thought Ginge was going to get our goal, Geoff reckoned Lanzini. Had he had the courage of his convictions with Bet365 he could have turned a cheeky fiver into £530. But, of course, he knows the golden rule that decrees backing West Ham to win will always result in defeat. Those Fates, I ask you! I really don't know what our club has done to upset them, but they really don't like us.

On leaving the ground Geoff checked his phone and noticed that David Blackmore had posted: 'Tottenham Hotspur: last team to lose the league at Upton Park. First team to lose it at the London Stadium.' Not strictly true, of course. But a good line nonetheless.

All around us there were happy Hammers in full voice. 'It's happened again, it's happened again, Tottenham Hotspur, it's happened again.' There were a couple of choruses of 'Bubbles', but on the whole those of us in claret and blue preferred to remind our north London rivals that in 2017, as in 2016, they would not be Premier League champions after all.

The singing continued as we headed towards the station. We were seriously happy. But you know what happiness is like – there's always some goon with a stop-go board who wants to dilute it a little. So it shouldn't have come as any surprise when our way was blocked at the end of Stratford Walk. To be precise, it was only Geoff and me who were stopped – Di had got past the stewards before they formed their human barricade. Geoff politely asked if we could join her on the other side, but his perfectly reasonable request was flatly refused. As a result I found myself standing eyeball to eyeball with a humourless individual ('I'm only doing my job, mate') who felt that my personal safety and the protection of others was best served by me being prevented from taking another step in the direction of Stratford International until I had his permission. It was not a view I shared.

Curiously, and for the only time in the season, when we had arrived prior to the game there were stewards on the platforms regulating the flow of people on to the escalators, which does make some sort of sense in health and safety terms. Again, Geoff and I had been briefly parted from Di, as she was told to wait while we went ahead. What this all has to do with the price of fish is anyone's guess, but I thought you'd like to know.

At Stratford International, as was the annoying custom laid down by those in charge of security arrangements, we were forbidden from using the nearest entrance and made to walk all the way round to the far end before being allowed access – only to then have our passage blocked once more (which, as any stand-up comedian who specialises in cheap innuendo will tell you, is not what you want on a Friday night following an eight o'clock kick-off). One supporter was particularly annoyed. 'Come on,' he urged the police, 'let us on the train. My wife's at home waiting to give me a celebratory leg-over!' Encouraged by the laugh he raised, he turned his attention to the law enforcement officers preventing us going through the ticket barriers. 'You don't have to listen to them,' he told us. 'They're not real police – they're just community knobheads.' It was all incredibly good-natured. Even the community knobheads were smiling.

The short train journey back to St Pancras was easily the most joyful of the season. 'Tottenham Hotspur, it's happened again,' echoed around the carriage before a philosopher among us summed up exactly how we all felt. 'It's not right, is it?' he asked of no one in particular. 'Life just shouldn't be this good when you support West Ham.'

Boleyn Ground
Saturday 7 May 2016
Kick-off: 3.00
Final score: West Ham 1–4 Swansea

The penultimate game at the Boleyn Ground could not have offered a greater contrast to the corresponding fixture in Stratford. Swansea were due to be our final opponents at the old place, but the extended FA Cup runs of both ourselves and Manchester United put paid to the plans of the league's fixture computer. Which, while being hugely welcomed by supporters, was a blow to headline writers everywhere who would almost certainly have been unable to resist the temptation of 'West Ham Swan Song'.

On the pitch it was more like a duck shoot – with West Ham as the target. It turned out to be the heaviest home defeat Bilić had to endure as manager at Upton Park, and it ended any lingering hopes we may have had about scraping into the Champions League places.

To be fair, it didn't look like we were going to lose 4–1 in the opening twenty-five minutes, then Wayne Routledge converted Kyle Naughton's low cross and the rout began. Six minutes later André Ayew – the man who was to become our record signing a few weeks later – doubled the lead six minutes afterwards before Ki Sung-yueng put the result beyond doubt early in the second half. A Stephen Kingsley own goal gave us a glimmer of hope but substitute Bafétimbi Gomis sealed the deal with Swansea's fourth in time added on.

If nothing else, the game proved the folly of playing Michail Antonio at right back. In Slav we trust and all that, but Bilić's insistence of persevering with the lad in defence was already being questioned. After this humbling, the answer was plain for all to see.

Let me say straight away, no blame should be attached to Antonio, who has more than proved his qualities in an attacking role. But he's not a defender by trade and asking him to do a job that he clearly wasn't cut out for was a major blunder by the manager.

He was cruelly exposed for each of Swansea's first three goals. First he was caught far too high up the pitch, next he was beaten for pace, then he was hoodwinked by a clever turn that a proper defender would not have let themselves be embarrassed by.

Furthermore, it wasn't just Antonio who had an off day. Payet was well below par, as was Lanzini. Kouyaté and Noble never got hold of central midfield while Carroll and Sakho posed little threat up front. It wasn't the first time at Upton Park that the boys in claret and blue left the pitch to howls of derision. But I am happy to report that it was the last.

We headed off to the Overdraft with Barry and Eddy, sorely in need of a pint. It was our second visit of the day.

On the way to the game we had received some sad news. Paris, one of our two family cats, had died at the vets after a short illness. We knew she wasn't in great shape but, even so, the news came as a terrible blow. I'm not the world's greatest animal lover, but I did have a soft spot for Paris. Think of the picture on the Felix cat food boxes and substitute the cheery smile with a grimace – that was Paris. She was a nervy little thing who never really did get to trust humans. It seemed she always knew that life was out to get her, and one day it did. We had originally got the cat for our daughter Katie when she was seven. Fourteen years later Katie had a home of her own, but Paris remained with us. She never would have put up with moving.

Di was too upset to speak. I volunteered to ring Katie and tell her the sad tidings. Hearing how shocked she was made me feel even worse.

Meanwhile, and in no way comparable to the loss of our cat, Brighton and Hove Albion – the team we would follow if we weren't dyed-in-the-wool Hammers – were contriving to blow their hopes of automatic promotion in a televised game at Middlesbrough. So we weren't exactly in the best of spirits before the game, and the battering we took at the hands of Swansea didn't make us feel any better.

The idea was not to linger in the pub. We'd have a couple, then hop on the Tube at East Ham. With luck the Hammersmith &

City line would take us to Baker Street, from where Geoff could walk to Marylebone and catch his train to Leamington. Di and I would then head to Victoria where we would catch our train back to Brighton. That, at least, was the plan.

The Overdraft is an unusual pub, or it was on match days at the Boleyn Ground. By all accounts it used to be a branch of NatWest Bank, hence the name. Unlike other pubs, where groups of friends chat among themselves, everybody in the Overdraft seemed to know everybody else. And if you didn't know someone when you went in, chances are you would have been introduced to them by the time you left.

It's generally not a good idea to talk politics in pubs, but the subject did come up from time to time. When it did, people would tell us how their parents had always voted Labour but the party had no relevance for them now. Jeremy Corbyn was particularly unpopular. When Di and I made a case for a left of centre solution to the nation's ills we were politely humoured, but changed no one's mind. Which makes me wonder why, after the Swansea game, we tried so hard to once again make the case for Remain.

The referendum was a little over six weeks away, and it appeared just about everybody in the Overdraft had decided which way they were going to vote. No one seemed very interested in talking about the match we'd watched that afternoon, so we talked about Brexit. We were still discussing the subject at closing time. Geoff had, very wisely, said his goodbyes some time beforehand, but Di and I were determined to battle on and make the case for sticking with the EU. At one stage Di was at the far end of the bar holding forth, while I was at the other end arguing equally passionately. And all the time the beers kept coming.

I have no idea how much I drank that night. I do recall that I had taken so much Guinness on board that I couldn't face another pint – which is when I switched to red wine. At Di's end of the bar, the pints of cider awaiting her attention were stacking up at an alarming rate. I like to think we bought our fair share of rounds and our credit card bill, when it turned up, was pretty tasty. But the generosity of the people in that pub was extraordinary. They may have thought we were talking nonsense, but that didn't stop them buying us drink after drink and fully engaging in the conversation. I'm certain that no one in there would have appreciated being called 'Comrade', but the place truly was comradely.

It's hard to believe that after your football team has been hammered and your cat has died you can look back fondly on the day. I have the good people of the Overdraft to thank for that. The move to Stratford means we don't go there any more, and I miss it. Beating Tottenham is great. Being made to feel welcome in a proper East End pub is even better.

21

A tale of two seasons

London Stadium
Sunday 14 May 2017
Kick-off: 2.15
Final score: West Ham 0–4 Liverpool

A GLORIOUSLY SUNNY day, shirtsleeve football and illustrious opponents. What more could any supporter want for the last home game of the season? Just one small problem though: we turned up, but the players didn't. Certainly not the West Ham players, who simply laid down, rolled over and allowed their tummies to be tickled in the most humiliating way imaginable.

Sorry, but I can't actually find it in myself to describe what we had to sit through that day. It was pathetic. The team didn't try and most of the crowd couldn't be bothered either. The London Stadium – home to some of the most passionate supporters in world football – felt like a county cricket ground on a somnolent Sunday afternoon.

It could not have been more different to the previous home game against Tottenham. But it was certainly more typical of our season overall. Disappointing results, lacklustre performances and apathy in the stands: Welcome to Stratford.

Most years, finishing eleventh with forty-five points would be considered a reasonable effort. But not this time. Is that, I wonder, partly down to the expectation that went with the move? There were always going to be teething problems, of course. And no one could have predicted the Dimitri Payet saga, which cast a long shadow over much of the season. But it's hard to describe the first season at our new home as anything but dispiriting.

Admittedly, it didn't help that much of the campaign resembled an extended version of *Casualty*. If we had finished as high in the Premier League as we did in the table of injuries compiled by PhysioRoom.com we'd have qualified for the Champions League.

Aaron Cresswell set the tone for what was to follow by sustaining a knee ligament injury in a not-so-friendly pre-season encounter with German club Karlsruher FC. He didn't return to the starting XI until mid-October.

In the first League game of the season at Chelsea, André Ayew limped off with a thigh injury after barely half an hour. It was the end of October before we saw him again – coincidentally against the hated Chelski once more, this time in the League Cup.

Diafra Sakho was on the point of moving to the Hawthorns in the summer but the deal fell through following concerns about his fitness. It was hotly denied that he had failed a medical, but after returning to London the Senegal international missed the first three months of the season due to a back injury. He managed two appearances in November and actually scored at Manchester United, where he suffered a hamstring problem which ruled him out until December – when his back trouble struck again and he underwent surgery. He remained out of action until April, when he finally made a couple of appearances as a sub. This, you will recall, is the man who scored nineteen goals in his first fifty appearances for West Ham.

Andy Carroll appeared in just eighteen Premier League games, starting sixteen of them and scoring seven goals. Given his track record it shouldn't have come as a big surprise that he spent so much time in the treatment room, but his fabulous goal against Palace showed just what we lack when he doesn't play.

Angelo Ogbonna was sorely missed after he had to undergo surgery in January, as was Pedro Obiang, who sustained a knee injury in the defeat to Leicester.

Even the squad players struggled to stay fit – Gökhan Töre, Arthur Masuaku and Álvaro Arbeloa all had injury problems, although it's fair to say the Spanish World Cup winner looked about as fit as I am on the few occasions he actually made an appearance (and Töre looked about as skilful).

Kouyaté, Noble and Reid were all sidelined at one time or another, and the team looked vulnerable without them. But perhaps the hardest injury of all to take was Michail Antonio's. He sustained a serious hamstring injury in the home game against Swansea and we didn't see him again. Not that the setback prevented him from being rightly named Hammer of the Year, and the fact that he agreed a new four-year deal is an encouraging sign for the future.

In the stands, some supporters settled in more readily than others. Thankfully, the infighting – mainly between those who want to stand and those who like to sit – that marred the early games appears to be a thing of the past. It seems the popcorn and ice cream are here to stay, however.

Oh yes, and there's the running track. That's obviously going to be with us for some while yet, too. If there's one single change that could be made to the London Stadium that would improve it for football supporters it is to forget all the Olympic legacy nonsense and get rid of that track. The present owners will never do it, but maybe one day someone will come up with the cash and the clout to change the terms of the lease.

Paris Saint-Germain, for example, are now effectively owned by Qatar. If countries are starting to buy football clubs, perhaps we could interest one. North Korea, maybe? If nothing else, Kim Jong-un might like to reinstate the nuclear facility at Stratford. He might even try to persuade the Ercan Fish Bar to leave the Barking Road and move there instead. They could sell fission chips.

What does need to change is the pricing policy. There are many seats at the very back of the stadium that are listed as band one and two, and priced accordingly. Having sat in those seats, I can testify they really are not worth that sort of money.

What should worry the West Ham management is that some supporters were not prepared to renew their season tickets after experiencing life at the next level. Among those people are none other than Graeme Howlett, founding editor of the hugely influential Knees Up Mother Brown website and a supporter so committed to the cause he is actually a bond-holder. I asked him why he'd taken such a radical step.

It's been a while since I attended my first game at the Boleyn Ground. Perhaps preparing me for future setbacks, of which there would be many, West Ham lost 2–1 to goals from Charlie George and Bruce Rioch. It was February 1976. Ever since then I've been a regular visitor to Upton Park and a season ticket holder for the past twenty years or so – as I was right up until the day the ground closed following the Hammers' famous 3–2 win against Man Utd in May 2016.

It was the last competitive match to be played there, and for many long-term, long-suffering fans that was the end of their association with the club (financially, if not spiritually). Hundreds, maybe thousands, ditched their season tickets in protest at a move to a stadium that some felt had been forced upon us.

Not for me, they decided.

Many thousands more renewed their tickets – often at increased prices – for the first season at the new arena, curious to see whether Karren Brady's promises of a 'world class stadium' would materialise. I was part of this expectant horde.

Some have seen their dreams realised. West Ham now play in what is often referred to as an 'iconic' stadium. Yet having experienced it for a season myself, I'm not one of them.

The reasons I decided to hang up my boots at the end of last season are many and varied, and certainly not all related to the stadium itself (though more on that later). Too often I find myself both dissatisfied with and disappointed by modern football. Whether that be as the result of Sky moving yet another match at late notice with little or no consideration for travelling fans, players generating ludicrous transfer fees or West Ham trying to rinse every last penny out of their supporters – usually referred to as 'customers' or 'clients' these days – it leaves me cold.

This, of course, is nothing new – we have been subject to all these issues for a number of years. However, as far as I was concerned, the stadium was the icing on the cake.

We arrived at the new ground in the summer of 2016 full of expectation and hope: the team had qualified for the Europa

League at the end of the previous campaign and introduced a dozen or so new players to the squad (nearly all of whom have since left, but that's another story).

The considerably longer twenty-minute walk from station to stadium that we'd prepared ourselves for seemed fine in the summer when the sun was shining and everyone was in positive mood. It wasn't so much fun on a Monday night in January however, when being herded back to the Underground at Stratford by temporary staff waving 'Stop' placards in your face as the freezing rain fell about you.

Things began to turn sour pretty quickly. My young son, in his first year as a season ticket holder (with us having taken advantage of the club's much-maligned plus-two scheme), was far from happy about the sporadic outbursts of violence that erupted between supporters at regular intervals as fans struggled with the no-standing policy the operators of the stadium seemed keen to enforce. So much so that by our third or fourth visit he said he no longer wished to go. (Fortunately he returned eventually, though only after some heavy coaxing and a little bit of bribery.)

Then it became farcical. The police informed us that they would have no presence inside the stadium as the radio system was defunct. It seemed incredible that such a vast arena, in the centre of the capital, was allowed to operate this way, given the terrorist incident that had occurred at the Stade de France some months before.

Structurally, the retractable seating promised by our vice-chair materialised as a network of scaffolding, to be moved at great cost (some £8m) at the end of every season to allow the running track to be used. However the biggest problem, from my own perspective, was the strange feeling of being disconnected from the game that was taking place in front of me. Although present in the stadium, being so far away from the action rendered it an entirely different experience to that of the Boleyn Ground.

In the old stadium I sat directly behind the dugout in the West Stand – an absolutely fantastic seat where I could hear the subs and staff discuss their next moves. You could almost touch the players by leaning forward, and the kids in our section of the ground had no trouble filling their programmes with autographs. What a contrast to Stratford.

Even though seated in the lower tier of the East Stand, some twenty-six rows from the front, I could barely see the subs bench from the opposite side of the pitch – let alone learn what they'll be doing after the game has finished!

In the end, I spent much of the season asking the chap a row or two above me to confirm which substitute was about to come on. He, you see, had the prescience to purchase a set of binoculars before the season began.

I should perhaps stress that this was partly my fault having missed my original appointment at the club's temporary offices in Westfield. By the time I had the opportunity to visit again a week later, the equivalent seats to those at the old stadium had been snapped up.

But the fact remains that wherever you are situated in the London Stadium, you are still a country mile away from the action. And while that may be fine for the occasional fixture – say perhaps a cup final at Wembley – it most certainly is not nineteen-plus times per season, especially when you have paid more than a grand for the luxury.

After some thought I decided enough was enough and that I wouldn't be renewing for a second season. Of course, I wasn't alone – in excess of 5,000 season ticket holders decided not to return. That's enough fans to have filled the East Stand at the Boleyn Ground. Potentially it could have been many more, but some fans were tied into two-year contracts so we'll only know the true extent at the end of the second season.

I should stress that I don't rule out a return eventually. Perhaps when I've rediscovered my footballing mojo I'll look forward to going to Stratford every week. However for this season, at least, I shall be watching West Ham's home games on TV – as will many thousands of my fellow lapsed supporters.

Many thanks for that Graeme. So, it's not just me then.

Boleyn Ground
Tuesday 10 May 2016
Kick-off: 7.45 (delayed to 8.30)
Final score: West Ham 3–2 Man Utd

History, they say, is written by the winners. Well, West Ham United won their final game at the Boleyn Ground. We wanted an encounter that did justice to the glorious 112 years that preceded it, and that is exactly what we got. I know I promised a comprehensive match report in an earlier chapter, but I can't write it. Not for the same reason I won't write about the Liverpool game at the London Stadium – quite the opposite, in fact. The football was fantastic and the excitement was unbearable at times. But I don't have the words to do it justice.

Take the final goal – the last ever goal at the Boleyn Ground. There were just ten minutes left and the score was tied at 2–2.

We had only just levelled through Michail Antonio, who had produced a great header at the far post after Payet had picked him out with another incisive cross. The French playmaker found himself on the ball again – this time at a set-piece. He whipped in the free kick and Winston Reid was first to it, powering a header back across goal. De Gea got a despairing hand to it, but couldn't keep it out. The stadium erupted.

It's what happened, but a mere description of the events doesn't begin to convey the emotion that underpinned it all. It was, quite simply, one of the most extraordinary moments of my life.

In the same way, recording that in the 2015/16 season West Ham finished seventh with sixty-two points hardly scratches the surface of the real story. The team had served up some beautiful football, much of it really was a joy to watch. Supporters turned up expecting to be entertained, and we were rarely disappointed. As a result we regularly generated a great atmosphere. Missing out on the top four was disappointing, but actually being in contention was a real treat. Who knows, we might even have made it had we got the benefit of the doubt from referees more often than we did. We came bottom of a table compiled by teamtalk.com which demonstrated how each Premier League team had sinned – and been sinned against. The table, compiled over the course of the season, numbered the crucial decisions that had gone against us as eighteen, with only seven going in our favour. The net score of minus eleven was the worst in the division. Top of the table were Man Utd, with a score of plus nine.

It was billed as the season of farewell, but I think there was more to the celebrations of times gone by than meets the eye. Yes, it was great to see the club's legends brought back to Upton Park for various games and the closing ceremony. Was there anything other than simple nostalgia behind the invitations, though?

New management, when it takes over, generally prefers not to have the old guard hang around any longer than it has to. The London Stadium is West Ham's Ground Zero. Acceptance of the new order involves forgetting about the Boleyn Ground as quickly as possible – and that means jettisoning its heroes and creating some new ones. Monsieur Payet was supposed to have fitted that particular bill, but he obviously didn't get the email. Still, even without new champions, the old ones from E13 might well find they have no place in E20. I fear that the 'Farewell Boleyn' programme wasn't 'see you later' – it was 'clear off and don't come back'. But maybe I'm just getting cynical in my old age.

I wondered when I first started writing this book whether or not I would ever go back to Upton Park. Well, I did – eventually. It was an emotional day. I went with Di – who else? Once we got past Tower Hill on the District Line the stations came thick and fast. Aldgate East; Whitechapel; Stepney Green; Mile End; Bow Road; Bromley-by-Bow; West Ham; Plaistow: every name almost as familiar to us as those of our kids. Next stop was Upton Park. We speculated about what had become of the signs pointing the way to West Ham United Football Club. They had been masked, but it was obvious where they once were. You can't airbrush history that easily.

We stayed on to East Ham. As we alighted from the Tube there was the usual announcement about reporting anything suspicious. We joked about suspecting that someone had stolen our football ground. Di wondered if it was worth checking with lost property.

Once in the High Street we wanted to confirm that, in this

ever-changing world, the Overdraft was still there. Having satisfied ourselves that it was, we strolled south, with Di outlining some of the myriad changes that had occurred since the days long ago when she would go shopping there with her parents. No one had heard of mobile phones and money transfer back then.

We'd been told that the Denmark had closed following the club's move from the area. We were so pleased to find it hadn't that we stopped off and had a pint for old times' sake. You don't realise exactly how big that pub is until you find yourself in there with just two other people and the bar staff. The hanging baskets were past their best. But at least the place was still going. As we left, preparing to head west along the Barking Road, Ian Dury was inviting us to hit him with our rhythm stick.

We'd seen a report that the Central had been a victim of the changing times. Sadly, this turned out to be true. Sociologists will have fun picking through the bones of all this in years to come. We took a slight detour and checked for signs of life at the Working Men's Club and the adjacent Supporters' Club. Alive, but hardly kicking.

We turned back into the Barking Road and walked the final few yards to the junction with Priory Road. There was a glimpse of the good old days as a giant mural of Billy Bonds and Trevor Brooking looked down on us from the side wall of Ercan's. Then we stared oblivion full in the face. Where the Boleyn Ground had once stood, there was a void. Nothingness. A vacuum. The cathedral that I had worshipped in for more than fifty years and the cornerstone of the area that Di grew up in no longer existed.

In its place was a building site, surrounded by high fencing. Reluctantly, we made ourselves peer through a hole in the fence to see the full extent of the destruction. In front of us was a large muddy pool. It reminded me of the goalmouths when I was a kid. Only now the goals had gone, along with the rest of the stadium. We had to move to allow a lorry on to the site, so we stepped back to view the desolation from the spot we'd so often stood in to queue for hotdogs and bacon rolls and burgers and cups of tea. The pounding of the machinery wreaking its devastation on the other side of the fence was the only noise to break the silence as Di and I looked on in silent despair. We both had to wipe away unexpected tears.

'Bastards'. It was me who spoke first. 'How dare they!' An Ian Dury song popped into my mind, but it wasn't 'Hit Me With Your Rhythm Stick'. I repeated the opening lyrics to 'Plaistow Patricia' – that's how I felt about the people who were responsible for the sacrilege that we were witnessing. They had no right. Just because you are lucky enough to own something very precious, you are not entitled to destroy it.

I loved the Boleyn Ground. Always did and always will – and it seems I'm not alone. I came across a Facebook post that sums up precisely what the old place meant to so many people. It's from respected journalist and lifelong West Ham supporter Charles Whebell, who was working abroad the night we played Man Utd in the final match at Upton Park. I'm grateful to Charlie for allowing me to reprint it in full:

I know there will be many who think I'm pathetic but tonight will be an extremely emotional time for me. My team will be playing at the Boleyn Ground for the very last time. How I wish I was there. But I will be watching on TV. Remembering the times when my nan lived in a prefab just yards from the Chicken Run. Where me and the other local children used to collect the balls that were kicked over the tin roof into the road and rush to give them back at the turnstiles. And twenty minutes from the final whistle when the gates were opened to let people out we used to creep in.

I will remember when my dad thought I was old enough to see ninety minutes and made a little box for me to stand on so I could see over the Chicken Run wall. I had a wooden rattle which I lovingly painted claret and blue and painted the names of my heroes on it. Every fortnight it was my church. My love. Me and my dad together, holding hands as we walked home discussing how on earth we lost yet another match.

I'll remember when my dad was ninety and I took him to his last match. VIP treatment all the way. Private box, lunch, beer, and photographs taken with some of the players. 'Blimey, that was all right wasn't it,' he said as we went to my car parked in the private car park.

I'll remember taking my son, Daniel. Watching his face as we lost yet another game. But like my grandad – who went to Wembley in 1923 for the FA Cup final (another defeat) in his wheelchair, he lost his legs in World War I – that passion, that love, has never wavered.

I'll remember the smell of hamburgers and the look of joy on my dad's face when we did actually win a match. The hugs he gave me. I'll remember hugging Daniel when we scored a goal. I'll remember the tears I shed when I laid flowers outside the ground when Bobby Moore died. You might call it pathetic but I'm sure my Daniel, and my other 'pathetic' West Ham friends and thousands of other West 'am fans – never trust anyone who pronounces the 'h' in Ham – will be just like me tonight. It's a family, a congregation.

The last time I went to the Boleyn was with my son for a victory last Christmas. When I asked him if he was going to try to get a ticket for tonight he replied: 'My first game there was with you and I want my last game there to be with you too.' Pathetic? Yes I'll be emotional tonight, watching the game in an Abu Dhabi pub, but I'll be happy with my memories.

Will the London Stadium ever be written about with such poignancy? I very much doubt it. The key difference is that it can never be the soul of the community in the way that the Boleyn Ground was. It is in the middle of the Olympic Park – it is not at the heart of a residential district and never will be.

I understand that the ethnic make-up of the area around the old ground has changed markedly over the years, and the vast majority of West Ham supporters no longer live near Upton Park. But that's not the point. And while the emigration of the East End to Essex and Kent made it easier for the owners to convince people of the merits of relocating to Stratford, the move to the new stadium was never about reconnecting with the fans in their heartland. It was about branding. It was about attracting the new wave of here-today-gone-tomorrow support. It was about television. It was about money.

Build it and they will come. West Ham's field of dreams is a concrete wasteland, yet the supporters will keep coming nevertheless. Whether or not they will live for Saturday afternoons in the way I once did remains to be seen. I only hope the view from the next level is as exciting as it was from the Chicken Run.

So, it seems I was grieving for the loss of a football ground and all that goes with it after all. Yes, I've certainly gone through the first four stages of grief. As for acceptance – well, I'm working on it. I just need a little more time. One hundred and twelve years should be about right.

Acknowledgements

Books, I have discovered the hard way, do not write themselves. So I am eternally grateful to everyone who has helped with this one. In no particular order, I would like to thank Seonaid Redden and Nick Fletcher for their thoughts as away supporters, Dee Searle for her insight on moving grounds, Geoffrey Williams for his recollections of the Bournemouth game and Jacqui Hughes for her memories of Mark Noble's testimonial. Their contributions, alongside those of Graeme Howlett, Ashley Gray and David Blackmore have, I believe, elevated this tome to the next level. Sean Whetstone's take on West Ham's finances was invaluable, as was the historical background provided by John Powles and Charles Korr.

I am also indebted to the awesome West Ham Statistics and TheyFlySoHigh websites for the vital information that is freely and readily available from both. Furthermore, I'd like to thank Colin Milne for the offer of swapping seats when he thought I was so fed up I might stop going to the London Stadium, and

Robert Banks for his eagle eye and encyclopaedic knowledge. A special word, too, for Charlie Whebell, who was kind enough to allow me to reprint his moving Facebook post but, tragically, did not live long enough to see it published in this book. Finally, I want to take this opportunity to thank my family for putting up with me whenever I moan and groan about West Ham United. Di, Geoff and Katie – you will always be the first names on my team sheet.

About the author

Brian Williams is a retired journalist. After qualifying for a senior railcard, Williams decided the time had come to call it a day at the *Guardian*, where he had worked for twenty-seven years, and spend more time annoying his wife Di in the home they share in Brighton and Hove. They have two grown-up children and joint custody of a cat. Williams is also the author of *Nearly Reach the Sky: A Farewell to Upton Park*, which is published by Biteback.